University of Kansas Publications
Humanistic Studies, 41

MANTILLAS IN MUSCOVY

The Spanish Golden Age Theater in Tsarist Russia 1672-1917

Jack Weiner

Lawrence: University of Kansas Publications, 1970

Library of Congress Catalog Card number: 73-630136
Printed in Lawrence, Kansas, U.S.A.
by the University of Kansas Printing Service

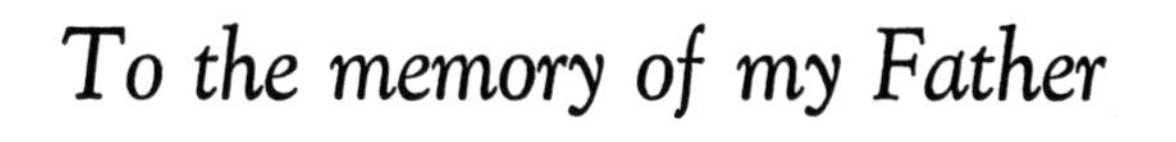

To the memory of my Father

Contents

Preface

This book is a revised version of my doctoral dissertation (Indiana University, 1968), and would not have been possible without the help of many people, institutions, and favorable circumstances, and to mention everyone (although I have forgotten none), who in one way or another assisted me, would be impossible to do here. Nevertheless, I would like to mention some of them.

I thank very much those who comprised my dissertation committee: Willis Barnstone, John C. Dowling, William B. Edgerton, Miguel Enguídanos, and Walter Poesse, of Indiana University; as well as Mikhail P. Alekseev of Pushkinskii Dom (Leningrad) and Zakharii I. Plavskin of Leningrad University who helped me so much during my stay in the Soviet Union (Spring, 1965). To Evelynne F. Meyerson of Johns Hopkins University I am especially indebted and grateful. I also thank Martha Masinton for helping me to prepare this manuscript for publication, and Nancy E. MacClintock for the preparation of the index.

Many are the institutions and libraries both abroad and in the United States whose staff warmly received me and offered generous assistance: The All Russian Theatrical Society (Moscow), British Museum, Central State Archive of Art and Literature (Moscow), Columbia University Library, Folger Library (Washington, D.C.), Helsinki University Library, Johns Hopkins University Library, Leningrad Public Library, Leningrad State Theater Library, Leningrad State Theater Museum, Leningrad University Library, Library of Congress, and The Lenin Library (Moscow).

I am most grateful to Indiana University for offering its fine faculty and facilities as well as generous financial assistance in the form of fellowships and research grants. I offer my unlimited gratitude to the Inter-University Committee on Travel Grants without whose help this work would have been impossible.

And last but by no means least I thank my mother whose extraordinary self-sacrifice and love have always been a great inspiration in my life.

I: Genesis and Development (1672-1801)

Spanish Golden Age plays first appeared in Russia during the reign of Peter the Great (1689-1725) after passing through translations and adaptations in France and Germany. Two Spanish plays were performed on the Russian stage in the early eighteenth century, and one in 1785. That a work of literature should pass through two or even three languages before becoming known to a people is a considerable handicap. Notwithstanding this obstacle, Russia's intellectuals became acquainted with Spain's Golden Age drama in the eighteenth century, and her later playwrights and producers made use of Spanish plays to reflect Russia's social and intellectual interests at various periods in her history.

Russia's sporadic contacts with Spain were, until the eighteenth century, commercial and political. These contacts date back at least to the tenth century, when for example the Arabic traveler Massudi speaks of Russians who journeyed to Spain on business;[1] and many Russians had traveled to Spain before the end of the eighteenth century.[2] The idea of trade and closer ties with Spain and her colonies had been proposed to Russia as early as 1651, when Jan de Gron, a doctor of theology and sea captain, on a sojourn in Moscow suggested that Russia build ships for sale abroad and to carry on trade with western Europe and South America.[3]

The need for mutual aid against the Turks stimulated contacts between Spain and Russia. Diplomatic relations had been first established during the reign of Philip I,[4] and again in 1521, when Vasilii III sent a diplomatic mission to treat with the Spanish throne.[5] Diplomatic relations were renewed in 1667 when the Hetman Doroshenko surrendered portions of Ukrainian territory to Megmet IV.[6] Seeing herself again threatened by the Turks, Russia sought alliances with several European powers; and a mission headed by Peter Ivanovich Potemkin, arrived in Madrid on March 8, 1668.[7]

Potemkin's mission in Madrid was essentially military and economic,[8] and it is unfortunate that his visit coincided with a period in which the Spanish theater suffered from the effects of a ban on public entertainment occasioned by the death of Philip IV in 1665.[9] All available sources indicate that there were no performances of any play on the Madrid public stage during the Russian embassy's stay in the Spanish capital.[10] This was particularly unfortunate in view of Tsar Alexis' apparent interest in the theater after 1660.

Potemkin left Madrid for Paris on June 17, 1668,[11] and in Paris he attended performances of François Le Metel's *Les coups de L'Amour et de la Fortune, ou l'Heureux infortuné,* and Molière's *Amphitrion,*[12] which he described at great length. At least one of the plays, Molière's *Amphitrion,* was performed in Russia before the end of the seventeenth century.[13]

During the first quarter of the eighteenth century, Peter the Great augmented diplomatic relations with Spain and commerce between the two countries became more firmly established.[14] Commercial contacts between Spain and Russia figured largely in Peter's long-range plans for his country's progress, and ranged from shipbuilding to the importation of products from Spain and her colonies.[15] After Peter's death, diplomatic and economic relations between Spain and Russia languished until the reign of Catherine the Great.[16]

The increasing contacts with Spain paralleled the process of westernization in Russia, and a part of westernization was the establishment of a theater.[17] In the sixteenth century, mercantile interests opened the way for diplomatic and cultural relations between Russia and her western neighbors. German, Swiss, and Italian physicians, architects, engineers, and artisans formed a colony in Moscow, and these foreigners constructed many of her churches, palaces, and public buildings. Important influences from the west made themselves felt in all aspects of Russian life.[18] The seventeenth century marked an intensification of this process, as Russia sought to establish arts and trades and adapt western ideas to Russian needs.[19] By the end of the century a select group was receptive to cultural importations, including the theater.

The beginning of the reign of Tsar Alexis Mikhailovich (1645-1676) was not propitious to the introduction of the theater, however, for by 1646, the second year of his reign, the tsar had fallen under the influence of the monk Nikon, who in 1652 became Patriarch of Moscow and the tsar's first minister. Alexis was a man of deep religious conviction who turned to his father confessor for advice and guidance on temporal and spiritual matters, both public and private. As a result, the period is characterized by extreme asceticism and piety. In 1648, in the third year of his reign, Alexis issued a proclamation which forbade public entertainment of any kind, thereby converting the country into what one historian has described as an "enormous, silent monastery."[20] Twenty-four years later the tsar completely reversed his attitude toward public entertainment. In 1672 he permitted the first cycle of theatrical performances in Russia.

A combination of factors appears to have contributed to Alexis' decision to establish the theater. When he led his troops through occupied territory during the Polish War (1654-1667), many theater buildings were pointed out to him, for Poland had a long tradition of western theater. He was aware, too, that German comedies were regularly performed in the *Nemetskaia Sloboda,* Moscow's predominantly German foreign colony.[21] In 1659, Alexis' ambassador to Florence, Vasilii Bogdanovich Likhachev, brought back glowing reports of stage performances in Italy.[22] The tsar appears to have been impressed, for the following year he commissioned an Englishman, John Gebdon, to get in touch with foreign theatrical groups for the purpose of establishing a theater in Moscow.[23] Whether by chance or as a result of Gebdon's efforts, in 1661 the Grand Duke of Tuscany sent to Moscow a troupe of actors who performed Italian plays before Tsar Alexis.[24]

In 1671, Alexis married Natalia Naryshkin (who became the mother of Peter the Great), a ward of Artamon Sergeevich Matveev. Having lived abroad and married a Scotswoman, Lady Hamilton, Matveev had become staunchly pro-Western. He was a great admirer of the French theater and under the tutelage of Matveev and his wife, Natalia became acquainted with the traditions of Western theater and shared her guardians' enthusiasm. After her marriage to the tsar, she prevailed upon him to establish a theater at the Moscow court.[25]

In 1669, Matveev replaced the Patriarch Nikon as the tsar's first minister. Church opinion augured well at this point for the establishment of the theater in Russia. When members of the church expressed their disapproval of the antics of the *skomorokhi* (jesters), Alexis turned to his confessor, Father Andrei Savinov, for his opinion of the Western theater. Savinov replied that had such spectacles been sacrilegious and immoral, God-loving rulers of other lands would not have allowed them to be performed.[26]

Having come to a decision as a result of these various influences, Alexis took definite steps in 1672 to implement his resolution. On May 15, 1672, he commissioned Colonel Nicholas von Staden, a German member of his court, to journey to the Baltic Duchy of Kurland, then under Polish suzerainty. Among other charges, he was to enlist the help of Duke Jacobus in bringing back to Russia a group of actors and directors, for Jacobus had been active in developing the Kurland theater.[27]

Matveev suggested to the tsar that there was already a man in Moscow who was capable of putting on theatrical productions, Johann Gottfried Gregory.[28] Gregory was pastor of the Lutheran Church in Moscow and director of a free school for children, in which the German curriculum called for the regular presentation of school plays. Within a few months, the German pastor assembled and rehearsed a company, mostly foreigners living in Moscow.[29] At the same time Alexis had a special theater built at his residence in the village of Preobrazhenskoe, near Moscow, and on October 17, 1676, Gregory's group produced the Biblical story of Esther.[30]

After Alexis' death in 1676 there was a general lull in theatrical activity partly because of recurrent Church and some conservative elements' opposition. Nevertheless the possibility of using the stage as a means of establishing new patterns of thought was not wasted on Peter the Great, who came to the throne in 1689. His general program of westernization gave a new impetus to the theater.[31] He brought a Danzig theatrical company, headed by Johann Christopher Kunst, to Moscow in 1701.[32] Peter saw great value in the theater as a medium of spreading his own doctrines to the people, and he moved the theater from Preobrazhenskoe to a state theater constructed on Red Square.[33] To encourage attendance, he lifted the evening curfew during the performances. Translators were engaged to render foreign plays into Russian, and Russians were trained and encouraged to become actors in them.[34]

Peter's niece, the Empress Anna Ioannovna (1730-1740), former Duchess of Kurland, and her German favorite, Biron, preferred the German theater, and during her reign many German plays were performed.[35] In the reign of Elizabeth Petrovna (1741-1762), when Russia was at war with Germany, and allied with France, the German theater gave way to the French, which dominated Russian taste well into the nineteenth century.[36]

Under Catherine the Great (1762-1796), the Russian theater flourished. The empress constructed the Bolshoi Theater in 1773 and six years later established the Imperial Theatrical School for the training of actors, singers, and dancers. She strengthened her control over the theater when she established a special Administration of the Theater in 1783.[37] All theaters, except those privately owned by the aristocracy, came under the direct control of the Crown, and those who worked in them became government employees.[38] As a result of the French Revolution, Catherine established official theater censorship in 1791.

Although there were some original plays in the eighteenth century, the Russian theatrical repertoire consisted mainly of foreign plays, or adaptations of them, and the theater depended heavily on performances by French, German, and Italian troupes. By 1710, several important Spanish themes reached the Russian stage, marking the beginning of Hispano-Russian drama relations.

Some Spanish writers were known and translated in Russia early in the reign of Peter the Great. A foreigner, Andrei Dikenson, translated from a 1655 German edition,[39] the *Empresas políticas, o Idea de un príncipe político-cristiano* of Diego de Saavedra Fajardo, one of seventeenth-century Spain's moralists and political philosophers. At the end of the seventeenth century, Feofan Prokopovich (1681-1736), one of Peter the Great's advisors, translated the same work of Saavedra Fajardo from the Latin,[40] for he believed that Saavedra Fajardo's wisdom had much to offer a ruler interested in governing well. In 1739 a certain Sergei Volchkov translated Baltasar Gracián's *Oráculo manual y arte de prudencia* into the Russian from Amelot de la Houssaye's 1702 French translation.[41] Cervantes' name appears in Russia as early as 1720,[42] but the first work translated into Russian, from the French, *Las dos doncellas,* did not appear until 1763.[43] In 1769, *Don Quijote* appeared in Russian for the first time, in an anonymous translation from the French.[44]

During Catherine's reign the opinions of Voltaire and the French philosophers were sacrosanct to Russia's intellectuals, all of whom, like their French counterparts, considered Spain a country of ignorance and religious fanaticism. Most eighteenth-century thinkers held that the Enlightenment never reached Spain at all, and the Russian writer Nikolai Ivanovich Novikov (1744-1818) expressed the opinion of many when he wrote that Spain was a country where the clergy, "gorge themselves on the best fruits and mystic celebrations dim the minds of the state. They build altars to superstition, calling it religion, in order to spread ignorance among the people."[45]

Russian producers, avid imitators of the French, took a similar view of Spanish drama. Other genres of Spanish literature were highly regarded and were, in fact, much better known to the Russian reader. For example, although the Russians were acquainted with Cervantes' prose fiction, he was unknown as a dramatist until the nineteenth century.[46] There was but a very brief interval between the appearance of a Spanish work in France and its appearance in Russia.

Despite this tendency to ignore the Spanish theater, Russian neoclassicists do mention Spanish playwrights. Lope de Vega appears in Russia for the first time in 1735. Vasilii Kirilovich Trediakovskii (1703-1769) includes Lope among the foremost poets of Europe.[47] Alexander Petrovich Sumarokov (1718-1777) in his *Epistola II,* "Epistle," (1747) refers to Lope and rhymes his name with Pope, "There is Tasso and Ariosto and Camoens and Lope/ Fondel and Guinter and the clever Pope." Sumarokov then remarks, "Lope, a glorious Spanish dramatist, died on August 24, 1635, at the age of 72. He was a knight of Malta and composed three hundred comedies."[48] Other eighteenth-century men of letters in Russia refer to Lope and to Calderón, and one mentions that Sumarokov's *Epistola* was the only material available on them in Russian.[49]

In 1792, a Moscow journal published a Russian translation of François Arnaud's essay, "Lettre sur le Théâtre Espagnol"[50] which had appeared in *Variétés littéraires* twenty-two years before. Arnaud's essay states the neo-classicist opposition to the Spanish Golden Age theater, and helps to explain Russia's attitude toward, and limited knowledge of, the Spanish comedia:

> What amazes us most about Spanish playwrights is how prolific some of them are. One cannot but be overwhelmed when he learns that Lope de Vega wrote 1800 plays. But when he sees the quality and structure of these plays he can explain this phenomenon. The Spaniards possess many chronicles, hagiographies, songs, etc. In them there are historical anecdotes, entertaining adventures full of the folk superstitious situation: The writer selects one of these adventures, rewrites it any way he pleases, and composes a dialogue based on the tale. He calls his composition a comedia. In these comedias the writer depicts either a person's entire life, from birth to death, or some historical incident, which lasts forty to fifty years; there is no structure, care, or relationship to reality; the action, without rhyme or reason, suddenly shifts from one part of the world to another. A great number of Spanish plays are composed in this style.[51]

Arnaud's essay contains a plot summary and analysis of two Spanish plays which he considered to be among Spain's best: Lope's *Los Benavides* and Moreto's *El ricohombre de Alcalá*. Arnaud's comments on Lope's ability to depict Spanish popular traditions and customs were of little interest to the eighteenth-century Russian, but these elements played an important role in the nineteenth-century revaluation of the Spanish theater.[52]

The Russian editors added a comment which indicated that by the end of the eighteenth century the Russian reader, with his limited knowledge about Spain, had not been interested in learning about her theater:

> We have heard much about Spanish customs and authors, but is much really known about them? We know little about that distant people, except that their pride and laziness have become legendary. But in general we know little about Spanish literature, and therefore hope,

especially for the friends of the theater, that our short work will not have been a waste of time.[53]

Long before Arnaud's essay appeared in Russia, however, some Russians had encountered Spanish Golden Age plays. Between 1702 and 1709, having undergone transformations in France and Germany, two plays of Spanish origin appeared in Russia: the first based on Tirso de Molina's *El burlador de Sevilla,* and the second on Calderón de la Barca's *El alcaide de sí mismo.*[54] Both plays were among the most popular productions of a group of strolling German actors managed by Johann Velthen. Not wishing to lose them to other troupes, as often happened, Velthen never wrote out the complete plays in manuscript form. Instead he distributed the individual parts to the actors, who performed them in a modification of the improvised style of the commedia dell' arte.[55] When Velthen died at the turn of the century and his company was disbanded, many of the players were invited to perform for Peter the Great. They brought with them the German versions of both Spanish Golden Age plays.[56]

Tirso's *El burlador de Sevilla* first appeared in Spain around 1621. An Italian, Onofrio Giliberti da Solofora, made an adaptation of it entitled *Il convitato de pietra.*[57] Having adapted the work to the needs of the commedia dell' arte, wandering groups of players performed the play and brought it to France. In 1658, the French actor Dorimon translated it into the French play *Le Festin de Pierre, ou le Fils criminel.* The error in the title may be accounted for by his having mistaken *convitato* (guest) for *convito* (feast), and the word *pietra* (stone) for the name Pietro. Thus it was that Tirso's commander became Pierre in France and Don Pedro in Russia. The success of this play in France caused still another Parisian actor, Claude Deschamps de Villiers, to rearrange the theme in 1659.[58] This arrangement, with many changes and omissions, was the basis for the German version which made its way into the Russian theater.

The central theme of Tirso's play is religious and moral. The play deals with man's responsibility for his sins, and with the struggle between good and evil, between the desires of the flesh, and the moral necessity of controlling these desires. Sooner or later man will die and God will judge him. But Tirso's hero, Don Juan Tenorio, is a believer whose answer to repentance is that he has much time left to pay for his sins, "Tan largo me lo fiáis!"

God has established a universal order which requires man to obey a code of behavior based on respect for religious, royal, and paternal authority. Don

Juan respects none. He offends God because of his sexual appetite, which leads him to dishonor woman and thereby defile the holy sacrament of matrimony. He defies royal authority by defiling the king's palace and betraying the king's confidence. He dishonors his own family name, thus showing disrespect for his father. His seduction by trickery of Isabela, Tisbea, and Aminta also shows his disrespect for the rules of hospitality; the king's as well as the peasant girls'.

Perhaps Don Juan's greatest virtue, and at the same time his greatest vice, is heroic pride. It manifests itself in his defiance of death in the presence of the commander's statue. In his heroism, he assumes godlike proportions and God permits no one to be His equal.

Yet in other ways Don Juan is a perfect caballero. With his male peers he is a man of honor, for otherwise he would not have accepted the statue's invitation. So great is Don Juan's trust in the statue's good intentions and personal honor that Don Juan accepts his handshake in good faith. He is also a generous host who cares for his guest's comfort and culinary pleasure.

Don Juan serves another function in Tirso's play; that of punishing others who are guilty of unbecoming conduct: Doña Isabela, Doña Ana, Tisbea, and the Marqués de la Mota all receive their just deserts.

Catalinón—a name which suggests the coward according to Américo Castro—is still a faithful and prudent servant who has his own virtues and vices.[59] He constantly reminds his master that time is running out and that he must improve his ways. Catalinón's role is made even more important because it is he whose description of Don Juan's descent into Hell puts a lightning-like end to the polyphonic final scene.

The Villiers play, which is the basis for the first Russian version on the Don Juan theme, differs in several respects from Tirso's *El burlador de Sevilla*. Villiers adapts the forms of the play to the rules of French neo-classic drama. The play consists of 1800 alexandrines divided into five acts, but differs from neo-classic rules in that it lasts two days instead of the prescribed twenty-four hour period. Both plays take place during the reign of Alfonso XI (1312-1350); Tirso's in Italy (Naples) and Spain (Tarragona and Seville), Villiers' in Seville and environs. Villiers also reduces the number of principal characters. For example, Amarille takes on the roles of both Isabela and Ana de Ulloa and the abducted peasant replaces Tisbea and Aminta. The plot is simple and has no secondary themes because Villiers reduced the importance of the Spanish theme of conjugal honor. In contrast to Tirso, Villiers generally avoids mixing comic and tragic elements, and with the exception of the scene in which Dom Juan's servant Philipin (a name which Villiers gives to the servant in his other plays)[60] frightens away the pursuing palace guards (I, vii, 665-682), there is almost no humor. Tirso emphasizes the moral theme implicitly, although Don Juan's father, uncle, and servant do admonish him from time to time; Villiers makes the moral message explicit throughout the play in the form of constant admonition to Dom Juan from a majority of the characters.

Whereas Tirso's Isabela and Ana permit certain liberties to their fiancés, in Villiers' work the love between Amarille and Philippe is pure, romantic, and chaste, serving as a contrast to Dom Juan's perverse sensuality. Even when Amarille permits Philippe to visit her at night, he may not enter her room, but must stand outside her window.

The Villiers' Dom Juan differs in many ways from Tirso's. From the outset Dom Juan manifests an uncontrollable violence and rebellious disrespect for any authority, be it divine, royal, or paternal. "Je ne veux plus souffrir de Père, ny de Maîstre; / Et si les Dieux vouloient m'imposer une Loy, / Je ne voudrois ny Dieux, Père, Maîstre, ny Roy" (307-310). Tenorio merely disregards his father's admonition, (186-376) but Dom Juan actually strikes his father, who subsequently dies from this shame. (765-770)

Dom Juan obtains his desires through violence and threats. He tries to rape Amarille and kills her father Dom Pierre, Seville's governor, when he intervenes. He later abducts and rapes a peasant bride on the eve of her wedding. In attempting to escape capture, he forces a pilgrim to exchange clothes with him, thereby mistreating a servant of God. His pleasure comes not from possession of a woman, but from depriving someone else of the pleasure of honorable love.

Not only is Villier's Dom Juan capricious, egotistical,[61] and more dangerous than Tenorio, he is treacherous as well and has no concept of honor. While dressed in the pilgrim's garments he meets Dom Philippe, who has sworn to avenge Dom Pierre's death. Convincing Dom Philippe that it is sinful to pray to God when armed, Dom Juan kills him as he kneels, unarmed, to pray. Dom Juan's vices and immoralities are so numerous that Georges Gendarme de Bévotte calls him "une sorte de monstre ou de caricature."[62] Yet Amarille, unlike Tenorio's conquests, is still attracted to her father's murderer.

Another significant difference between the two protagonists is that Dom Juan is introspective and seeks self knowledge. One such dialogue between Dom Juan and his servant Philipin is found in verses 1020-1097. Tenorio "does not analyze himself at length in intimate soliloquies or in confidential dialogue (as Molière's Don Juan is wont to do)."[63]

The first play on the Don Juan theme performed in Russia was *Don Pedro, pochitannyi shliakhta i Amarillis, doch' ego ili komediia o Done Iane i Done Pedro,* "Don Pedro the Honorable Nobleman and Amarillis, his Daughter, or a Comedy about Don Juan and Don Pedro."[64] Only a sketchy fifth act of this play has survived, but it is almost the same in theme, plot, and character as the fifth act of Villiers' play. The act consists of six short scenes. In Scene i Don Ian and his servant Filipin anxiously await the arrival of Don Pedro's ghost. In Scene ii Don Pedro's ghost comes and extends an invitation to Don Ian, to visit his tomb at midnight. Scene iii depicts a wedding feast. In Scene iv Don Ian abducts the bride. In Scene v he forces the frightened Filipin at swordpoint to accompany him to the tomb of the ghost. Scene vi depicts Don Ian's death and condemnation to Hell.

All three protagonists—Spanish, French, and Russian—search for sexual satisfaction. They bear no social or class prejudice toward woman, for woman, regardless of her social standing, is desirable, and to be enjoyed to the utmost. Isabela, Ana, and Amarille are equal in Don Juan's opinion to the peasants Tisbea, Aminta, and the abducted peasant bride. The Russian protagonist resembles his French counterpart in that he does not achieve his goals through cunning and trickery, but rather through force and rape. Both, by the abduction and rape of a peasant bride on her wedding night, violate the laws of hospitality and the holy sacrament of marriage.

Like his Western counterparts, Don Ian is defiant of death, and his attitude toward the commander's ghost reflects this. When Don Pedro tells Don Ian not to fear, Don Ian answers, "I did not fear you when you were alive and I do not fear you now that you are dead" (p. 243).

Another characteristic of Don Ian and Dom Juan, but not of Tirso's Don Juan, is the desire to eat, drink, and be merry. In Tirso's play neither Juan nor the commander eats earthly food, and the snakes and scorpions served at the commander's table are symbolic of the horrors of hell. Don Ian is a splendid host and takes great care in preparing a fine table of meat and wine for his guest.

Although the three plays differ in important aspects, the Russian work maintains the moral atmosphere and religious message of the French and Spanish plays. The Russian Don Juan is aware that he should give up his evil ways. Don Pedro asks, "Don't you want to repent before heaven, or are you ready to be condemned to hell? For the sake of this, take care. Time is growing short." Don Ian answers, "If you want to preach go to your tomb. We have gotten together to make merry. Listen, Filipin, serve us a glass of Rhine wine!" (p. 244)

When time does run out, Don Pedro says, "Repent, cursed man. Heaven has long been watching your evil doings." And Don Ian in his last moments on earth shouts, "Stop preaching, I ask neither heaven, nor hell, nor the Devil, nor his mother for anything." Don Pedro answers, "Fine. When no teaching is useful, then take the award which you deserve. (Both descend.)" (p. 248).

The roles of Philipin and Filipin are similar but at times are different from Catalinón's. Tirso's servant, despite his fear in the presence of the statue, is a moral and honest friend who does his utmost to lead Don Juan along the straight path. Both Philipin and Filipin are gluttons and faithless cowards who place their stomachs and safety before duty and loyalty to their masters.

Filipin feels no sorrow when he loses his master, and his final comments do not reflect the play's religious and moral message:

> What a nice trip they are having. They obviously are going to live in peace with everyone. If someone strikes me on one cheek, I'll give him the second. And if he strikes it I'll give him the third cheek. And if someone approaches my wife I shall lock them up in a room and not let them out until he pays two *grivnas* [an old Russian unit of money equivalent to the old English pound] for my patience. (pp. 248-249)

Villiers' work ends on a very moral note:

> Enfans, qui maudissez souvent et Pere, et Mere, Regardez ce que c'est de bien vivre, et bien faire; N'imitez pas Dom Juan, nous vous en prions tous, Car voicy, sans mentir, un beau miroir pour vous. (1797-1800)

Although the chief source for the Russian Don Juan play is Villiers' work, other sources undoubtedly provided material. Several expressions appear in the Russian play which are not in the French. The words of the ghost to Don Ian, "I do not require mortal food, I only came to see whether you wish to put aside your evil and immoral deeds" (p. 244), are found in a German puppet show from the early eighteenth century entitled, *Don Juan and Don Pietro oder das Steinerne-Todten-Gastmahl*: "Jüngling, ich bin nicht gekommen, irdische Speisen zu essen, sonder um Dich mit den ewigen zu erquicken."[65] The same expression also appears in a work attributed to Cicognini, *Il con-*

vitato de pietra: "Non ha bisogno di cibi terreni. . . ."[66] These words do not appear in Tirso's original play on Don Juan.

In both the Russian play[67] and the German puppet show[68] the time is set at midnight for Don Ian's rendezvous with the ghost, whereas no specific time is given in either the Spanish or the French play. The only actual allusion to Germany, however, is the mention of Rhine wine (p. 240). While no particular locale is named in the closing act of the Russian play, nor any Spanish color provided, neither does it appear to have Russian details. The title of Don has not been converted to its Russian equivalent nor have the names Ian and Pedro. Actually the name Dom Pierre in the Villiers play appears only once, in the list of characters.[69] In the text, Amarille's father is Dom Pedre. Nevertheless in the Russian Dom Pedre becomes Don Pedro, the Spanish form.

The Polish words in the title are enigmatic despite the absence of Polonisms in the text. *Shliakhta* is the Polish word for nobleman and perhaps equivalent to the Spanish word *don,* which (to the best of my knowledge) had no equivalent in the Russian language early in the eighteenth century. Also difficult to explain is the word "Ian," the Polish name for Juan, where one might expect Ivan or Ioann to be used. A Polish translation of the Villiers work is plausible, though no such work has been found.

Within a few years the second play of Spanish origin appeared on Peter's stage, the Russian version of Calderón's *El alcaide de sí mismo,* called *Prints Pikel-Giaring, ili Zhodelet, Komediia, samyi svoi tiur'movyi zakliuchnik,* "Prince Pickelhering, or Jodelet, His Own Jailer, a Comedy." The title itself reveals its provenance, for in France the name Jodelet was added and in Germany, the name Pickelhering. Jodelet was the stage name of one of the most popular comic actors of the seventeenth-century French theater, Julien Bedeau. The success of many plays was attributed to his talent alone, and French playwrights wrote works especially for him. The inclusion of the actor's name in the title virtually assured success to such plays as Scarron's *Jodelet, ou le Maître-Valet,* and D'Ouville's *Jodelet Astrologue.* In 1655, Thomas Corneille adapted the Calderón play to Jodelet's talents, calling it *Jodelet Prince, ou le Géolier de soymesme.*[70] In 1680, Corneille's play was presented in Hamburg as a German opera entitled *Sein Selbst Gefangener, oder der närrische Prinz Jodelet.* In adapting the opera to his play, Velthen included the popular German comic figure Pickelhering and added his name to the title. The Russian adaptation retained both the French and German names in the title.[71] Both Jodelet and Pickelhering correspond to Calderón's comic figure Benito.

The setting for Calderón's play is Naples. Federico, a prince of Sicily, has killed Pedro, the nephew of the King of Naples, in a tournament and has fled into the countryside. To avoid capture he discards his armor in the woods, and eventually finds himself at Belflor, the country estate of the king's niece, Elena. Here he passes himself off for a Catalan merchant who was robbed of his clothes and other possessions. At Belflor he is given food and shelter, and subsequently becomes chatelain of the castle. Meanwhile, Benito, a peasant, chances upon Federico's armor in the forest and puts it on. Thereupon the king's guards take him for Federico and arrest him. The guards have also captured Federico's loyal servant Roberto, who, in order to protect his master, acts as if Benito really were Federico. Benito is imprisoned in Belflor Castle, where Federico becomes his jailer. At the end all true identities are revealed, Benito is freed, Federico is forgiven, and marries the king's daughter Margarita, with whom he has been in love from the play's beginning.[72]

The theme of Calderón's play is the love triangle between Margarita, Federico, and Elena. Margarita's love for Federico conflicts with her sense of duty and obligation toward her father, her slain cousin Pedro, and her homeland. The kingdoms of Sicily and Naples have long been enemies and Federico has killed a possible pretender to her hand and her country's throne. Fortunately Margarita's father learns of her love for Federico and relents in his hatred for him. Elena, unaware that Federico has killed her brother, falls madly in love with Federico. Federico is in love with Margarita, but feels a great responsibility and gratitude to Elena for her warm and generous hospitality.

Calderón set this love theme in a somber and melancholy atmosphere of knighthood with its tournaments and pageantry. The tone is courtly, refined, and distant from reality. It is a play in which Calderón's Italian noblemen are very Spanish in their sense of honor, love, and passion. The work contains no social or class strife. On the other hand it does contain many elements of Spanish folklore centered mainly around the peasant Benito's speech and songs. Benito's inability to pronounce erudite words provides a humorous contrast to the somber atmosphere. He confuses, "Nerón, Sardanápalo, and Matusalén" with "enerón, sardina de palo, and Mateo de Allén" (p. 808). He mistakes Federico de Sicilia for Fueborrico de Cecilia (p. 817) and Fraile-rico de Cecina (p. 818). Nevertheless, Benito principally serves as a contrast for Federico. Spanish audiences doubtless laughed at anyone who could take

Benito for a prince. Calderón was laughing at a king (in this case not a Spaniard) who would not see immediately that Benito is not a nobleman.

Thomas Corneille's version greatly resembles the Calderón original. The principal theme still centers around Frédéric's predicament following the tournament and his love entanglement with Laure (Margarita) and Isabelle (Elena). And as in the Spanish, Corneille's work is characterized by a lachrymose and melancholy atmosphere.[73]

Although the theme of chivalrous love is the principal one, almost equal importance is accorded the role of Jodelet, for whom Corneille added several scenes and augmented others. Jodelet is no longer the simple fun-loving peasant of the Spanish original. He is cunning and clever enough to take advantage of his new surroundings at the Belflor castle. Even before his imprisonment he tells friends that he is a marquis (p. 23), and at Belflor he plays the role of a prince enjoying the pleasant food and surroundings (p. 66). Jodelet also considers himself a lady-killer and does not refrain from courting any lady who comes by (p. 57). While at Belflor he tests his ability on Isabelle, but without success.

In contrast to Benito, Jodelet does not want to relinquish his role of Frédéric. When Edouard, Infante of Sicily, seeks his brother's release, the guards bring Jodelet to him. Naturally, Edouard, upon seeing that Jodelet is not Frédéric, wants to see his real brother. Jodelet insists that he is Frédéric (p. 195). The element of humor is augmented by Jodelet's bragging about his nobility and his talents with women. One of the most comic scenes in the French (which is greatly expanded in the Russian version)[74] describes Jodelet's capture by the king's guards, who are afraid of Jodelet because they recall how brave and skilled Frédéric was in the tournament. They expect, but do not encounter, resistance from Jodelet.[75]

The Russian version follows the plot of Calderón and Corneille. In contrast to the Russian Don Juan play, we have a full length five-act work.

The atmosphere and emphasis in the Russian play are in sharp contrast to the Spanish and French. The love element and chivalrous setting, although present, are reduced to a position of secondary importance. Since the German text from which the Russian play comes is not extant, it is impossible to determine which changes the Germans made and which changes (if any) Peter's translation made. The Russian play gives Zhodelet a greatly increased role. The scenes in which Benito and Jodelet appear in the Spanish and French versions are considerably lengthened in the Russian and new scenes are created for Zhodelet, for example, Act I, Scenes ii-iv, in which Zhodelet dons Friderikh's attire and is subsequently apprehended by the king's soldiers.

Zhodelet is not the naive Benito. He resembles his French counterpart, whose traits he carries to a greater extreme. If Jodelet is a polite lady's-man, Zhodelet is an ungentlemanly one. Zhodelet's role is characterized by its vulgarity, coarse speech, and slapstick antics. His speech contains many pornographic expressions and phallic allusions (p. 110). Zhodelet is constantly referring to his sexual prowess and at Belflor makes vulgar overtures to the chatelaine (p. 150). He uses many Russian curses throughout the play, not only to his social peer, Pashkal, (I, ii-iv., p. 110, p. 116, p. 175) but also to the king and other members of the nobility (p. 136).

The theme of political peace found in the Spanish and French plays is very important in the Russian version. In Act IV, Scene iv, the king's guards confront Zhodelet, still believed by Naples to be Prince of Sicily, with the choice of ending the hostilities between the two countries or losing his head. Zhodelet answers that he has no desire to fight and wants peace. Friderikh agrees that the war should end (p. 177). The king of Naples wants to secure peace by giving Izabella in marriage to Friderikh. And the play closes on a peaceful note as Friderikh says hopefully, "Mars and his cruel army will stay far away" (p. 195). This expression is present only in the Russian version, and one may conjecture that at the time Peter was trying to instill in his people a desire for peace with a neighboring power.

A little Russian color is woven into the play, even though the scene is set in Naples. "Sidor and Karp in the Crimea" are Zhodelet's tailors (p. 120), and the money he uses he designates by the Russian name for a small coin, *altyn* (p. 122).

A study of the three versions of this play reveals several curious points. In a comic attempt to show the audience how he would address a lady, Zhodelet speaks in apostrophe to Margarita (p. 114). She is the heroine of the Calderón play but does not appear in the Corneille work. There are sections of the Russian text which were virtually lifted out of the Calderón play, but which are not in the French. In the Spanish, after donning Federico's armor, Benito says to his friend Antona, "Pues Antona, ¿qué dirá? Que so con figura extraña, San Jorge mata-la-araña." (p. 813). In the Corneille play, when Jodelet appears for the first time, he is already, "armé des mesmes armes que Frédéric auoit portees au Tournoy." The scene in which he actually puts on Frédéric's gear is omitted and there is no mention of St. George. The Russian version, however, reproduces the original Spanish; Zhodelet dons the hero Friderikh's armor and says to his friend Pashka, "Look at me now. Don't I look like the Knight George who killed the dragon?" (p. 117). The internal evidence of the Russian play proves that the translator of either the German or the Russian version consulted the original Spanish, though his rendering of "San Jorge mata-la-araña" suggests a misunderstanding of the Spanish folk expression.[76]

The Russian play differs importantly from the Spanish and French in that it contains material critical of the nobility. Peter intended to reform a profligate and indolent nobility, and to teach his people that nobility does not come from ancestry but from merit and reward based on labor and contribution to a progressive society. Zhodelet defines the aristocracy as "anyone who wears velvet pants" (p. 143). When the king and his court take Zhodelet for a prince, despite his vulgar speech and uncouth manners (p. 138), the implication is that the nobles of Peter's Russia are themselves little better than vulgar bumpkins.

Not until the end of the eighteenth century do we encounter another Spanish play, again by Calderón, in Russia. The adapter was the monarch herself, Catherine the Great. Catherine took interest in writing for the stage, having composed three lyrical dramas, eleven comedies, an imitation of the *Merry Wives of Windsor,* and five operas.[77] In 1787, she began an adaptation of Calderón's *El escondido y la tapada.*[78] She uses as her text Simon Linguet's prose version in French, *Le Cloison,* first published in the 1770 Paris edition of his *Théâtre espagnol* (4 vols.).[79] Catherine's title *V chulane* corresponds in meaning to the name of Linguet's work.

Catherine's plays, many of which were performed on the Hermitage stage, fall into two periods, 1772-1776 and 1786-1790. She wrote comedies of manners describing the Russian middle class and lesser nobility.[80] They were moralistic and sought to instruct. Her aim in presenting these plays is inscribed on the Hermitage Theater stage, "Ridendo castigat [sic] mores," "Correct manners by laughter,"[81] adapted from the motto which the French poet Santeuil devised for the seventeenth-century Harlequin Dominique. According to the Soviet theater historian, S. Danilov, "The rules governing her plays were that they should be funny, but not insulting, contain jokes but not offense, should have salt but neither bile nor bitterness."[82] By the time of her second cycle (1786-1790), she had also become interested in western comedies of manners, which she adapted to Russian surroundings. It was during this period that she wrote *V chulane.*[83]

Like Peter the Great, Catherine used the theater to further her social and political aims of strengthening the existing class structure. The legislation passed during her reign guaranteeing the institution of serfdom was one of the mainstays of this rigid social structure. Because Russia had witnessed two peasant uprisings, Stenka Razin in 1670 and Emilian Pugachev in 1773, the aristocracy was haunted by the spectre of mass revolt and consequently no play depicting social upheaval could find endorsement in Catherine's Russia. As the Soviet theatrical historian Liubov' Gurevich put it, "A tragedy depicting opposition to the nobility, with heroes ready to stake their lives not only for their country but for freedom as well, and for a limited monarchy, now became a thing of the past."[84] Catherine's adaptation of *El escondido y la tapada* reflects her theatrical and political ideas.

In the Calderón play César is in love with Lisarda, who does not return his love. In a vain attempt to forget her, he courts Celia whom he does not love. Nevertheless, César becomes jealous when he sees Celia walking with Don Alonso, Lisarda's brother, and kills him in a duel. He flees Madrid for Portugal to escape execution. While there César receives a letter from Celia who says she loves him very much. She also feels responsible for César's plight because her association with Alonso helped provoke the duel. Celia offers him asylum in her second-story apartment during her brother Félix's military tour of duty in Italy. César accepts the opportunity to see Lisarda.

Meanwhile Félix, having heard about Celia's involvement in Alonso's death and preoccupied with his family's honor, has secretly returned to Madrid and has nailed down all windows in his home. (Catherine's adaptation—some 550 lines—ends here.)

Félix and Juan de Silva, Lisarda's cousin and fiance, plan to murder César, but Celia hides César and Mosquito in a secret place in her house. This hiding place gives the title for Linguet's and Catherine's plays. It opens on to Celia's bedroom, and César (the "escondido" in Calderón's play) and Mosquito remain there until the end of the play.

Meanwhile, Félix and Juan kill a man, mistaking him for César, and Félix and Celia must give up their apartment. Lisarda's father decides to rent the apartment and he, Lisarda, and Juan de Silva, unaware of the secret hiding place and of César's presence, come to live there. Celia, hiding her identity by wrapping herself in a cloak, asks Don Diego to grant her asylum because of an affair of honor. Celia is the "*tapada*."

The remainder of the play is equally complicated. Félix returns to look for his sister, and Lisarda's inevitable marriage to Juan makes César despair. Soon all are aware that someone else is in the house and they search time and time again. Don César finally leaves his hiding place to protect Celia's honor. All is forgiven. César marries Celia and Juan marries Lisarda.[85]

With the exception of a few name changes Linguet's prose version is the same as the Spanish, although it does not possess the poetic qualities of the original.[86] Catherine's adaptation differs significantly from the Linguet version.

Catherine moves the place of action from Madrid to Moscow. In the Spanish and French versions, the heroes ride mules; in the Russian they ride horses because there are no mules in Great Russia (p. 389). In the Spanish, Félix serves in Italy; Felov was in the Caucasus (p. 395). In some cases Catherine Russifies the names slightly: Diego-Diegin, Félix-Felov, César-Sevin, Mosquito-Moise. In others she substitutes purely Russian names: Isabelle-Pulkheria, Inés-Arina (p. 396).

There is no reference to violence in Catherine's play. The killing of the brother is reduced to a mere exchange of words for which the hero is banished from Moscow by his own father. Catherine avoids reference to public execution, which she theoretically banned by her Nakaz of 1767.[87]

In *V chulane* Catherine emphasizes the loyalty of the servant for his master. Moise says to his master, "You did not want to take me with you but I, loving you, have accompanied you." (p. 390) She also adds lines which suggest her desire to strengthen serfdom. Moise is resigned to his fate, "I, my lord, was born to serve you. I was trained and reared to it" (p. 389). This subservient tone is missing in the French and Spanish versions.

Catherine chose to adapt *Le Cloison* because it reflects her theatrical as well as her political interests. The play is a western comedy of manners, a genre to which her second cycle of plays belongs. It contains no social message or protest, nor does it have a religious or mystical theme; the empress disliked superstition and mysticism.[88] Interestingly enough, the play which immediately precedes *Le Cloison* in Linguet's edition is *Le viol puni,* "El alcalde de Zalamea," a work completely incompatible with Catherine's political and social views.[89]

Linguet's *Théâtre espagnol* provided the source of another Russian adaptation of a Spanish play. A. F. Malinovskii in 1785 presented *Sel'skii mudrets,* a version of Lope de Vega's *El villano en su rincón.* Malinovskii used a French adaptation published in the Hague in 1782 by Jean Baptiste Dalainval and performed in a local French theater on September 19 of that year. Dalainval in turn had based his work on Linguet's 1770 edition of *Théâtre espagnol.*[90]

The production history of *Sel'skii mudrets* illustrates the changing attitude of Catherine. It was performed on the Petrovskii Theater stage in Moscow in 1785, but a scheduled performance in 1790 was cancelled. Lope's play depicts a proud but loyal subject to the king, the prosperous peasant Juan Labrador. It was perhaps because of Labrador's loyalty that Catherine permitted the 1785 performance, but in 1790, because of the fear engendered by the outbreak of the French Revolution, she probably found Labrador's personality excessively independent.[91] On his own property Labrador considers himself equal to the king, and such thinking was unacceptable in the Empress' eyes. The fact that Lope's play takes place in France may have made the work even more distasteful to her.

At the end of this period an author feigned a translation of a Spanish play in order to disguise the criticism he was making. In 1794 there appeared in Moscow a play entitled *Don Pedro Prokodurante, ili Nakazannyi bezedel'nik*, "Don Pedro Prokodurante, or the Punished Loafer," which was attributed to Calderón de la Berca [sic]. Actually, it was an original Russian work by I. P. Chaadaev, whose son was the author of the *Filosofskie Pis'ma*, "Philosophical Letters." Purportedly set in Barcelona, the story portrayed the life of a dishonest government official, and its aim was to criticize the bureaucracy of Tsarist Russia.[92]

The end of the eighteenth century brings to a close the long period of sporadic contacts between Russia and Spain, and initiates closer ties which develop very early in the nineteenth century. In spite of a resounding lack of interest of the part of Russian intellectuals, three Spanish plays had reached the Russian stage under the auspices of Russian rulers. Both Peter and Catherine, though primarily interested in economic and social ties with the West, had been able to understand the educational possibilities of theater, and they had initiated a practice which would become characteristic of Russian theater, that of making dramatic works a vehicle for the reinforcement of prevailing social or political ideas. The particular nature of Spanish drama would, in the nineteenth century, make it readily adaptable to such a purpose.

Notes

Chapter I was previously published in *Annali dell'Instituto Universitario Orientale: Sezione Romanza* XI, 2 (1969), 193-223. Certain material in this book previously appeared in the author's "Russian and Soviet Criticism of the Spanish *Comedia*," *Yearbook of General and Comparative Literature*, XVIII (1969), 48-69.

1. V. I. Lamanskii, "O slavianakh v Maloi Azii v Afrike i v Ispanii," *Uchenye zapiski imperatorskoi akademii nauk, vtoroe otdelenie, Kniga V* (1859), 222.

2. Mikhail Pavlovich Alekseev, *Ocherki istorii ispano-russkikh literaturnykh otnoshenii XVI-XIX vv.* (Leningrad, 1964), pp. 5-18.

3. Richard A. Pierce, "Source Materials on a Project for Russian Colonization in South America, 1735-1737," *California Slavic Studies,* I (1960), 183.

4. Alekseev, p. 8.

5. Jack Weiner, "Sobre el origen de las palabras Moscovia y Moscovita," *Hispania,* XLVII (1964), 135-136.

6. T. K. Krylova, "Otnosheniia Rossii i Ispanii v pervoi chetverti XVIII veka," *Kul'tura Ispanii* (Leningrad, 1940), p. 326.

7. Gabriel Maura y Gamazo, *Carlos II y su corte* (Madrid, 1911), I, 308.

8. Konstantin Derzhavin, "La primera embajada rusa en España," *Boletín de la real academia de la historia,* XCVI (1930), 880-882.

9. Emilio Cotarelo y Mori, *Ensayo sobre la vida y obras de Don Pedro Calderón de la Barca* (Madrid, 1924), I, 322. See N. D. Shergold, *A History of the Spanish Stage From Medieval Times Until The End Of The Seventeenth Century* (Oxford University Press, 1967), p. 331.

10. Maura y Gamazo, I, 310. See *Drevniaia Rossiiskaia Vivliofika* (Moscow, 1790), Chast' IV, p. 390. See Jack Weiner, "The Death of Philip IV of Spain (1665) and the Early Russian Theatrical Repertoire (1672-1686)," *Theatre Research* (1970).

11. Maura y Gamazo, I, 313. See Ada Mae Coe, *Catálogo bibliográfico y crítico de las comedias mencionadas en los períodicos de Madrid desde 1661 hasta 1819* (Baltimore, 1935), passim.

12. A. Popov, "Russkoe posol'stvo vo Frantsii v 1668 godu," *Russkaia beseda,* I (1856), 78.

13. Nikolai S. Tikhonravov, *Russkie dramaticheskie proizvedeniia 1672-1725* (St. Petersburg, 1874), I, xliv.

14. Krylova, p. 326. D. M. Lebedev, *Geografiia v Rossii petrovskogo vremeni* (Moscow, 1950), p. 281.

15. Vladimir A. Ulianitskii, *Istoricheskii ocherk russkikh konsul'stv za granitsei* (Moscow, 1899), II, cvii.

16. "Pis'mo grafa (kniazia) A. A. Bezborodka k S. S. Zinov'evu (Poslanniku v Ispanii)," *Russkii arkhiv* (1862), 210-214. In 1785 Catherine the great was interested in establishing trade with Spain, toward whom she was very well disposed because their national interests did not conflict. Angel Grisanti, *Miranda y la Emperatriz Catalina la Grande* (Caracas, 1928), pp. 14, 16.

17. Pimen Arapov, *Letopis' russkago teatra* (St. Petersburg, 1861), p. 5.

18. Derzhavin, 877-896.

19. P. Medovikov, *Istoricheskoe znachenie tsarstvovaniia Alekseia Mikhailovicha* (Moscow, 1854), p. 45.

20. Liubov' Gurevich, *Istoriia russkogo teatral'nogo byta* (Moscow, 1935), p. 8.

21. V. V. Kallash and N. E. Efros, eds. *Istoriia russkago teatra* (Moscow, 1914), I, 56.

22. Gurevich, p. 7.

23. Kallash and Efros, I, 56.

24. Ivan Nosov, *Khronika russkago teatra* (Moscow, 1883), p. 2. Also, Gurevich, I, 7.

25. Kallash and Efros, I, 58.
26. Ibid., I, 59.
27. S. K. Bogoiavlenskii, "Moskovskii teatr pri tsariakh Aleksee i Petre," *Chteniia v obshchestve istorii i drevnostei rossiisskikh pri imperatorskom moskovskom universitete* (Moscow, 1914), II, iv.
28. Boris V. Varneke, *History of the Russian Theater,* trans. Boris Brasol (New York, 1951), p. 25.
29. Bogoiavlenskii, loc. cit.
30. Varneke, loc. cit.
31. Marc Slonim, *Russian Theater From the Empire to The Soviets* (New York, 1961), p. 23.
32. Kallash and Efros, I, 70.
33. Slonim, loc. cit.
34. Varneke, p. 37.
35. Kallash and Efros, I, 99.
36. Slonim, p. 25.
37. Ibid., p. 28.
38. Ibid., p. 29.
39. A. I. Sobolevskii, *Perevodnaia literatura Moskovskoi Rusi XIV-XVII vekov* (St. Petersburg, 1903), p. 383.
40. Alekseev, p. 31.
41. Ibid., p. 82.
42. Ibid., p. 62.
43. *Migel' de Servantes, Bibliografiia russkikh perevodov i kriticheskoi literatury na russkom iazyke: 1763-1957,* comp. A. D. Umikian (Moscow, 1959), p. 11.
44. Ibid., p. 46.
45. Alexander I. Nezelenov, *Literaturnye napravleniia v Ekaterinskuiu epokhu* (St. Petersburg, 1889), p. 354.
46. Alekseev, p. 78.
47. V. K. Trediakovskii, *Stikhotvoreniia,* ed. A. S. Orlov (Leningrad, 1935), p. 151.
48. Alexander Petrovich Sumarokov, *Izbrannye proizvedeniia* (Leningrad, 1935), p. 117.
49. Alekseev, pp. 79-80.
50. *Chtenie dlia vkusa, razuma i chuvstvovanii,* V (1792), 126-185.
51. Ibid, 127-128.
52. Ibid., 153.
53. Ibid., 127.
54. Tikhonravov, I, 240-249, 105-194.
55. Pavel Osipovich Morozov, *Ocherki iz istorii russkoi drama XVII-XVIII stoletii* (St. Petersburg, 1888), p. 255.
56. Ibid., p. 255.
57. Oscar Mandel, *The Theater of Don Juan* (Lincoln, University of Nebraska Press, 1963), p. 126. Georges Gendarme de Bévotte, *Le festin de pierre avant Molière* (Paris, 1907), p. 365. A play by the Italian Cicognini was written before 1650 and precedes da Solofora's work.
58. Mandel, pp. 105-106.

59. Gerald E. Wade, "*El Burlador de Sevilla:* Some Annotations," *Hispania,* XLVII (1964), 751-752.

60. Gendarme de Bèvotte, p. 160.

61. Gendarme de Bèvotte, *La légende de Don Juan* (Paris, 1906), p. 125.

62. Ibid., p. 116.

63. Tirso de Molina, *El burlador de Sevilla and La prudencia en la mujer,* introduction and notes by Raymond R. MacCurdy (New York, 1965), p. 16.

64. Tikhonravov, I, xlvi.

65. Johann Scheible, *Das Kloster* (Stuttgart, 1846), III, 723.

66. Gendarme de Bèvotte, *Le festin,* p. 418.

67. Tikhonravov, II, 246.

68. Scheible, p. 123.

69. Gendarme de Bèvotte, *Le festin,* p. 160.

70. Morozov, pp. 254-255.

71. Ibid., p. 255.

72. Don Pedro Calderón de la Barca, *Obras Completas,* ed. Angel Valbuena Briones (Madrid, 1960), II, 801-834.

73. Thomas Corneille, *Le Geolier de Soy-Mesme, Poemes Dramatiques* (Rouen, MDCLXI), II, 1-112.

74. Tikhonravov, II, 120-126.

75. Corneille, 27-29.

76. Gonzalo de Correas, *Vocabulario de refranes y frases proverbiales* (Madrid, 1924), p. 443.

77. Slonim, p. 25.

78. A note to her translation says, "A free adaptation of a dramatic composition by Calderón de la Barca," *Sochineniia Ekateriny II* (St. Petersburg, 1901), III, 389-395.

79. The Linguet edition was in the library of Count Sheremetev. M. M. Stasiulevich, *Opis' biblioteki nakhodivsheisia v Moskve na Vozdvizhenke v dome Grafa D. N. Sheremeteva do 1812 goda.* (St. Petersburg, 1883, p. 198.

Catherine visited the Sheremetev theater at Kuskovo near Moscow at approximately the time she did the Calderón adaptation, according to Nikolai Drizen, *Materialy k istorii russkago teatra* (Moscow, 1913), p. 65. Voltaire's library, which arrived at St. Petersburg in 1779, also contains several Golden Age plays, e.g. Calderón's *Lances de amor y fortuna,* translated by Voltaire (p. 223, N. 609); Moreto's *La misma consciencia acusa* (p. 640, N. 2524), and Belmonte Bermúdez *El príncipe perseguido.* Biblioteka Vol'tera,ed. M. P. Alekseev (Moscow, 1961).

80. Kallash and Efros, I, 326.

81. Varneke, p. 132.

82. Sergei Danilov, *Ocherki po istorii russkogo dramaticheskogo teatra* (Moscow, 1948), p. 96.

83. Kallash and Efros, I, 331-333.

84. Gurevich, I, 243.

85. Calderón de la Barca, 673-709.

86. Simon Nicholas Henri Linguet, *Theâtre espagnol* (Paris, 1770), II.

87. "Nakaz imperatritsy Ekateriny II": ed. N. D. Chechulin, *Pamiatniki russkago zakonodatel'stva 1649-1832* (St. Petersburg, 1907), pp. 61-62.

88. Kallash and Efros, II, 331.

89. Linguet, II.
90. *Dramaticheskii slovar'* (St. Petersburg, 1880), p. 123.
91. *Lope de Vega, Bibliografiia russkikh perevodov i kriticheskoi literatury na russkom iazyke: 1735-1961,* comp. Zakharii I. Plavskin (Moscow, 1962), p. 7.
92. N. N. Smirnov-Sokol'skii, *Rasskazy o knigakh* (Moscow, 1959), pp. 174-180.

II: From Romanticism to Realism (1801-1855)

During the first half of the nineteenth century—the reigns of Alexander I (1801-1825) and Nicholas I (1825-1855)—the tsars were haunted by the spectres of the Napoleonic War and the Decembrist uprising of 1825. The Polish revolt of 1831 and the revolutions of 1848 served to confirm Nicholas' apprehensions.[1] As a result, censorship, long knit into the fabric of Russian life, became more severe. In 1826 Admiral Alexander Semenovich Shishkov (1754-1841), Nicholas' archconservative Minister of Education, codified the so-called "iron-clad" censorship laws. Theatrical censorship received particular attention.[2] Moscow's Governor-General Alexander Andreevich Bekleshov (1745-1808) set the pattern in 1805 for the distinction between printed books and theatrical performances when he prohibited a play based on Lesage's *Gil Blas*. He reasoned that, while, "the book does not contain many daring expressions and thoughts against the government and rulers, the average person reads to himself alone, while a theatrical performance is attended by the masses."[3]

In Nicholas' time the tsar's internal security section controlled all plays so that censorship was under the direct aegis of the monarch himself.[4] Nicholas looked upon literature as a means of moral edification, and the function of the theater as he saw it was to concern itself with morality, patriotism, and the confirmation of established values.[5] After Shishkov's successor, Sergei Semenovich Uvarov (1786-1855), in 1833 proclaimed orthodoxy, autocracy, and nationality as the aims of the government, the tsar and his censors scrutinized theater performances even more closely.

They required that the monarch and religion be treated with particular respect. Religion was not to be discussed in plays, members of the clergy were not to be portrayed on the stage, nor were religious images to be used in the theater.[6] Like Philip II of Spain, Nicholas did not care to see the figure of the monarch shown on the stage. From time to time he permitted foreign sovereigns to be represented but only if the plays showed them in a favorable light. Similarly, the censors did not tolerate social criticism of any kind[7] and they permitted no mention of serfdom on the stage, so that a play that dealt with social unrest or lacked decorum did not receive their approval.[8]

As a result of the restrictions laid down by Nicholas and by Shishkov's censorship law, the plays produced during his reign fell into two general categories; the patriotic and the melodramatic.[9] Since there were no theaters operating outside the Imperial monopoly during Nicholas' reign, all performances were bound by the strictest controls. In fact, two of Russia's greatest plays were not performed during the playwrights' lifetime: Pushkin's *Boris Godunov* and Lermontov's *Maskarad,* "Masquerade."[10] The work which best exemplifies the tsar's ideal was an insipid melodrama glorifying the Romanovs, *Ruka Vse vyshniago Otechestvo Spasla* (1834), "The Almighty's Hand the Fatherland Has Saved," by Nestor Vasilevich Kukol'nik (1809-1868).[11]

Thus while Spanish Golden Age drama was becoming known in Russia through books and articles, both the publication and the performance of plays were subject to the limitations of tsarist censorship.[12] The religious proscriptions in the censorship laws precluded a great number of Calderón's major works; while censorship against social protest and the violation of authority excluded from the Russian stage such Spanish plays as *La vida es sueño, El alcalde de Zalamea, Fuente Ovejuna, El purgatorio de San Patricio, El mejor alcalde, el rey,* and many others, which, in subsequent years, with the relaxing of censorship, were performed for the Russian public.[13]

Most of the Spanish plays which were performed during Nicholas' reign were produced under the beneficiary system, under which the actor or actress, known for this performance as the beneficiary, had the privilege of choosing the play he wished to act in, provided, of course, that it had been passed by the censor. The beneficiary usually played the leading role in his chosen play; he received the net proceeds from the box office on opening night and was permitted to sell tickets among his friends and acquaintances, who often added a personal donation. The proceeds from the benefit performance formed an important part of the actor's annual income.[14]

The Peninsular War created a new image of Spain and altered Russia's attitude toward her literature and culture. Locked in combat with Napoleon, the Spain which the men of the Enlightenment had scorned as a country of ignorance and superstition became a symbol of loyalty and heroic courage.[15] The Russian press published reports of the Peninsular War, and Spain became the object of sympathy, admiration, and respect. The resistance of the Spanish *guerrilleros* against the French, the battle of Bailén, the heroic resistance of the Spanish during the sieges of Gerona and Zaragoza were familiar to the Russian people, to the limited reading public as well as to the illiterate masses.[16] Praise and prayers for the Spanish struggle intermingled as the Russians came to look upon Spain as a nation true to its king, church, and homeland. In the words of Admiral Shishkov:

> In the breasts of the people there burned a holy flame of faith, freedom, homeland, and the ancient honor of the Spaniards and Visigoths, their forefathers. . . . In their brave hearts there was only a sweet feeling of revenge, which aroused them, in burning ardor, to spare neither possession, wealth, health, nor their lives.[17]

S. S. Uvarov later transformed these words into the rigid tsarist policy of "autocracy, orthodoxy, and nationality,"[20] under which revolutionary activity seethed.

Russia's sympathy for Spain on the battlefield generated a new interest in her language and culture. At the beginning of the nineteenth century, the Russian intellectual interested in Spanish culture was dependent for the most part upon French, German, and English translations. There were exceptions, of course. In 1791, Fedor Vasil'evich Karzhavin (1745-1812), the noted translator and linguist, provided, in his *Kratkoe izvestie o dostopamiatnikh prikliucheniiakh kapitana d'Sivilia,* "A Brief Account of the Memorable Adventures of Captain d'Sivilia," a pronunciation chart for Spanish words in Russian transliteration.[19] But there were few such Russians until Napoleon Bonaparte invaded Spain.

Russia's writers and journalists praised Spain lavishly during the Peninsular War and in the decade that followed. They published studies comparing Spanish and Russian virtues.[20] In the journals they demanded a revaluation of Spain's contribution to world thought. The poet Gavriil Romanovich Derzhavin (1743-1816) satirized the French army in Spain.[21] Denis Vasil'evich Davydov (1781-1839), the poet and partisan leader of the Russian forces against Napoleon, credited Spanish *guerrillero* tactics with having aided Russia in repulsing Napoleon.[22]

In 1811, Iakov Langen published a Spanish grammar based on the rules of the Spanish Academy. In its review of this grammar, the *Sankt-Peterburgskie vedomosti,* "St. Petersburg News," summarized the changed attitude which was then coming into vogue:

> For a long time now the study of Spanish has been disregarded, owing to unjust and prejudicial concepts of Spain. But since dependable contemporary writers have shown that excellent country from a positive point of view, it is now honorable to become acquainted with

> such a wealthy, expressive, and melodious language. It is the wish of the editor if not to reinstate, so to say, a neglected language, at least to help those who wish to become acquainted with it.[23]

In 1812 the journal *Syn otechestva,* "The Son of the Fatherland," published from the English, S. L-ch's *Osada Saragossy,* "Siege of Saragossa."[24] That same year *Vestnik Evropy,* "European Herald," published an article which contrasted Spain's past with her present:

> French writers of the eighteenth century had little respect for Spanish letters because Spain had for a very long time failed to participate in any intellectual development and had fallen into oblivion. Nations from which she had completely cut herself off had long forgotten the monuments to her glory. But now they are asking what Spanish letters are like, how they differ from others, what might the Spanish be proud of, and in what way do they merit the respect of other nations.[25]

Political and military relations between the two monarchies contributed to this interest. At Paris on October 4, 1801, and Velikia Luki on July 20, 1812, Spain and Russia signed mutual defense treaties and became political as well as spiritual allies. At Madrid on September 1, 1812, during the Duke of Wellington's temporary occupation of the capital, Spain and Russia signed still another treaty.[26]

On May 13, 1813, some twelve hundred Spanish soldiers, conscripted by Napoleon to fight against Russia and there taken prisoner, swore an oath of allegiance to Ferdinand VII. The Spanish ambassador in St. Petersburg administered the oath in the presence of Alexander I and thousands of spectators.[27] On July 17, in a farewell celebration, these Spanish soldiers performed a consecration of the flag ceremony. Alexander was their protector and the two battalions were named in his honor. The event received wide coverage in the Russian press; a poem by Count Dmitrii Ivanovich Khvostov (1756-1835) commemorated the affair.[28] Leo Tolstoy in his *War and Peace* mentions Spanish soldiers forced to fight for Napoleon against Russia.[29]

Alexander had appointed Prince Alexander Alexandrovich Shakhovskoi (1777-1846) as his special representative in charge of this group of Spanish soldiers.[30] Perhaps this close contact was responsible for the development of his interest in Spanish culture, for it was Shakhovskoi who, in the late 1820's, wrote plays in the Spanish style and translated and had performed Rojas Zorrilla's *Del rey abajo, ninguno.*

Alexander's ambassador in Spain from 1815 to 1821, Dmitrii Pavlovich Tatishchev (1767-1845), enjoyed great influence at the court of Ferdinand VII. From St. Petersburg came valuable gifts, cordial correspondence, membership in orders, and decorations for the Spaniards, while members of the Russian royal family in turn received Spain's Toisón de Oro.[31] Tatishchev, too, received this honor, and when he returned to Russia, he took with him many Spanish books and paintings.[32]

Other Russian travelers and diplomats left reports of their stay in Spain. Dmitrii Ivanovich Dolgorukov (1797-1867), a member of the Russian Embassy staff, became well-versed in Spanish culture. Although he knew no Spanish on arriving, he undertook at once to study the language and soon after wrote his brother Mikhail that he was "assiduously learning Spanish and beginning to read Calderón and Lope."[33] Dolgorukov's correspondence from Madrid reflects his great enthusiasm for Spain, his knowledge of the Spanish way of life, and his love for Calderón and Lope, whose works he found to be "remarkably beautiful."[34]

During his three years in Madrid he became a close friend of Washington Irving. The American author respected Dolgorukov's knowledge of Spain sufficiently to consult the prince on details of Spanish life and culture for his *Tales of the Alhambra.*[35]

Events in Spain also affected the thought of Russia's intellectual revolutionaries. The Riego rebellion of 1820 gave a new direction to Hispano-Russian relations.[36] In 1812, during Napoleon's occupation of much of Spain, the Cortes of Cádiz proclaimed a constitution which gave greater freedom and civil liberties to the Spanish people. When Ferdinand returned to Spain from his detention in France in 1814 he suspended this constitution and a period of political repression began. On January 1, 1820, a revolt against Ferdinand erupted. Two of its most important leaders were Rafael de Riego, a colonel, and General Antonio Quiroga. This uprising, although initially successful, was later suppressed and though Quiroga escaped with his life by fleeing temporarily from Spain, Riego was captured and hanged on October 16, 1823.

The enlightened and progressive elements among the Russian intellectuals considered the rebellion a struggle against despotism and tyranny, and regarded it as one with their own struggle. As a result both Riego and Quiroga became heroic figures among these progressive Russians. Peter Iakovlevich Chaadaev (1793-1865), the author of the *Filosofskie Pis'ma,* "Philosophical Letters," wrote to a friend:

> Here is some news for you which will have repercussions throughout the world! The revolution in Spain is over; the king was forced to sign the 1812 Constitution. The entire nation is in arms. A revolution carried out in eight months, and moreover, not one drop of blood, no slaughter, no destruction, a complete absence of force—in short, nothing that could blemish such a beautiful deed. What do you have to say about that? The event will serve as an excellent example for the good of revolution. In all of this there is something which concerns us more closely. Need I say more?[37]

The Russian press followed the Riego rebellion closely and many liberal writers praised the heroic struggle and lamented its suppression. Pushkin, while still in exile, took a great interest in this event. In a letter to Alexander Ivanovich Turgenev (1785-1846) of July 14, 1824, Pushkin recalls his early days of exile in Kishinev, many of which he spent in conversation with the Governor-General Ivan Nikitich Inzov (1768-1845):

> Old Inzov would put me under arrest every time I gave a Moldavian boyar a beating. True. But on the other hand the good mystic at the same time would come to visit me and chat with me about the Spanish revolution. I do not know whether Vorontsov would put me under arrest, but he certainly would not come to discuss the Constitution of the Cortes.[38]

Mikhail Semenovich Vorontsov (1782-1856), the Governor-General of the provinces of New Russia and Vice-Regent of Bessarabia, was the object of a number of Pushkin's most critical and vitriolic epigrams.[39] One such poem addressed to Vorontsov has, as its central theme, Riego's execution.

To Vorontsov

They once told the tsar that at last
The mutinous leader Riego was suppressed.
"I am very glad," said the enthusiastic
  flatterer,
"The world is free of still another scoundrel."
Everyone became silent and cast their glances
  downward
Everyone found the hasty sentencing funny.
Riego was guilty in Ferdinand's eyes,

I agree. That is why he was hanged.
But tell me whether it is courteous
To curse so quickly the executioner's victim?[40]

This poem resulted from a statement that Vorontsov made to Alexander I when Riego's capture was announced. Vorontsov was quoted as saying, "What wonderful news, your highness."[41]

Alexander saw the Riego affair as a threat and looked with alarm lest it spread. The Riego rebellion made the tsar more and more reactionary and as Admiral Shishkov recalls, "The events in Spain and Naples completely changed his way of thinking. He began to stop thinking about giving freedom to the people."[42] The Decembrist trials proved that the court's concern was well founded. The leader of the Southern Society, Colonel Pavel Ivanovich Pestel (1792-1826), in a statement made after his arrest on December 14, 1825, declared that the events in Spain had a profound influence on him and "affirmed me very strongly in a republican and revolutionary mentality."[43]

As a result of the Riego rebellion, the Russian court frowned upon Spanish thought and any indication of sympathy for revolutionary Spain was held suspect. Works on Spain by western writers such as Byron and some of the French romantics were considered dangerous.[44] This attitude represented a complete change in Russian court opinion, but despite all the efforts of the tsarist state to eradicate such a revolutionary example, portraits of Quiroga and Riego were exhibited in a St. Petersburg store on the eve of the Decembrist uprising.[45]

The Riego rebellion caused the Russian intellectual revolutionary to take an even keener interest in Spanish literature. Literature became the vehicle for expressing political beliefs, and the Spain that was forbidden as a topic for political discussion became a topic for literary debate.[46] The development of the Spanish theater in Russia from this period onward must be viewed against the background of the nineteenth-century socio-political struggle, on the one hand, and in the ambiance of German romanticism, on the other.

Russian interest in the Spanish Golden Age theater during the early nineteenth century is related to the popularity of the ideas of the German romantics, especially the Schlegel brothers, August Wilhelm (1767-1845) and Friedrich (1772-1829). By the 1820's they had reversed the general literary attitude toward Spain's classical theater. Consequently, the nineteenth century, in contrast to the eighteenth, was well disposed toward Spain's great seventeenth-century dramatists.

The German romantics turned their eyes to the past for their aesthetic and philosophic values. In their "opposition to anything rational, their *Sehnsucht* for the unknown," and despite the Protestant origin of many, they were attracted by the Catholic church.[47] The Schlegel brothers, looking backward toward what they considered to be the medieval ideal, were drawn to the God-oriented qualities of Spanish literature. To these two men, the Spanish Golden Age plays presented "an ideal picture of the Middle Ages . . . in a background of picturesque splendor."[48]

The German romantics translated many Spanish plays, particularly those of Calderón,[49] and August Wilhelm Schlegel praises the art of Calderón in his *Lectures on Dramatic Art and Literature*.[50] "If the Spanish theatre consisted only of the works of Lope and a few of his more eminent contemporaries," Schlegel maintained, ". . . we should have to praise it rather for grandeur of design and promising subject than for mature perfection. But Don Pedro Calderón de la Barca now made his appearance, a writer so prolific and diligent, a poet, if ever a man deserved the name." With Calderón the Spanish theater took on perfection, "for only the noblest and most exquisite excellence could satisfy him."[51]

Schlegel's writings on the Spanish theater influenced many Russian writers, critics, and university professors. Professor Ivan Ivanovich Davydov (1794-1863) gave a series of lectures at Moscow University on the history of the Spanish theater based on the Schlegel work.[52] Nikolai Alekseevich Polevoi (1796-1846), the playwright and historian, whose liberal journal, *Moskovskii Telegraf,* "Moscow Telegraph," did much to develop Romanticism in Russia, likened the Spanish theater to that of the Greeks in its immeasurable wealth, and accused the Italians, French, and English of using Spanish works without showing their sources.[53] Orest Somov, the romantic critic, declared: "The Spaniards, it seems, were the founders of romantic taste in dramatic poetry. Lope de Vega, Calderón de la Barca, and other poets adhered to neither tradition nor rules."[54]

One of the first Russian writers to follow the German lead in extolling Calderón was Faddei Venediktovich Bulgarin (1789-1859). A Pole by birth and a soldier of fortune by temperament, he claimed he fought in Napoleon's army in Spain and in 1821 published part of his recollections of the campaign (the veracity of which has been questioned by several important scholars).[55] In the same year he published a work on Spanish literature.[56] Like Professor Ivan Davydov, he was influenced by the Schlegel *Lectures* and praised highly the German contribution.[57] Bulgarin, tracing the development of Spanish theater, notes that:

> Some German scholars consider Calderón greater than all other writers of modern times. He truly deserves to occupy an excellent place among the writers and poets of all nations; and the title of King of the Spanish theater, given to him by his contemporaries, is very just.[58]

Bulgarin follows the lead of Schlegel in praising Lope as a prodigious writer with an inimitable imagination, while pointing out that his verse is "sometimes heavy, bombastic, and careless" and that the "fanaticism, inhumanity, and perverted morality which marked the horrible reign of Philip II are everywhere mixed with the poetic beauty of Lope's compositions."[59] In Bulgarin's view, Lope's theatrical compositions lacked an orderly plan and could not serve as models for any type of composition, their principal virtues being the "customs presented in the most vivid colors."[60]

The poet and dramatist Alexander Sergeevich Pushkin (1799-1837) was attracted by the strong element of national identification which characterized German Romanticism. "There is a way of thinking and feeling," he wrote in 1826, "there is a host of customs, beliefs, and habits which belong exclusively to a given people. Climate, form of government, religion, give each nation its special appearance and are more or less reflected in the mirror of its poetry."[61] He called this national character *narodnost'*, and he particularly detected it in Spanish Golden Age literature.

In giving literary expression to the national self-consciousness which followed in the wake of Napoleon, Pushkin attempts to define *narodnost'* in his essay entitled, "O narodnosti v literature," "On National Character in Literature,":

> For a good while now it has become the custom in our country to speak of national character, to demand national character, to complain about the absence of national character in works of literature—but no one has thought of defining what he means by the word national character.
>
> One of our critics suggests that national character consists of choosing subjects from national history; others see national character in words—they are happy if one uses Russian expressions when speaking Russian....
>
> National character in a writer is a quality which can be wholly appreciated only by one's countrymen; for others it either does not exist

> or may even appear as a defect. An erudite German is indignant at the courtliness of Racine's heroes; a Frenchman laughs on seeing Calderón's Coriolanus challenge his opponent to a duel; however, all of this bears the mark of national character.[62]

In his essay, "O narodnoi drame i drame *Marfa Posadnitsa,*" [Mikhail Petrovich Pogodin (1800-1875)] "On Popular Drama and the Drama *Martha the Governor,*" (1830), Pushkin points out that no matter what theme the great dramatic writers choose, national characteristics appear in their works; thus we have Roman consuls who retain the traits of London aldermen in Shakespeare or of Spanish noblemen in Calderón.[63]

The outstanding literary figure of his day, Pushkin had, in fact, an extensive knowledge of Spain;[64] he knew her theater, which he considered "lyrical, realistic, and replete with *narodnost',*"[65] and he had read and translated from Cervantes.[66] Several of his works have Spanish themes.[67] The critic Nikolai Gavrilovich Chernyshevskii (1828-1889) said that it was Pushkin's great interest in Russian *narodnost'* in literature which led to his interest in foreign works that embodied this quality, among them those of Calderón.[68] Spain's playwrights figure importantly in Pushkin's views on world literature and he discusses them at length in several of his critical writings. To Calderón, however, he assigns a place of enviable eminence, shared only by Shakespeare and Racine, "at an inaccessible height, and their works comprise an eternal subject for our study and delight."[69]

While some Russians were attracted by the aesthetic qualities of Calderón's plays, members of the revolutionary Decembrist groups discovered in his works a message of social protest which served to further their progressive ideas. Vil'gelm Karlovich Kiukhel'beker (1797-1846), the Decembrist writer and poet, took a special interest in Calderón. He taught literature at St. Petersburg Lyceum and at that time counted among his students Konstantin Petrovich Masal'skii (1802-1861), later an author and literary historian, the first to translate *Don Quijote* from Spanish into Russian (1838).[70] Pushkin also was one of Kiukhel'beker's friends.

Kiukhel'beker's initial interest in Spain was political, and in 1820 he published a series of historical essays on contemporary Europe. After the manner of Montesquieu in his *Persian Letters,* Kiukhel'beker employed the device of imaginary letters and travelers to write of Spain's struggle against Bonaparte and the Riego uprising. During his political exile after the Decembrist uprising he read Robertson's *The History of the Reign of the Em-*

peror Charles the Fifth.[71] In 1823, apparently using a French translation, he collaborated with the composer Aleksei N. Verstovskii (1797-1862) in writing an opera, *Liubov' do groba ili grenadskie mavry,* "Love until the Grave, or The Moors of Granada," based on Calderón's *Amar después de la muerte.*[72] Calderón's play depicts the *morisco* uprising near Granada in 1568 which was brutally put down the following year by Don Juan de Austria.[73] Calderón is very sympathetic toward the *moriscos,* because Philip II had deprived them of their rights and liberties, converting them to Catholicism and forcing them to give up their language and customs. The *moriscos* in the Spanish play are brave and have a high sense of personal and national honor. The Russian libretto follows the Calderón plot very closely, although the love interest between the hero, Tuzani, and Clara is reduced in importance.

Kiukhel'beker translated the play to reflect the Russian progressive's desire to combat the despotism of Alexander I. Despite attempts by Peter Andreevich Viazemskii (1792-1878), a friend of both Kiukhel'beker and Pushkin, however, the libretto never passed the censor.[74]

Kiukhel'beker's religious inclinations and love for the Bible and Koran were another reason for his interest in Calderón. Kiukhel'beker speaks of Calderón's religiousness and the other similarities which the Spaniard, in his opinion, shared with the Russian classicist Prince Sergei Alexandrovich Shirinski-Shikhmatov (1802-1846). In a commentary on the Prince's epic poem *Petr Velikii,* "Peter the Great," Kiukhel'beker comments:

> In both we encounter the same strict, constant lay wit and devotion to the faith of their forefathers; in both the same knowledge of religion, the sacraments, and ecclesiastical ritual; both souls are nourished by the Bible and the holy fathers. Their flowery language bears the same stamp of Eastern luxury, their colors are flaming, their thoughts are refined . . . like the poets of Asia, both love to play with words.[75]

Calderón's most important influence on Kiukhel'beker is seen in *Izhorskii, Misteriia,* "Izhorskii, A Mystery Play," (1827-1841).[76] In the "Predislovie," "Prologue," to the first edition of Act I, Kiukhel'beker explains that he has structured the play very much after the Spanish tradition by dividing it into three parts or "khornady in the way the Spaniards divide their dramatic compositions."[77] In *Izhorskii,* though there are no formal act divisions, the three *jornadas* represent earth, hell, and heaven, previously represented by the three-tiered stage used for Medieval mystery plays. Kiukhel'beker applies the theme of the one-act *autos sacramentales* (Man the sinner is saved through the Eucharist, the symbol of Christ's supreme sacrifice).[78] The concepts of earth, hell, and heaven correspond to Izhorskii's fall (brought on by his pacts with the demons, Kikimora and Shishimora), his subsequent suffering because of his lonely existence and evil deeds, and his final salvation through repentance and ascension into heaven.

Kiukhel'beker professes his love for both the Spanish Golden Age and the Romantic Theater with their mixture of the comic and serious, folklore, and popular and religious elements of drama.[79]

In *Izhorskii* Kiukhel'beker includes elements of the supernatural, numerous characters from Russian mythology and folklore, such as Rusalka, Kikimora, Buka, and Russian folk songs and traditions. He even created a demon called Shishimora, a Russian variation of Mephistopheles, according to the critic Vissarion Grigor'evich Belinskii (1801-1848).[80]

Like many Spanish Golden Age plays, *Izhorskii* has two basic levels of interpretation: the romantic and the religious. Izhorskii, a nobleman thirty years old, returns to St. Petersburg after five years of wandering throughout the world. He is bored, disgusted with life, and incapable of loving anyone. He has experienced so many of life's sensations and pleasures that he seeks perversion to satisfy his jaded appetite. At the moment when he contemplates suicide, Buka, the Russian bogy-man and king of the evil spirits, has just condemned two disobedient demons, Kikimora and Shishimora, each to spend a year with Izhorskii in order to bring about his fall (p. 103).

In *jornada* I (Earth), Izhorskii signs a contract with the first devil, but is unaware that Kikimora wants his soul in exchange. Kikimora gives him a philter which causes him to fall in love with Lidiia, the vain and capricious ward of Prince Pronin. Lidiia rejects his love and Izhorskii turns to Shishimora, who promises to win the girl's love for him. Izhorskii does not know that the philter which had made him love Lidiia will, if his love is returned, cause him to stop loving not only Lidiia, but all mankind as well. Thus, in *jornada* II (Hell), after Shishimora has obtained Lidiia's love for him, Izhorskii begins to hate, and, thereafter, to lead an exceedingly dissolute life. He demands that Lidiia consummate their relationship, and she, by refusing, ceases to function as a temptress and becomes instead a Mary figure. He then kills his best friend, Vesnov, and, indirectly, Lidiia. In *jornada* III (Heaven), Izhorskii comes to repent his sins and he attempts to expiate them through good works. Finding this not enough, he sets out on a journey to find God, and he is finally saved through the heavenly intervention of Vesnov and Lidiia.

Kiukhel'beker makes no specific reference to the Spanish Golden Age plays on which he based *Izhorskii.* Nevertheless, there are two Calderón *autos sacramentales (El año santo en Roma* and *El año santo en Madrid)* which bear a very close resemblance to *Izhorskii.* In these two *autos sacramentales* the protagonist is Man, depicted as a wandering pilgrim who, in his youth, has followed the easy path of sin and pleasure, and now is standing on the verge of perdition. He is eventually saved through his own repentance and God's unlimited mercy. The pilgrim's journey represents the life of Man, and is full of allegorical figures such as fame, vice, and appetite, Lucifer's instruments of temptation and condemnation. The pilgrim at first is misled by these sins, but later repents when he realizes that the basic truths of life are faith and love of God.

Izhorskii is given over to pride, appetite, and libertinage. And yet finding nothing to satiate his desire, he wallows in despair and melancholy. His contemplation of suicide reflects his despair and lack of confidence in God. Thanks to the prayers of his two victims, Lidiia and Vesnov, who symbolize the forgiveness of sins and the regaining of Divine Grace, Izhorskii dies reconciled with God.

Lidiia and Vesnov correspond to Calderón's Truth and Good *(El año santo en Roma),* the hero's spiritual brothers, who are faithful and seek the pilgrim's salvation despite his misunderstanding and rejecting them. In *El año santo en Roma,* there is a scene similar to the one in which Izhorskii repents and ascends to heaven.

Although Calderón occupied an important position among the Russian Romantics, Lope also had his followers, who were concerned because so few scholars were aware of his contribution to world theater. They also liked Lope because he was interested in everyday life and people, characteristics which they did not attribute to Calderón's theater.

In 1829 Lope was praised in an article that appeared in *Atenei,* "Atheneum," on the Spanish theater:

> With Lope de Vega a great genius appeared who, like Shakespeare, helped establish a national theater. . . . Lope had greater influence on foreign nations; and France, obligated to him more than others, should repeat with Lord Holland that just praise: without Lope de Vega perhaps the fine creations of Corneille and Molière would not exist and Lope would then be considered the greatest dramatist in Europe.[81]

Pavel Alexsandrovich Katenin (1792-1853), a Decembrist who was well acquainted with Spanish literature and who had translated into Russian Herder's version of the Spanish ballads of the Cid, expressed his preference for Lope. In his essay "O poezii ispanskoi i portugal'skoi," "On Spanish and Portuguese Poetry," published in 1830, Katenin protests against the Calderón vogue launched by the German Romantics. Of Lope and Calderón, Katenin says:

> Cervantes was not successful because the public preferred Lopes [sic] de Vega and Calderón to him and placed them side by side on the theatrical throne. For a long time they sat there without insulting one another and sharing equally the plaudits of their admirers. Lopes [sic], enjoying longevity, even occupied the place of honor when Schlegel and the Germans dared to attack him by trying to remove him and give more room to the younger brother.[82]

He read Calderón, but saw little merit in his plays when compared with those of Lope:

> But not believing anyone and wanting to see for myself, I obtained a two-volume edition of Calderón's selected works. I found eight plays: three comedies, *Los empeños de un acaso, Dicha y desdicha del nombre, La desdicha de la voz;* a pastoral play, *Eco y Narciso;* and four tragedies, *La vida es sueño, La devoción de la cruz, El príncipe constante, La gran Cenobia.* The comedies seemed to me better than the rest, although in them the characters have no personality. They differ only in age and social position; for example, old men, lovers, servants, etc. . . . All people of the same social position are identical. On the other hand, the plot is clever and quickly introduced and their dialogue is more natural than the pearly-voiced shepherds and the characters in the exaggerated tragedies. . . . *La gran Cenobia* is so confused that it is difficult to make out what is going on.[83]

In the opinion of the Soviet scholar Mikhail Pavlovich Alekseev, it was not Calderón's religious themes which attracted Katenin to the Spanish theater, but the humanistic and popular qualities of Lope's historical dramas and comedies of manners.[84]

The conservative elements as well as the revolutionaries approached Spanish themes by way of their interest in German Romanticism, and in the ideas of Schlegel and Herder on the development of individual, racial, and national characteristics.[85] Shishkov praised the Spaniards for precisely these traits.

Schlegel too had written: "If a feeling of religion, loyal heroism, honor, and love be the foundation of romantic poetry, it could not fail to attain its highest development in Spain."[86] Indeed, Uvarov's trinity of autocracy, orthodoxy, and nationalism were embodied, in the Russians' opinion, in the basic characteristics of Spain and were portrayed in the Spanish Golden Age theater. The conservatives could therefore quite freely interpret many aspects of Calderón's work as an expression of their own aims.

Two of the staunchest supporters of official nationalism at this time were Mikhail Pavlovich Pogodin (1800-1875) and Stepan Petrovich Shevyrev (1806-1865).[87] These future Slavophiles both taught at the Moscow University and jointly founded and edited the conservative journal, *Moskvitianin,* "The Moscovite," and the pro-German Romantic journal, *Moskovskii vestnik,* "The Moscow Herald," (1827-1830). They saw the Romantic movement as a guide in the development of Russian nationalist consciousness and wanted to adapt the idealistic philosophy and Romantic aesthetics of the Germans to the intellectual needs of Russian society. During the early days of its publication, *Moskovskii vestnik* announced that Johann Georg Keil's 1827-1830 Leipzig edition of *Las comedias de Don Pedro Calderón de la Barca* in Spanish was appearing and that the first of four volumes had already been received by the editors. This comment accompanied the announcement: "One must recall that in Russia Calderón is known by few, and even then by name only. The editors would like to try to acquaint the Russian reading public with Calderón as soon as possible through the works of Schlegel."[88]

In 1828, *Moskovskii vestnik* published Pogodin's translation of Schlegel's *Lectures on Dramatic Art and Literature,*[89] and a few months later Peter Vasil'evich Kireevskii's (1808-1856) translation of the first act of Calderón's play, *Casa con dos puertas mala es de guardar.* "We consider it our duty to make the following announcement to lovers of letters," the editors wrote on publishing the Calderón play, "P. V. Kireevskii, to whom we are indebted for this piece, plans to translate all of Calderón's best works. Such events are rare in Russia, and surely all our readers, seeing his successful beginning, will wish him success."[90] Apparently Kireevskii changed his plans. He does not appear to have completed the translation, going instead to Germany in the summer of 1829.[91] The poet Nikolai Mikhailovich Iazykov (1803-1846) wrote, however, that Kireevskii was engaged in translating Calderón's *El mágico prodigioso* during 1832 and 1833, and in private papers after his death in 1856 several incomplete translations of Calderón dramas were found.[92]

On January 7, 1831, Vasilii Andreevich Karatygin (1802-1853), a student of Shakhovskoi[93] who had also been director of the repertory section of the Imperial Theater since the reign of Alexander I, chose a Spanish Golden Age play for his benefit performance.[94] In the range and versatility of his roles, Karatygin was considered one of the greatest tragic actors of his time. He excelled in Shakespearean drama and was best known for his Hamlet and Othello.[95] He chose for his benefit performance Calderón's *El médico de su honra,* which he adapted from the German translation of J. D. Gries.[96] Karatygin's abridged version entitled *Krovavaia Ruka,* "The Bloody Hand," underwent several changes.

Calderón's play takes place in the XIV century during the reign of the Spanish king Pedro I. A short while after the marriage of Don Gutierre, an important nobleman from Seville, and Doña Mencía, Don Enrique, King Pedro's brother, appears. Enrique had been in love with Mencía before her marriage and tries to seduce her. Mencía rejects him completely. Nevertheless, Gutierre, obsessed with a mixture of honor and jealousy, soon suspects his innocent wife of infidelity. One night Gutierre blindfolds and kidnaps a surgeon whom he forces to bleed Mencía to death. Upon his release after the foul deed has been done, the surgeon leaves a bloody imprint of his hand on the portal, thereby identifying simultaneously the scene and the perpetrator of the deed. This action inspired the title of the Russian version of the play. When Pedro finds out about this murder, he not only condones it, but suggests that Gutierre marry Doña Leonor, his former fiancée.[97]

In Spanish criticism there are two schools of interpretation for this play. One group believes that Calderón approved of Gutierre's conduct because it would urge women to be faithful to their husbands.[98] A second group believes that the work is a protest against the inhuman and pathological cruelty of which Calderón's contemporaries were capable.[99] Obviously the Spanish public understood the play and learned something from it, and was not surprised by Mencía's death. Dmitrii Konstantinovich Petrov, the Russian Hispanist, has argued that such murders were a reflection of Spanish reality.[100]

In translating the work, Karatygin, whether to avoid the censor's veto or because of his own moral sense, changed the ending of the Calderón play. Whereas in the Spanish original Gutierre marries Doña Leonor and continues his life at court, in the Russian version Gutierre falls upon his sword in remorse, as the final curtain comes down.[101] Murder for any reason is usually punished in Russian literature, either by the state or the murderer's own conscience; but this change in Karatygin's version may have been because of official censorship. In 1835, for example, Lermontov's play *Masquerade,* a work on the Othello theme, did not pass the censors because the protagonist Arbenin went unpunished after murdering his wife.[102]

While the Spanish public could understand the Calderón play, the Russians could not because of "the gloominess of the plot."[103] The Russian critic for the journal *Severnaia pchela,* "The Northern Bee," was horrified by Gutierre's crime:

> A powerful jealousy overcame Gutierre. His mind and reason thought only of bloody revenge. And Gutierre went through the streets of the Castillian [sic] city of Seville and found a surgeon. Blindfolding him very tightly, he brought him to his palace and, threatening him with certain death, he ordered him to bleed Mencía to death—an unheard of evil deed![104]

King Pedro's reaction and attitude toward the murder also were unintelligible to the Russians. Pedro, instead of punishing the crime, praises it. As the critic said, "The king judged the criminal and the sentence was unheard of: Gutierre was to marry Isabella!" [sic][105] Because of Nicholas' attitude toward the presentation of the king on the stage, *Krovavaia ruka* constitutes an anomaly. One can only wonder how it passed the censors.

Alexander Vasil'evich Nikitenko (1805-1877), the Crown Censor instrumental in bringing about the reforms of the censorship code under Alexander II, has provided us with a spectator's opinion of the Calderón play, which he saw as a young man. His opinion differs radically from the review in *Severnaia pchela.* Apparently he was well enough acquainted with Calderón's work to compare one play with another, for he noted in his diary:

> I was at the theater and saw the new play, *Krovavaia ruka,* a tragedy by Calderón, translated by Karatygin. Because of its theme, this play does not attain Calderón's usual heights. It is based on one human passion: jealousy, which is described, however, with all the power of the great writer. Frenzies of jealousy—that is the basis of the whole tragedy. Our public received the play quite coldly, in spite of Karatygin's magnificent performance. This is natural, since we are not capable of loving, consequently we are not capable of being jealous. We cannot understand the fire of the Spaniard whose honor and heart have been simultaneously offended. Alas, the concept of honor is too knightly for us.[106]

While it is true that Russia experienced nothing like the Western concept of chivalry and knightly honor,[107] Nikitenko's observations seem remarkably naïve and inconsistent with Russian society. He was apparently either unaware of or unwilling to admit that the Russian attitude toward conjugal honor was more humane than the Spanish. The Russians rarely, if ever, killed an unfaithful wife, and the killing of a wife on the grounds of mere suspicion was completely incongruous with the society in which Nikitenko lived. The point of honor was an affair between the husband and the offender, and of course such duels were frequent. On the other hand, they were not acts of vengeance against an innocent victim, but rather an affair of justice against a guilty man. Perhaps the finest example of such a concept of personal and conjugal honor was Pushkin's fatal duel.[108]

In 1839 Iakov Grigorevich Brianskii (1790-1853) presented for his benefit performance Calderón's *El postrer duelo de España,* translated into Russian as *Posledniaia duel' v Ispanii.* Calderón's play, based on an event from the early reign of the Spanish monarch Charles V, has a simple plot.

Two young noblemen from Zaragoza, Don Pedro Torrellas and Don Jerónimo de Ansá, are in love with Doña Violante, who prefers the former. In a secret duel for Violante, Torrellas drops his sword, but Ansá offers his opponent a chance to save his life. Torrellas accepts the offer provided Ansá tells no one. A peasant, Benito, secretly witnesses the duel and tells everyone that Torrellas accepted Ansá's offer to live. When this news reaches Violante's ears she accuses Torrellas of being a dishonorable coward and demands that he challenge Ansá to a public duel. Carlos V, who is passing through Zaragoza, suggests that they fight in Valladolid where the emperor is going. When all the preparations for the duel have been made and the two nobles are ready to start, Carlos V stands up and declares that the duel is over and that from then on there will be no more dueling in Spain.[109]

Just as he opposed dueling in *El alcalde de sí mismo* because of the suffering it brought, Calderón wrote *El postrer duelo de España* in protest against dueling. Brianskii's choice of this particular play is intriguing, because it was his first opportunity to select his own play since Pushkin's death in a duel of honor with the French emigré Georges d'Anthès on January 29, 1837.[110] Brianskii was a friend and admirer of Pushkin; he had performed his play *Motsart i Salieri,* "Mozart and Salieri," for his benefit performance of January 7, 1832. His choice of the Calderón work may well have been a protest against Pushkin's death and a plea to Nicholas to enact and enforce legislation against dueling.

Dueling, although frowned upon in Russia at that time, was, nevertheless, a common occurrence, and little was done by the authorities to prevent it. Pushkin's death was cause for national mourning in Russia and many protests were voiced by his countrymen. Lermontov's poem, "Smert' Poeta," "The Death of a Poet," was a direct plea to Nicholas to punish the evildoers. Nicholas punished Lermontov instead, exiling him on the ground that he dared address his plea to the tsar instead of through the proper channels.[111] Brianskii's method of protest, if such it was, was certainly more discreet.

Pushkin's contemporaries were very much aware of his highly developed sense of personal honor; he and his compatriots carried this concept of honor to the realm of marital infidelity. In connection with these two Calderón plays some comments should be made on this theme in Pushkin's life and creative art.

Although in many of his earlier works, Pushkin's heroines are unfaithful, after his marriage to the flirtatious Natal'ia Goncharova on February 18, 1831, the poet emphasizes conjugal fidelity. The best examples of this change are Zemfira in *Tsygane,* "The Gypsies," (1824), and Tatiana, the faithful wife in *Evgenii Onegin,* "Eugene Onegin," (1833).

In many ways Pushkin resembled Don Pedro Torrellas, the hero of *Posledniaia duel' v Ispanii,* especially in his highly developed sense of honor. He was, however, utterly different from Calderón's Don Gutierre. The Spaniard's lack of faith in his wife and almost religious fanaticism in his attitude toward his honor border on the pathological. Pushkin was convinced of Natal'ia's fidelity and innocence. The person to punish was the culprit, d'Anthès. This is the essential difference in the concept of honor and conjugal faithfulness of seventeenth-century Spain and nineteenth-century Russia.

Posledniaia duel' v Ispanii was given on January 10, 1839, at the Alexandrinskii Theater and received a highly favorable review from the theater critic of the *Literaturnye Pribavleniia k Russkomu invalidu,* "Literary Supplements to the *Russian Invalid.*" The public was treated to Spanish music and dancing as well as to the ritual and pomp of what it believed to be medieval knighthood and pageantry: "This play . . . ," the reviewer wrote:

> has many fine qualities, especially for the Russians, who did not participate in medieval tournaments and are not familiar with all the customs and rituals which constituted knighthood's glorious age. In this play, Calderón poetically depicted to the smallest detail all the rituals observed in public tourney.[112]

The reviewer gives a detailed plot summary and, after praising the performers, he closes the review with a few remarks on the poet: "There are extremely funny and terribly touching scenes in the play. Calderón, like Shakespeare, loves contrast. He often softens with light humor a moving moment produced by a tragic scene."[113]

Another critic, Faddei Bulgarin, in contrast to his previously expressed opinion of Calderón, took an opposite view of the play. In a sarcastic and disparaging review he reported that "the audience strongly disliked the play and showed its displeasure." The play itself had "a weak plot, contradictions, improbabilities, and continual anachronisms." He also belittled the acting.[114] Bulgarin was one of Pushkin's bitterest enemies, and to judge from his review of *Posledniaia duel' v Ispanii,* one might well believe that he had reason to think Brianskii had indeed chosen it as a protest against Pushkin's death.

Another Golden Age play, Francisco de Rojas Zorrilla's *Del rey abajo, ninguno,* was performed at the Alexandrinskii Theater in St. Petersburg from December 19 to 23, 1837, and January 3 to 16 of the following year.[115] It was translated by Shakhovskoi, [116] who had dedicated his time and efforts to introducing Western plays to the Russian public. A firm believer in Uvarov's concept of official nationalism, he often adapted his productions of foreign works to contemporary tastes and tsarist censorship; Russian proverbs and popular expressions often replaced those of the original work, and his translations differed in detail if not in essence.[117] Shakhovskoi translated from both the English and the French,[118] and, in 1821, he wrote *Bakalavr Salamanskii,* "The Bachelor from Salamanca," which he took from the play on a Spanish theme by Lesage entitled *Le Bachelior de Salamanque.*[119] From this period on he became interested in what the Soviet specialist on Shakhovskoi, A. A. Gozenpud, calls "chivalrous and exotic themes."[120]

Some scholars have attributed to Shakhovskoi the first adaptation of a Spanish Golden Age play (from Calderón) during the first half of the nineteenth century.[121] The play, given as a benefit performance by the actress Ezhova on October 28, 1829, was entitled: *Roza i Rozaliia ili kak na svete vse prevratno, romanticheskaia komediia-vodevil' v 3 sutkakh v podrazhanie Ispanskomy teatry,* "Rosa and Rosalia, or How Wrong Everything is, a Vaudeville Comedy in Three Acts, an Imitation of the Spanish Theater."[122] A single review appeared in the press, according to which not more than a score of friends chose to attend and those perhaps less by choice than out of obligation to the beneficiary. "The less said, the better," commented the anonymous critic in *Severnaia pchela,*[123] adding that the best part of the play was the Russian proverbs Shakhovskoi employed.

The play's title page does not correspond to any Calderón play either in the names of the characters or the place of action. The director of the Leningrad State Theatrical Library, Nadezhda Vladimirovna Piatkova, quotes Gozenpud as saying that it is an original work by Shakhovskoi and consequently has no relationship with any Calderón play.[124]

Rojas Zorrilla's play deals with important themes in Spanish Golden Age theater—profound loyalty to the king and a deep sense of conjugal love and honor. It appears likely, however, that it was the former theme which prompted the monarchist Shakhovskoi to adapt the play and have it performed.

The play describes the vicissitudes of García del Castañar, one of Alfonso XI's most loyal subjects. During an incognito visit by the king to García's home, one of the king's aides, Don Mendo, falls in love with and tries, unsuccessfully, to seduce García's wife, Blanca. García mistakes him for the king and, because of his loyalty to the king, does not intervene. When García marches off with Alfonso's army, Mendo returns to García's home to continue his pursuit of Blanca. García returns home also, and, rather than be dishonored, burns his house and tries to murder his innocent wife. Fortunately, he recognizes Mendo and kills him instead.[125]

The Shakhovskoi production introduced Spanish songs and dances, accompanied by castanets, to the Russian stage. These innovations were an early attempt to provide an authentic background.[126] The critic of *Severnaia pchela* gave a brief resumé of the Spanish Golden Age theater in general:

> There is no doubt that of all European dramatic literature, the Spanish is the most fecund. The treasures of the Spanish theater have become proverbial, and many of the greatest writers of France and Germany became famous by using Spanish sources. . . . Very few people know the Spanish theater, which in spirit, form, and origin differs greatly from what is understood by drama in other countries.[127]

Then the reviewer praised the talent of Shakhovskoi in adapting Spanish plays to the requirements and conditions of the contemporary Russian stage and spoke highly of the performances.[128]

The work of still another Spanish Golden Age playwright appeared during the reign of Nicholas I. On January 29 and February 2, 1834, the St. Petersburg Mikhailovskii Theater presented Agustín Moreto's *El desdén con el desdén,* which in Russian was called *Donna Diana.*[129] In the nonpolitical Moreto work Diana is a spoiled and pampered society girl who finds all her suitors unfit. She finally falls in love with Don Carlos, a suitor who overcomes her disdain with his disdain.[130]

The play was adapted from a German translation made by Shreyvogel West, director of the Vienna Burg Theater.[131] It met with scant success, receiving but one review, which was unfavorable:

> The play's weaknesses consisted of the long-winded scenes and stiff dialogues. The play was created in Spain and adapted in Germany, and this version was the source of the Russian rendition. Doubtless no one would ask us our opinion on the translation, but the dignity of the play, which depends upon the roles of Donna Diana, Don Cesar, and Perrin, is still palpable in the Russian version.[132]

By the end of Nicholas I's reign many articles had appeared discussing Spanish literature from its origin to the present. The aim of these articles was to give to the limited reading public a general idea of the nature of Spanish literature. For the most part, the articles were translations of French, Spanish, English, and German studies and were usually of a rather general nature. Their authors did not intend to make original contributions, for original research on Spanish literature did not appear in Russia until the end of the century. However, they increased the interest and curiosity of the Russian intellectual and led to more profound studies in Spanish literature.

On the other hand, works by Russian writers dealing with other aspects of Spanish life and history, as well as plays and novels based on Spanish themes, became widespread and eventually laid the foundation for further interest in the theater. The greatest influence on Russia's understanding of Spain was Vasilii Petrovich Botkin's (1810-1869) *Pis'ma ob Ispanii* (1845), "Letters about Spain."[133] Botkin wrote these epistolary essays while traveling in Spain during the Carlist Wars. They are a classic of their kind because of Botkin's penetrating insight into the history and culture of Spain.[134]

The composer Glinka gathered musical themes during his Spanish travels and greatly influenced future Russian writers and composers by his predilection for Spain. Glinka's interest in Spain's culture was not limited to music. Like many of his contemporaries, he was attracted by the classical theater, especially by Calderón and Lope. In a letter from Madrid written to his brother-in-law, in November, 1845, he said: "Si j'ai une certaine facilité à parler l'espagnol je suis bien loin de posséder la langue. A Granada je prendrai un maître de langue, pour m'aider à lire des poètes anciens dramatiques, tels que Calderón de la Barca, Lope de Vega."[135]

Alexander Ivanovich Herzen (1812-1870), the well-known Russian intellectual and political thinker, was very much impressed by the Spanish concept of justice. Having read a French translation of Calderón's *El Alcalde de Zalamea* a few years before his exile, he noted in his diary on July 9, 1844: "Great is the Spanish peasant if in him exists such a concept of justice, an element which is not at all developed in us, either among our peasantry or among any of us. In Russia, one either bears an injury like a slave or avenges it like a mutinous serf."[136]

Ivan Sergeevich Turgenev (1818-1883) became interested in Spain and her literature early in his career and maintained this interest throughout most of his life. This was first indicated by his short play entitled *Neostorozhnost'*, "Indiscretion," (1843), which dealt with Spanish customs and was written in the manner of Prosper Merimée's *Théâtre de Clara Gazul* (1825).[137]

On October 28, 1843, the twenty-five-year-old Turgenev met Louis Viardot, the noted Hispanist and translator of Cervantes, and, a few days later, Viardot's young wife, Paulina García, a leading singer with the Italian Opera of Paris, on tour in Russia.[138] Later, while in Paris, Turgenev entered the García-Viardot circle, where new horizons opened for his interest in Spain and her culture. Paulina García-Viardot was the daughter of the famous Spanish tenor Manuel García, whose family had taken up residence in Paris. The Spanish community of Paris and the García-Viardot library greatly facilitated Turgenev's knowledge of Spanish. Turgenev and the García-Viardot's were intimate friends until the writer's death.[139]

From among Spain's writers Turgenev showed a marked preference for Calderón and Cervantes. His interest in the former stems from the general Russian interest in Calderón and in Hegel, Feurbach, and Goethe, men very much influenced by the Spanish playwright. Turgenev studied these Germans during his university days in Berlin (1838-1839).[140] In his personal library there was a copy of an 1838 Paris edition of *Teatro escogido de Calderón de la Barca*.[141] In 1860 Turgenev wrote his famous essay on Hamlet and Don Quijote,[142] and in 1866 he translated Cervantes' short novel *Rinconete y Cortadillo*.[143]

During one of his trips to Paris, Turgenev undertook to learn the Spanish language. He wrote to Madame Viardot on December 19, 1847:

> Je lis maintenant Calderón avec acharnement (en espagnol, comme de raison); c'est le plus grand poète dramatique catholique qu'il y ait eu, comme Shakespeare, le plus humain, le plus antichrétien. Sa *De-*

> *voción de la Cruz* est un chef-d'oeuvre. Cette foi immuable, triomphante, sans l'ombre d'un doute ou même d'une réflexion, vous ecrase à force de grandeur et de majesté, malgré tout ce que cette doctrine a de répulsif et d'atroce. Ce néant de tout ce qui constitue la dignité de l'homme devant la volonté divine, l'indifference pour tout ce que nous appelons vertu ou vice avec laquelle la grâce se répand sur son élu—est encore un triomphe pour l'esprit humain; car l'être que proclame ainsi avec tant d'audace son propre néant s'élève par cela même à l'égal de cette Divinité fantastique, dont il se reconnaît être le jouet. Et cette Divinité—c'est encore l'oeuvre de ses mains. Cependant, je préfère Prométhée, je préfère Satan, le type de la révolte de l'individualité. Tout atome que je suis, c'est moi qui suis mon maître; je veux la vérité et non le salut; je l'attends de mon intelligence et non de la grace.[144]

On December 25, in another letter to Madame Viardot he says:

> Depuis la dernière lettre que je vous ai écrite, j'ai encore lu un drame de Calderón, *La vida es sueño.* C'est une des conceptions dramatiques les plus grandioses que je connaisse. Il y règne une énergie sauvage, un dédain sombre et profonde de la vie, une hardiesse de pensées étonnante, à côté du fanatisme catholique le plus inflexible. Le Sigismond de Calderón (le personnage principal), c'est le Hamlet espagnol, avec toute la différence qu'il y a entre le Midi et le Nord. Hamlet est plus réfléchi, plus subtil, plus philosophique; le caractère de Sigismond est simple, nu et pénétrant comme un épée; l'un n'agit pas à force d'irrésolution, de doute et de réflexions; l'autre agit—car son sang méridional le pousse—mais tout en agissant, il sait bien que la vie n'est qu'un songe.
>
> Je viens de commencer maintenant le "Faust" espagnol, *El mágico prodigioso;* je suis tout encalderonise. En lisant ces belles productions, on sent qu'elles ont poussé naturellement sur un sol fertile et vigoureux; leur gout, leur parfum est simple; le graillon littéraire ne s'y fait pas sentir. Le drame en Espagne a été la dernière et la plus belle expression du catholicisme näïf et de la société qu'il avait formée à son image.[145]

Curiously, outside of his correspondence with Madame Viardot, Turgenev mentions neither Calderón nor his works.[146] Nevertheless, an analysis of

Fathers and Sons (1862) and its nihilist hero Bazarov shows a certain resemblance to the figure of Eusebio in *La devoción de la cruz.*

One of the most important religious questions in Calderón's Spain centered on the problem of how one could achieve salvation. Some believed that salvation was possible only through good works. Others believed that man, regardless of his conduct on earth, could achieve salvation if he had an unfailing faith in God's mercy. The latter is the central theme of Calderón's *La devoción de la cruz.*

For Eusebio, God's mercy and forgiveness is symbolized by the cross; and his birth, life, death, and salvation are directly related to this symbol of Christ's sacrifice. Eusebio has a blind and unwavering faith in the cross which will save him despite his murders, rapes, and robberies.

He becomes an outlaw as a result of a duel in which he unwittingly kills his own brother, and later almost has incestuous relations with his beloved Julia who, unbeknownst to him, is his twin sister. Eusebio flees Julia's bed when he sees a cross, identical to his own birthmark, on her breast.

What makes Eusebio and Bazarov alike is their faith in a given system as a panacea for all of mankind's earthly ills. Eusebio believes in an irrational and subjective Christianity; Bazarov, the atheist who denies every tradition important to man, in rational and objective natural sciences. On several occasions Eusebio places a cross on his victims' graves in order to guarantee their salvation. And as Eusebio is about to die he speaks to his confessor Alberto:

> Ven a donde mis pecados/confiese, Alberto, que son/más que del mar las arenas/y los átomos del sol./Tanto con el cielo puede/de la Cruz la devoción![147]

Bazarov wants to help man achieve an earthly salvation through the sciences and the reformation of society. Odintsova remarks, "Then in your opinion, there's no difference between stupid and intelligent people, between good and evil?" Bazarov's answer:

> No, there is; just as there is between the sick and the healthy. The consumptive's lungs are not in the same condition as yours and mine, although identical in form. We know approximately what produces bodily diseases, while moral sicknesses are produced by bad education, by all the nonsense with which people's heads are crammed from infancy on—by the outrageous state of society, in brief. Reform society and there will be no sicknesses.[148]

When Turgenev, in his letter to Viardot on December 19, 1847, refers to Eusebio's faith, "Cette foi immuable, triomphante, sans l'ombre d'un doute ou même d'une réflexion, vous écrase à force de grandeur et de majesté, malgré tout ce que cette doctrine a de répulsif et d'atroce,"[149] he almost describes Bazarov's character as well.

Although Turgenev emphasizes mankind's earthly salvation through material progress, he also utilizes the theme of eternal salvation through the mysteries of the cross. This theme is presented in terms of the struggle between the spirit and the flesh, with the spirit, symbolized by the cross, the ultimate victor.

Turgenev's Princess R., like Calderón's Julia after she flees the convent, is given over to the pleasures of the flesh. But she is constantly tormented by a religious fervor equal in intensity to her carnal desires. One of her lovers, Pavel Petrovich, Arkady's uncle, gives her a ring, telling her, "That sphinx—is you."[150] The two soon separate for a decade and at the beginning of 1848 (the period of Turgenev's infatuation with Calderón) she dies on the verge of insanity. Soon, "a messenger brought him a package containing the ring he had given the princess. She had drawn the sign of a cross on the sphinx and ordered the messenger to tell him that the cross was the key to the enigma."[151] Calderón's Julia achieves salvation when she repents and is forgiven at the foot of the cross which covers Eusebio's grave.[152] Turgenev, in combining a spiritual and earthly theme in a single work, utilizes a technique characteristic of many Spanish Golden Age playwrights and adapts it to the Russian intellectual and political atmosphere.

By the end of the Crimean War many Russian intellectuals felt a certain affinity with Spain. Seeing Spain in a new perspective during the Peninsular War, becoming more and more aware of her cultural past, many Russians saw the possibilities of spiritual enrichment through her dramatic literature. Juan de Valera, the Spanish writer and critic, secretary to the Spanish Ambassador in Russia in 1857, wrote from St. Petersburg describing the extensive Spanish library of the Russian bibliophile, Sergei Aleksandrovich Sobolevskii (1803-1870);[153] the Real Academia Española edition of *Don Quijote* and other Spanish classics in the library of Prince Mikhail Alexandrovich Galitzin (1804-1860);[154] and the wealth of Spanish art in the Hermitage.[155] He then names paintings by Antolínez, Ribera, and Velázquez, and mentions canvases by Coello, Juan de Juanes, Baltasar del Prado, Ribalta, and many others. These paintings took on an additional significance in the Russian theatrical world in the following decades, for they were used as guides for authenticating Spanish dress used in the theater.

Nor was the image created by the Peninsular War forgotten; for some fifty years after the event, Valera wrote, "Many here have told me that the defense of Sevastopol can only be compared with that of Zaragoza."[156]

Notes

1. Daniel Balmuth, "Censorship in Russia: 1848-1855," (Ph. D. Diss., Cornell, 1959), p. 9.
2. Sergei Danilov, *Russkii dramaticheskii teatr XIX veka* (Moscow, 1957), I, 134.
3. Nikolai V. Drizen, "Ocherki teatral'noi tsenzury dvukh epokh (1801-1856)," *Istoricheskii vestnik,* LXXXI (July, 1900), 558.
4. Danilov, *Russkii,* p. 135.
5. Balmuth, p. 9.
6. Danilov, *Russkii,* p. 137.
7. *Sbornik postanovlenii i rasporiazhenii po tsenzure, 1720-1862* (St. Petersburg, 1862), pp. 170, 313.
8. Sydney Monas, *The Third Section* (Cambridge, Mass., 1961), p. 137.
9. Boris V. Varneke, *History of the Russian Theatre,* trans. Boris Brasol (New York, 1951), pp. 239-240.
10. Danilov, *Russkii,* p. 124.
11. Varneke, p. 241.
12. P. N. Stolpianskii, "Piesy ispanskago teatra na peterburgskoi stsene nikolaevskoi epokhy," *Ezhegodnik imperatorskikh teatrov,* I (1912), 48.
13. Nevertheless, the German actor Wilhelm Kunst performed Calderón's *La vida es sueño* in German at the Mikhailovskii Theater in St. Petersburg in 1841. *Repertuar russkago teatra* (1841), "Smes'," II, 29.
14. Varneke, pp. 159-160.
15. Mikhail Pavlovich Alekseev, *Ocherki istorii ispano-russkikh literaturnykh otnoshenii XVI-XIX vv.* (Leningrad, 1964), p. 101.
16. Ibid., pp. 101-103.
17. Alexander Semenovich Shiskov, *Sobranie sochinenii i perevodov* (St. Petersburg, 1827), I, 178.
18. Edward C. Thaden, *Conservative Nationalism in Nineteenth-Century Russia* (Seattle: The University of Washington Press, 1965), p. 20.
19. Alekseev, p. 96.
20. Stepan S. Volk, *Istoricheskie vzgliady Dekabristov* (Moscow, 1958), p. 271.
21. Gavriil Romanovich Derzhavin, *Sochineniia* (St. Petersburg, 1866), III, 433.
22. Denis V. Davydov, "Opyt teorii partizanskikh deistvii dlia russkikh voisk," *Sochineniia* (Moscow, 1861), I, 23-26.
23. Alekseev, p. 106.
24. *Osada Saragossy,* translated from the English, *Syn otechestva,* 1812, Part II, 21-33, 112-121, 206-216, 245-258.
25. Alekseev, p. 106.

26. Facundo Goñi, *Tratado de las relaciones internacionales de España* (Madrid, 1848), p. 151. Alekseev, p. 99.
27. Joseph de Maistre, *Correspondance Diplomatique* (Paris, 1861), I, 326-328, 332-333, II, 339.
28. Alekseev, pp. 109-110.
29. Leo Tolstoy, *War and Peace,* trans. Constance Garnett (New York, N.D.), Part 10, Chapter XXXVIII.
30. Alekseev, p. 111.
31. Alexander Trachevskii, *Ispaniia deviatnadtsatogo veka* (Moscow, 1872), p. 280.
32. *Russkii biograficheskii slovar' Brokgauza i Efrona,* XX, 347-349.
33. "Perepiska kniazia D. I. Dolgorukago," *Russkii arkhiv,* V (1915), 118.
34. Ibid.
35. Peter M. Irving, *Life and Letters of Washington Irving* (New York, 1862), II, 437.
36. Dmitrii Konstantinovich Petrov, *Rossiia i Nikolai I v stikhotvoreniiakh Espronsedy i Rossetti* (St. Petersburg, 1909), p. 6.
37. Peter I. Chaadaev, *Sochineniia i Pis'ma,* ed. M. O. Gershenzon (Moscow, 1914), II, 53.
38. *The Letters of Alexander Pushkin,* trans. and ed. J. Thomas Shaw (Bloomington, Indiana, 1963), I, 165.
39. William B. Edgerton, "Pushkin, Mickiewicz, and a Migratory Epigram," *The Slavic and East European Journal,* X (Spring, 1966), 1-9.
40. Alexander Sergeevich Pushkin, *Polnoe sobranie sochinenii v 10 tomakh* (Moscow, 1949), II, 242.
41. Ibid., II, 431.
42. "Zapiski A. S. Shishkova," *Chteniia v Obshchestve istorii drevnostei rossiiskikh pri imperatorskom Moskovskom universitete,* 7-9 (1869), 105.
43. Alexander Sergeevich Pushkin, *Eugene Onegin,* trans. and ed. Vladimir Nabokov (New York, 1964), III, 361.
44. Alekseev, p. 137.
45. Petrov, p. 53.
46. Alekseev, pp. 139-140.
47. Madelaine Ashton, "A Comparative Study of the Romantic Movement in Germany and France" (Ph. D. Diss., Urbana, Illinois, 1930), p. 10.
48. Leonard Ashley Willoughby, *The Romantic School in Germany* (Oxford: Oxford University Press, 1931), p. 64.
49. H. Breymann, *Calderón-Studien* (Munich, 1905), passim.
50. Arturo Farinelli, *Lope de Vega en Alemania,* trad. Enrique Massaquero, (Barcelona, 1936), p. 41.
51. August Wilhelm Schlegel, *Dramatic Art and Literature, Lecture XXIX,* trans. John Black, second edition (London, 1902), p. 494.
52. Ivan I. Davydov, *Chtenie LVI* (Moscow, 1838), 237-248.
53. *Moskovskii telegraf,* Chast' VII (1826), 321-322.
54. N. I. Mordovchenko, *Russkaia kritika pervoi chetverti XIX veka* (Moscow, 1959), p. 191.
55. Faddei Bulgarin, *Vospominaniia ob Ispanii* (St. Petersburg, 1823). Alekseev, p. 113.

56. Faddei Bulgarin "Vzgliad na istoriiu ispanskoi literatury," *Syn otechestva* (1821), Chast' 72, 289-321, Chast' 73, 3-21.
57. Ibid., Chast' 72, 289.
58. Ibid., Chast' 73, 6.
59. Ibid., 5.
60. Ibid.
61. Alexander Sergeevich Pushkin, *Polnoe sobranie sochinenii* (Moscow-Leningrad, 1937-1959), XI, 40.
62. Ibid.
63. Ibid., 177.
64. K. N. Derzhavin, "Zaniatiia Pushkina ispanskim iazykom," *Slavia,* XIII (1934), 114-120.
65. A. O. Smirnova, *Zapiski* (St. Petersburg, 1895), I, 157-158.
66. Jack Weiner and Evelynne Meyerson, "Cervantes' *La Gitanilla* and Pushkin's *Tsygane,*" *Indiana Slavic Studies,* IV (1964), 209-214 and *Nueva Revista de Filología Hispánica,* XVII (1963), 282-287.
67. Robert C. Stephenson, "The English Sources of Pushkin's Spanish Themes," University of Texas Publications, *Studies in English,* XVIII (1938), 85-111.

Pushkin's play on the Don Juan theme, *Kamennyi Gost',* "The Stone Guest," is mainly based on Molière's *Le festin de pierre.* Nevertheless, Boris Tomashevskii, the Soviet scholar, finds traces of Villiers' play also. See V. Z. Krzhevskii, "Ob obraze Don Zhuana Pushkina, Mol'era i Tirso de Molina," "On the Don Juan Figure in Pushkin, Molìere, and Tirso de Molina," *Stat'i o zarubezhnoi literatury* (Moscow-Leningrad, 1960), pp. 208-215. Alekseev, pp. 163-164. Boris Tomashevskii, *Pushkin i Frantsiia* (Leningrad, 1960), p. 289.

Pushkin did, however, know of Tirso's play. D. F. Fikel'mont, one of the visitors to the A. O. Smirnova's literary circle, suggested (1826?) to Pushkin that he read the Spanish Don Juan play. A. O. Smirnova, ,I 84. The Soviet Hispanist N. I. Balashov has discussed the possibility of indirect Spanish influence on Pushkin's *Boris Godunov.* In a detailed study, Balashov states that a play by Pushkin's contemporary, Andrei A. Zhandr, *Ventseslav,* was a source for *Boris Godunov.* Balashov bases his conclusion on the play's similarities in versification, dialogue, theme of popular revolt, and the criticism of tyranny.

Zhandr's play was adapted from the work of the French playwright Jean de Routrou, *Wenseslav,* which in turn is based on Francisco de Rojas' *No hay ser padre siendo rey.* This play deals with revolt against royal authority in early seventeenth-century Poland. N. I. Balashov, "Pushkin i ispanskaia drama XVII v. na slavianskie temy," *Russko-evropeiskie literaturnye sviazi* (Leningrad, 1966), pp. 27-38.

68. N. G. Chernyshevskii, *Polnoe sobranie sochinenii* (Moscow, 1949), II, 429-430.
69. Alexander Sergeevich Pushkin, *Polnoe sobranie sochinenii* (Moscow-Leningrad, 1937-1959), XI, 177.
70. *Migel' de Servantes, Bibliografiia russkikh perevodov i kriticheskoi literatury na russkom iazyke: 1763-1957,* comp. A. D. Umikian (Moscow, 1959), p. 47.
71. *Dnevnik V. K. Kiukhel'bekera* (Leningrad, 1929), p. 169.
72. V. A. Bochkarev, "Neopublikovannaia tragediia-opera V. K. Kiukhel'-bekera, "Liubov' do groba ili grenadskie mavry," "An Unpublished Tragic Opera

by V. K. Kiukhel'beker, *Life After Death or The Moors of Granada,*" *Izvestiia akademii nauk SSR,* otdelenie literatury i iazyka, XIX (November-December, 1960), vypusk, 6, 523.

73. Ibid.

74. Ibid., p. 527.

75. V. K. Kiukhel'beker, "Analiz poemy kniazia S. A. Shirinskago-Shikhmatova "Petr Velikii," *Syn otechestva,* CII (1825), 365-366.

76. K. V. Kiukhel'beker, *Dramaticheskie proizvedeniia,* ed. Iu. Tynianov (Leningrad, 1939), II, 473-474. Izhorskii is the name of Kiukhel'beker's Byronic hero. I would like to thank Professor Lydia Slavatinsky of Queens College (CUNY) and Professor Gabriela Roepke of the Juilliard School of Music for their generous help on the section about Kiukhel'beker.

77. Ibid., 474.

78. Bruce W. Wardropper, *Introducción al teatro religioso del siglo de oro* (Madrid, 1953), pp. 15-16.

79. Kiukhel'beker, *Dramaticheskie,* II, 475.

80. Vissarion Grigor'evich Belinskii, *Polnoe sobranie sochinenii* (Moscow, 1958), I, 230.

81. *Atenei,* Chast' 4 (1829), 130-131.

82. P. A. Katenin, *Literaturnaia gazeta,* II, No. 50 (September 3, 1830), p. 112.

83. Ibid.

84. Alekseev, pp. 157-158.

85. Thaden, pp. 5, 19.

86. Schlegel, p. 501.

87. Shevyrev considered Calderón to be greater than Shakespeare because the Spaniard, "Expresses the idea of the apotheosis of Christianity." *Istoriia poesii* (St. Petersburg, 1887), p. 53.

88. *Moskovskii vestnik,* Chast' V (1827), 108.

89. *Moskovskii vestnik,* Chast' IX (1828), 154-166, 287-294.

90. *Moskovskii vestnik,* Chast' XI (1828), 234-271.

91. M. O. Gershenzon, *Russkie Propilei* (Moscow, 1915-1919), I, 159.

92. *Pis'ma P. V. Kireevskogo k N. M. Iazykovu,* ed. M. K. Azadovskii (Moscow, 1935), pp. 21-22. "Iz perepiski N. M. Iazykova s V. B. Komovskim: 1831-1833," *Literaturnoe Nasledstvo,* XIX-XXI (Moscow, 1935), 75.

93. *Ezhegodnik imperatorskikh teatrov; prilozhenie* (1903-1904), p. 7.

94. Petr Andreevich Karatygin, *Zapiski* (Leningrad, 1930), II, 412.

95. E. Finkel'shtein, "O Karatygine," *Teatr,* N. 5 (May, 1941), p. 108.

96. Karatygin, loc. cit.

97. Don Pedro Calderón de la Barca, *Obras Completas* (Madrid, 1960), I, 313-348.

98. Don Pedro Calderón de la Barca, *El médico de su honra,* ed. C. A. Jones (Oxford: Oxford University Press, 1961), xii.

99. Ibid, xiii.

100. D. K. Petrov, *Ocherki bytovogo teatra Lope de Vegi* (St. Petersburg, 1901), passim. See his *Zametki po staro-ispanskoi komedii* (St. Petersburg, 1907), passim.

101. *Severnaia pchela,* N. 10 (January 14, 1831).

102. Marc Slonim, *Russian Theater From the Empire to The Soviets* (New York, 1961), p. 47.
103. Alexander Vol'f, *Khronika peterburgskikh teatrov* (St. Petersburg, 1877), I, 24.
104. *Severnaia pchela,* N. 10 (January 14, 1831).
105. Ibid.
106. A. V. Nikitenko, *Dnevnik* (Moscow, 1955), I, 98.
107. One Russian nobleman expressed a similar opinion to the Marquis de Custine, during his visit to Russia in 1839:

The Russians have not been molded in that brilliant school of good faith by which chivalrous Europe has so well profited that the word "honor" has for a long time been a synonym for fidelity to the word; and "word of honor" is still a sacred thing, even in France where so many other things have been forgotten! The noble influence of the Knights of the Crusades stopped in Poland along with that of Catholicism. The Russians are warriors, but for the purpose of conquest; they fight through obedience and through avarice; the Polish knights fought through pure love of glory. Marquis de Custine, *Journey For Our Time,* ed. and trans. Phyllis Penn Kohler (Chicago, 1951), p. 37.

108. The individual performances received a few brief comments from the critic of *Severnaia pchela.* P. G. Grigor'ev's performance was rewarded "by the audience's attention," and V. G. Brianskii's role of Pedro was "that of an intelligent and experienced artist. He did everything possible to enhance the role."
109. Calderón de la Barca, I, 1271-1311.
110. Varneke, pp. 226-227.
111. M. Iu. Lermontov, *Izbrannye proizvedeniia v dvukh tomakh,* ed., B. M. Eikhenbaum (Moscow, 1964), I, 678.
112. *Literaturnye pribavleniia k Russkomu invalidu,* N. 3 (January 21, 1839), 58.
113. Ibid., 64.
114. *Severnaia pchela,* N. 12 (January 10, 1839), 44-47.
115. Leningrad State Theatrical Library Catalogue.
116. Stolpianskii, p. 50.
117. *Severnaia pchela,* N. 133 (November 5, 1829).
118. A. A. Gozenpud, "Val'ter Skott i romanticheskie komedii A. A. Shakhovskogo, *Russko-evropekskie literaturnye sviazi* (Leningrad, 1966), p. 39.
119. Alexander Alexandrovich Shakhovskoi, *Komedii, Stikhotvoreniia,* ed. A. A. Gozenpud (Leningrad, 1961), p. 820.
120. Ibid., p. 55.
121. Alekseev, p. 145 and Stolpianskii, pp. 48-49.
122. *Severnaia pchela,* N. 133 (November 5, 1829).
123. Ibid.
124. Letter from N. V. Piatkova, September 6, 1966.
125. Francisco Rojas Zorrilla, *Del rey abajo ninguno,* ed. F. Ruiz Morcuende, Clásicos Castellanos, XXXV (Madrid, 1917).
126. *Severnaia pchela,* N. 28 (February 5, 1838), p. 111.
127. Ibid., p. 110.
128. Ibid., p. 111.
129. *Biblioteka dlia chteniia,* Number 2, otd., VII (1834), 47.

130. Agustín Moreto, *El desdén con el desdén,* ed. Willis Knapp Jones (New York, 1935).
131. *Biblioteka dlia chteniia,* Number 2, otd., VII (1834), 47.
132. Ibid.
133. Alekseev, pp. 171-206.
134. Although Botkin's main interest is not Spanish literature, he does make the following comment which includes Calderón:

Rich merchants established *mayorazgos* for their eldest sons by which they hoped to elevate them to the rank of hidalgo. The younger brothers, deprived therefore of their inheritance, on the other hand were ashamed to continue in their father's trade and joined the ranks of those beggar-gentlemen whom Calderón so marvelously brought to the stage as Don Mendo in *El alcalde de Zalamea.* V. P. Botkin, *Pis'ma ob Ispanii* (St. Petersburg, 1857), p. 233.

135. M. I. Glinka, *Literaturnoe Nasledie* (Moscow, 1952), p. 322.
136. Alexander Hertsen, *Polnoe sobranie sochinenii* (Moscow, 1954), II, 363.
137. *Teatr Turgeneva* (Leningrad, 1924), p. 108. Prosper Mérimée began his literary career with two successful hoaxes. First was his "translation" (1825) of the works of Clara Gazul, famous Spanish actress who had never existed. A pseudo-portrait of the actress was in fact one of Mérimée himself disguised under a mantilla, bare-shouldered, a golden cross on a necklace on "her" breast.
138. Alexander Zviguilsky, "Tourgénev et l'Espagne," *Revue de Litérature Comparée,* XXXIII (January-March, 1959), 51.
139. Richard Freeborn, *Turgenev: The Novelists' Novelist* (Oxford: Oxford University Press, 1960), p. 12.
140. Zviguilsky, 71-72.
141. I. S. Turgenev, *Polnoe sobranie sochinenii i pisem* (Moscow, 1961), *Pis'ma,* I, 578.
142. Freeborn, p. 89.
143. I. L. Rozenkranz, "I. S. Turgenev i ispanskaia literatura," *Slavia,* VI (1927), 612.
144. Turgenev, *Pis'ma,* I, 279.
145. Ibid., 281-282.
146. Zviguilsky, 75. See T. I. Bron. "Ispanskie tsitaty u Turgeneva," *Turgenevskii sbornik, materialy k polnomu sobraniiu sochinenii i pisem I. S. Turgeneva* (Moscow, 1964), I, 303-312.
147. Calderón de la Barca, I, 419.
148. Ivan Turgenev, *Fathers and Sons,* trans. Barbara Makanowitsky (New York, 1959), p. 81.
149. Turgenev, *Pis'ma,* I, 279.
150. Turgenev, *Fathers and Sons,* p. 27.
151. Ibid., p. 28.
152. Calderón de la Barca, I, 419.
153. Juan de Valera, *Obras Completas* (Madrid, 1958), III, 156. By 1828 Sobolevskii possessed several plays by Calderón. TsGALI (Central State Archives of Literature and Art) in Moscow. F. 450, Opis' I, Edinitsa khraneniia Number 4, page 7.
154. Valera, III, 98.
155. Ibid., 94.
156. Ibid., 79.

III: Calderón and Lope de Vega in Moscow (1855-1886)

With its defeat in the Crimean War, the Russian nation was more than ever aware of the need for change, for "reform from above," as Alexander II said; and the second half of the nineteenth century saw basic and rapid changes in the structure of the old Russian state. In the years between 1855 and 1870, there was some easing of conditions in the country's internal and political life. This period, which the poet Tiuchev called the "thaw,"[1] saw a relaxing in censorship controls, the granting of political amnesties, and changes in the socio-economic scene, as the old Russia slowly began her move from an agrarian society toward an industrial and artisan nation.

The intellectual and political group that helped to establish the socio-literary trend during these years was the *raznochintsy,* or men from the non-noble class who had a university education. Their prime interest was the emancipation of the serfs and the many problems which then ensued. This new stratum of society, which influenced all the arts, came into being by the emergence of educated men and women from all classes. From their ranks came many of Russia's scientists, technicians, professionals, artists, and revolutionaries. Holding that art had to serve a social rather than purely aesthetic function, they therefore preferred the literature that Gogol established in what the literary critic Belinskii praised so highly as the "Natural School."[2]

The existence of the *raznochintsy* helped to alter the nature of the theater audience. No longer did the stage belong exclusively to the aristocratic elite which was content with the romanticism and formal aestheticism of the past. The new social stratum required a literature which best depicted the Russian people's plight and its struggle for political rights and human dignity. The *raznochintsy* were in conflict with their parents and consequently refused to accept the socio-economic status quo and concepts they considered sacred and inviolable. The classic example of this struggle in Russian literature is Ivan Turgenev's novel *Otsy i deti,* "Fathers and Sons."

Shortly after Nicholas' death there arose the question of lifting the Imperial theater monopoly. Alexander's minister, Count Adlerberg, warned him against it,[3] however, and the Imperial monopoly of all theatrical performances for the public continued until the end of Alexander's reign.[4] On the other hand, Alexander was well aware of the problems presented by the aspirations of the rising *raznochintsy,* particularly the need for some means of expression.

His early liberality did bring a series of censorship reforms, most notably the recodification of 1865 by A. V. Nikitenko. These reforms paved the way for the performance of many Spanish Golden Age plays which otherwise would never have been seen on the Russian stage. Unlike his father, Alexander had little or no interest in the theater, and patronized it only in the capacity of a monarch fulfilling his obligation. Indeed, he rarely mentioned the theater.[5]

With the easing of censorship it was now possible to produce plays in which monarchs not only appeared on the stage but were portrayed with some attempt at historical accuracy. Aleksei Konstantinovich Tolstoy's (1817-1875), *Smert' Ionna Groznago,* "Death of Ivan the Terrible," and Alexander Nikolaevich Ostrovskii's (1823-1886), *Vasilisa Melent'eva,* for example, not only showed the monarch on the stage, but depicted him in his true colors; in both plays the dramatists portrayed Ivan as the murderer he was.[6] Performances were given of Pushkin's *Boris Godunov,* prohibited by Nicholas, as well as Mussorgskii's operatic version of the work. Religious restrictions were still enforced in the theater, but those concerning the image of court life and requiring an idealized picture of the monarch and his courtiers were considerably relaxed, and even plays depicting social unrest were seen on the stage during the reign of Alexander II. This easing of theatrical censorship freed the theater for such works as Lope's *Fuente Ovejuna* and *El mejor alcalde, el rey;* Calderón's *El alcalde de Zalamea;* and the anonymous *La Estrella de Sevilla,* which the Russians as well as most Western hispanists attributed to Lope. Any work showing the monarch in the role of murderer or conspirator, or the lower classes rising up against their master, could have been permitted only in a period of extreme liberalism.

The dramatic stage had two important Imperial theaters in Russia at this time, the Maly, "Little," Theater in Moscow, which was established in 1808;[7] and the Alexandrinskii Theater in St. Petersburg (1832). The productions of the Maly Theater had a cultural significance which the Alexandrinskii Theater never achieved. St. Petersburg was an imperial city, tsarist, official, and autocratic. Its principal theater-goers were important government figures. Its theater was a court theater. Nicholas I and Alexander III, the two most reactionary Russian rulers in the nineteenth century, not only were frequent spectators at the Alexandrinskii Theater, but also were regarded as its directors as well; consequently, the theater's repertory and policies were adapted to the taste of the royal household and its coterie.[8]

The Maly Theater had an entirely different atmosphere. It was away from high society, away from the pressure of foreign noblemen with whom St.

Petersburg teemed, and above all, far from the direct influence of the French theater, which had found a second homeland in St. Petersburg.[9] The Maly from its beginning attracted large audiences from all levels of society, and during the second half of the century, scholarly, literary, and social groups formed around it. Every cultivated Moscovite looked upon the theater as a part of his general education and unbringing.[10]

The Maly Theater reflected the tastes and aims of the social classes that it served. It presented works of Griboedov, Gogol, and Ostrovskii for the first time. Almost all European classical works as well as those of any contemporary writer of value received attention.[11] Its reputation for humanism, liberalism, and realism, and its serious classical repertory attracted Moscow's outstanding literary scholars and historians.[12] Personal friendships often united the most important actors with the most important scholars of the Moscow University, and the Maly Theater became the arena where the Russian intelligentsia found satisfaction for its artistic, literary, and social longings, where several generations received their education.[13]

The Maly group particularly esteemed Alexander Nikolaevich Bazhenov (1815-1867), the man responsible for introducing the cycle of Spanish Golden Age plays to Moscow during Alexander II's reign. A lover of the theater from early childhood, Bazhenov worked throughout his brief life to raise the aesthetic and cultural level of the theater. He began early by writing reviews of stage performances for Moscow's journals and newspapers, and in 1861 helped form the Kruzhok Liubitelei Dramaticheskogo Iskusstva, "The Amateur Dramatic Art Circle," an organization dedicated essentially to the performance of Western classical plays and the best Russian works. Alexander Ostrovskii, the best-known of Russia's playwrights of this period, was a member of the Art Circle, and its troupe produced many of his plays for the first time.[14]

Bazhenov's influence on the Maly Theater group was inestimable. As one of the members of the Art Circle wrote in his autobiography:

> I would in no way be exaggerating if I said that the Circle owed its serious atmosphere essentially to that man, to whom we must attribute its classical repertoire. Bazhenov's influence in that direction was overwhelming. We recall that thanks to him the plays of Shakespeare and Molière became part of the repertoire of the Imperial stage, and translations of other classic writers began to appear.[15]

In January of 1864, Bazhenov founded the theatrical journal *Antrakt,*

"Entr'acte." In it he followed the development of the theater, in Russia as well as the West, and became a competent scholar.[16] Because there were so few Russian plays of quality, and because Western drama offered such unlimited possibilities, his interest focused on the Western classical repertoire, and it was essentially because of this that the repertoires of Shakespeare, Molière, and Calderón all but eliminated the hegemony of French melodrama from the Russian stage.[17] In issue after issue Bazhenov took contemporary Russian writers to task for the quality of their work and praised such Western writers as Molière and Lope de Vega.[18] In viewing the European theater of his day, Bazhenov suggested that the only means of saving it from total eclipse was a return to the "eternally beautiful models of her classic theater."[19] For a true understanding of the dramatic art, Bazhenov advised his readers to "study the great masters: Shakespeare, Schiller, Molière, Gothe, Calderón, and Lope."[20]

In his journal *Antrakt* he gave attention to the performance of the actor, the authenticity of mood, and the faithful reproduction of scenery and costuming. He urged as realistic a reproduction as possible. In the ensuing years, this tradition became more and more important, not only with Spanish plays, but with other repertoires as well.[21] If the Maly Theater group of the 1860's was incapable of producing Western plays which recreated the original in tone, costuming, and setting, at least it set a goal to be reached in years to come.[22]

Bazhenov followed the theatrical reports issued by government committees, and his vast knowledge of the classical theater enabled him to recommend at once approved works he felt might lend themselves to easy and artistic performance by the Maly Theater group. In his article entitled "On the Coming Season," in the August, 1865 issue of *Antrakt,* Bazhenov recommended one of Calderón's plays:

> We recommend Iur'ev's recent translation of Calderón's tragedy *Za tainoe oskorblenie, tainoe mshchenie,* "A secreto agravio, secreta venganza." This tragedy, or rather this drama-tragi-comedy, as Calderón calls it, presents an interesting and lively spectacle which is pleasing to the eye because of its striking presentation of contrasts and its incomparably marvelous play of light and shadow. . . . One of the advantages of this play is that it is short, and in its three acts there is as much action as can be found in longer plays. In addition, it is easy to present; there are few characters and the four leading roles could become part of the repertoire of our best actors.[23]

Bazhenov in the same article reminded:

> Beginning September 1, theatrical censorship by the Third Section will be transferred to the activities of the Ministry of Internal Affairs, which from then on will decide what plays will be forbidden or allowed. As a result, we are encouraged to hope that many classical plays which have up to now been forbidden will come to the stage, since those conditions which caused their prohibition do not exist at present.[24]

Sergei Andreevich Iur'ev (1821-1888) translated a number of Spanish Golden Age plays, and on October 28, 1866, the Maly Theater presented his translation of Calderón's *El alcaide de sí mismo,* translated as "Sam u sebia pod strazhei," for the benefit performance of the director, A. F. Bogdanov.[25] Iur'ev translated the play in an easy, everyday conversational style; and the comic actor Prov Sadovskii carried off the role of the peasant Benito with perfection. Moscow's audience was delighted from beginning to end.[26]

"Contemporary playwrights have forgotten how to make people laugh,"[27] Bazhenov wrote in his review. After discussing humor in Shakespeare and Molière, he praised both the comic talent of Calderón as it is revealed in the language and figure of Benito, and the actors in their expression of that which is truly humorous.[28]

Nineteenth-century Russian actors read Bazhenov's reviews carefully. In addition to his analysis of the work itself, his reviews tended to provide constructive criticism by which he hoped the actors might benefit. Actors valued his criticism and he never wished to damage an actor's career by his words. He sought to raise the level of the actor's performance,[29] and to achieve authenticity and artistic expression on the dramatic stage.[30] Owing to their primitive execution and to technical difficulties, stage decorations, wardrobes, and settings were inferior until late in the century, and, because Russian dwellings were vary apt to resemble Roman or Gothic halls, little distinction was made between the size of a poor man's hut and a rich man's castle.[31] Bazhenov never failed to point out the anachronisms and inaccuracies which the Maly troup could avoid.

He was particularly distressed to see the minuet danced in Henry VIII's England in the next production of a Calderón play, *La gran cisma de Inglaterra,* translated as "Eres' v Anglii," which Glikeriia Fedotova chose for her benefit performance of November 4, 1866. Though barely twenty years old, Fedotova was one of the leading ladies of the group, a talented actress whose roles ranged from Shakespeare to the lighter comedies of Ostrovskii; she often chose from the classics for her benefit performances.[32] Perhaps in an effort to enhance the play's success, Fedovota asked the composer Alexander Dargomyzhskii to set verses from Acts I and II to music.[33] Dargomyzhskii was a close friend of Glinka, who instilled in him a love for Spain's music and culture,[34] and in that same year (1866) he wrote an opera on *The Stone Guest,* Pushkin's play on the Don Juan theme.[35]

In his review of *Eres' v Anglii,* Bazhenov provided the readers of *Antrakt* with a detailed historical background of the events themselves, the artistic merit of the work, and, after a criticism of the acting and technical imperfections, he noted that:

> . . . Mr. Samarin and Madame Fedotova very cleverly and expressively performed their extensive roles as Henry VIII and Anne Boleyn; we only regret that Madame Fedotova clings to her habit of bending the upper part of her body and affectedly turning her head and lifting up her face. Nor can we imagine how it entered her head to dance a minuet before the king. In the first place, the minuet could not have been known during Henry VIII's reign, since it was only invented and introduced during the reign of Louis XIV; and in the second, who could have advised her that the minuet was danced by one person?[36]. . .
>
> In spite of the length of the play, some imperfections in the translation, and some weaknesses in the acting, *Eres' v Anglii* was received by the public with great interest and enthusiasm. After each act, the principal performers were asked to take several bows. The public thanked the young actress, whose current repertoire is almost completely composed of classical roles, and who for the last two years has bestowed a classical play on our stage for her benefit performances. The success of *Eres' v Anglii* is decisive, and in our opinion it will guarantee the success of a more famous and worthier Calderón play, *El alcalde de Zalamea,*" "Salameiskii Al'kad," which will be performed at Mr. Samarin's benefit performance.

The second performance of *Eres' v Anglii* played to a full house, and Fedotova received a gold watch.[37]

The final Spanish play performed in 1866 by the Maly Theater was Calderón's *Salameiskii Al'kad,* produced for the benefit performance of the actor I. V. Samarin, on December 16.[38] The play did not measure up to expectations, and no one was more disappointed than the man who had so highly recommended it. Bazhenov wrote in his review:

> Last Friday, in the benefit performance for Mr. Samarin, Calderón's *Salameiskii Al'kad* was performed. We were quite sure that it would be a great success, especially after the triumph of *Eres' v Anglii*. However, it was not. What could have deceived us, and where are we to find the reasons for its failure on our stage? The reasons must be sought either in the play itself, the Russian translation, or in its performance. Were we wrong in a previous issue of *Antrakt* when we described the play as "remarkable" and full of merit? Hardly. And even after having seen its lack of success on our stage, we are unwilling to change our former opinion about it. Without a moment's hesitation we call this play remarkable for the daring concept of the author in basing it on class discord, on the clash of physical and moral strength, and the triumph of justice. All of this is shown with much brilliance, and developed with much force, in a rich and varied spectacle. Among the virtues of the play, we call attention to the artistic inventiveness and development of the plot, which gathers momentum from the very first scene of the drama, particularly ingenious is the ruse employed by Rebolledo to gain entrance into Isabel's room.[39]

Bazhenov attributes the play's poor success to the translation of S. Kostarev:[40]

> The translator did not do his job. Not having the slightest idea of versification, he rejected even the basic rules of Russian syntax. Almost everywhere one has sentences of the most impossible structure . . . as a result, we have stiffness and poor quality verse, in addition to dullness, error, and want of polish in the language . . . .[41]

Bazhenov concludes that while for the most part the actors performed very well individually, the play's failure was due to their inability to maintain a smooth, closely knit internal structure, which the Calderón work demands.[42]

In the years that followed, the Maly Theater continued to maintain its serious and classical repertoire. The didactic role of art continued to be emphasized, as well as its enormous social force and ideological content. But with the passing of Bazhenov in 1867, there was no one sufficiently interested in the Spanish plays themselves to continue the precedent set by him, until a decade later, when the translator of *El alcaide de sí mismo* and other Spanish Golden Age plays, Iur'ev, revived this interest.

As a young man, Iur'ev was interested in mathematics and astronomy; he wrote two works on the solar system while at the University of Moscow, but trouble with his eyes led him to abandon science.[43] He remained an accomplished mathematician and philosopher, however, and became as well a translator and theatrical historian. In addition to his work at Moscow University, he studied abroad, attending various universities' lectures on the literature and drama of the West. For the remainder of his life, he devoted himself to literature and dramatic art and counted among his friends such literary giants as Tolstoy, Dostoevskii, and Saltykov-Shchedrin.

All his life Iur'ev believed in truth, beauty, and goodness.[44] He was not a revolutionary; he believed in unity between the ruler and the ruled. In social and political opinions, he stood on the side of humane liberalism, sympathizing with any triumph for freedom, humanity, and truth, not only in his native Russia but everywhere in the world. He belonged with the men of the Renaissance in his concepts of independence of action and the development of the powers of the individual; these he considered not only a right but the supreme duty of the human being.[45] Iur'ev believed in freedom of conscience and expression and his most fundamental ideas of social conduct found their best expression in the works of Lope.

Like Rousseau, Iur'ev had a great faith in the common man and his propensity to good. When he returned from Western Europe in 1861, he established a school for the peasants on his estate, and built a theater for them where they could put on their own productions.[46] He believed in a bright future for mankind, and had a deep moral sense of history.

For Iur'ev art was holy, and its mission he conceived to be the vital personification of ideals, beauty, and truth. "Of art he demanded not the satisfying of coarse tastes but the awakening of the human spirit to a higher light."[47] As he expressed it in one of his articles on the importance of the theatre:

> The poet and the dramatist are sent to mankind to destroy evil with awareness, vice by laughter, and to enlighten national consciousness to superior ideals. From the stage, these elevated minds speak to the entire people, who are thereby elevated by the word, if one may so say, of a Prophet; and the artist himself is crowned with the wreath of his artistic creation. To carry his ideals to the national consciousness is an exalted achievement, a serving of the Holy: for poetry and art are holy in the life of the people.[48]

Iur'ev founded and edited the Slavophile journal *Russkaia Mysl'*, "Russian Thought," was the editor of both *Beseda,* "The Visit," and *Artist,* and served as the chairman of the Obshchestvo Liubitelei Rossiiskoi Slovestnosti, "The

Society of Lovers of Russian Letters." This organization had been revived at Moscow University in 1858, after the death of Nicholas I, and aimed at following the trends and events of the literary world and serving as its mirror and guide. The group published many literary translations, including those of Spanish plays.[49] They published works on literary and linguistic problems, organized lectures and distinguished gatherings, literary and musical evenings, and commemorated important cultural events, such as the unveiling of the Pushkin monument at Moscow in 1880. Through his journals and the Society, Iur'ev became one of the most compelling forces in the theatrical world during the second half of the nineteenth century.

The theater Iur'ev regarded as the lecture hall of the people. "We shall speak of the most powerful force on the human consciousness," he wrote, "the dramatic stage: the superior creation of poetry which speaks not only to the mind but to the whole spirit."[50] In the Spanish playwrights he found a reflection of his own idealized concept of art. He was attracted by the role of the people, by the mass movements, and the moral and social ideals that were found in the plays of Lope;[51] by the penetrating psychology of Calderón, and resolved to bring them to the Russian stage. "Iur'ev was so convinced of the necessity to acquaint the Russian public with the Spanish Theater that the names of Cervantes, Lope de Vega, and Calderón never left his lips,"[52] the actress Glama Meshcherskaia wrote in her *Memoirs*. Between 1865 and 1877, he translated nearly a score of dramatic works from Shakespeare, Tirso, Calderón, and Lope, which included *La Estrella de Sevilla, El castigo sin venganza, A secreto agravio, secreta venganza, Marta la piadosa,* and *Fuente Ovejuna*.[53] Of Lope he wrote:

> Lope de Vega loved the simple people with an ardent flame and defended their great importance and moral virtue. In powerful artistic images, he revealed their spiritual beauty, inner force, and noble pride. He has many dramas in which the main characters are taken from the peasantry, depicting with unusual force their pride in their way of life, vying with kings in moral virtue while bowing in respect before the royal person. In Lope's historical dramas, we are aware that the master of historical events is the people, that its desire and will, covertly or openly, control these events, and that in many of these dramas the collective personality has the prime position.[54]

In 1871 his translation of Calderón's *A secreto agravio, secreta venganza* was published.[55] In his introduction, Iur'ev refers to Calderón as:

> . . . a powerful and independent thinker, who wrote many dramas in which there unfolds before the reader a true picture of human life. In these plays he is a penetrating psychologist, a sober thinker who protests class prejudice and many other prejudices which are still with us today, a mighty champion of the rights of man and the inviolability of his person. In this sense, the great Spanish poet belongs to our own time.[56]

While his early translations of Spanish plays were made from the German, Iur'ev was forced to learn Spanish during the middle of 1875, as a result of a family quarrel. Iur'ev's brother-in-law was the translator N. M. Piatnitskii, who had studied in Spain under Aurelio Fernández Guerra y Orbe.[57] Piatnitskii was apparently never really able to master the Spanish language. While in Spain he had attempted a translation of Vélez de Guevara's picaresque novel *El diablo cojuelo,* with the help of Agustín Durán of the Royal Academy, but he abandoned the project because of his poor knowledge of Spanish at the time.[58] His translations of Lope ten years later, *El perro del hortelano* and *Los melindres de Belisa,* were unfavorably reviewed by the critics. Toward the close of 1874, Piatnitskii asked Iur'ev to read his translation of *La Estrella de Sevilla.* Iur'ev, who knew the work in German, found his brother-in-law's Russian version to be an unsatisfactory literal translation.

At a gathering of the Society for Lovers of Russian Letters on April 27, 1875, Iur'ev read his brother-in-law's work; but through an oversight Piatnitskii's name was omitted as translator. Although Iur'ev quickly corrected the error, his brother-in-law never forgave him the omission and their friendly relationship ended.[59] It would appear that Iur'ev had at least had recourse to his brother-in-law's knowledge of Spanish in the past when working on his own translations of Spanish works, for immediately after the rift Iur'ev took up the study of the Spanish language. The critic from the St. Petersburg newspaper *Golos* wrote the following:

> With the stoicism of the classical thinkers, he decided that it was never too late to study, and last summer began to study a Spanish grammar to learn the language of Cervantes, Calderón, and Lope de Vega. Iur'ev's efforts were rewarded with complete success; the translation of both *La Estrella de Sevilla* and *Fuente Ovejuna* were done by him without any outside help.[60]

While never an official member of the Maly Theater staff, Iur'ev's role, like that of Bazhenov, was that of unofficial director, consultant, and counselor. It was in this capacity that he exercised the greatest influence on the Maly Theater productions.

> The moral and artistic influence of Iur'ev on the Maly Theater was inestimable. . . . At a time when St. Petersburg was specializing in melodramas and the so-called semidramatic genre which was so characteristic of the eighteenth century . . . the Maly Theater continuously tried to achieve, and doubtless did, great results in the heights of true drama. Shakespeare, Hugo, Schiller, Lope de Vega, and others invariably adorned its repertoire. Iur'ev was a fanatical admirer of the Spanish drama and an untiring translator of classical Spanish plays.... The Maly Theater is indebted to him for the performances of *La Estrella de Sevilla,* and especially *Fuente Ovejuna* . . . a play which will long remain in the memories of Moscovites, thanks to its performance on the stage of the Maly Theater.[61]

Among the academic friends of the Maly Theater was Nicholas Il'ich Storozhenko (1836-1906). Professor of Western literature at the Moscow University, Shakespearian scholar, and translator of George Ticknor's *History of Spanish Literature,* Storozhenko was a highly esteemed friend of the Maly group. He was a close friend of Iur'ev and the rising young actress, Mariia Nikolaevna Ermolova. A member of the Society for Lovers of Russian Letters, Storozhenko had been present at the gathering of December 7, 1875, when Iur'ev read his new translation of *Fuente Ovejuna.* Since Storozhenko knew that Ermolova was looking for a play for her coming benefit performance, it occurred to him that she might be interested in the new Iur'ev translation. Storozhenko relates in his memoirs that after a brief conversation with Iur'ev regarding Ermolova, Iur'ev suggested that she play the principal role in his recently translated *La Estrella de Sevilla.* Ermolova was delighted and a meeting was arranged; but after hearing her read the part, Iur'ev excitedly exclaimed, "I have another role which is more suited to your talent, that of Laurencia in Lope de Vega's drama, *Fuente Ovejuna.* This is the pearl of his works and in it you will be magnificent. I am now working on its translation, and it will be ready for your benefit performance."[62] Iur'ev was true to his word. At the end of 1875 the drama was ready, and on March 8, 1876, it was staged with enormous success for Ermolova's benefit performance.[63]

Fuente Ovejuna was produced virtually under Iur'ev's direction. He attended every performance of the rehearsals and had more faith in Ermolova's ability to play the role of Laurencia than the actress had in herself. " . . . the role is magnificent, but will I do it well? See and judge. To tell you the truth, I am quite afraid," she wrote to Professor Shchepkin, a few days before the play opened.[64] But her performance was attended by a success that Moscow had not seen for a long time. Storozhenko recorded:

> The theater was full very early and the audience was highly excited. . . . Moscow was waiting to see its favorite in her first benefit performance. Deafening applause, shouts of "bravo" and hurrahs, and the waving of handkerchiefs, which did not stop for fully a quarter of an hour, greeted the actress. Overcome by nervousness, she had to leave the stage, but as the rumble of applause died down, she appeared for the second time.[65]

After the second scene of the third act, Ermolova was in considerable anxiety backstage concerning the next scene; she was convinced that she would be unable to render the difficult passages of Laurencia's monologue and thereby ruin the play.[66] Iur'ev agreed to her requested deletions, and listened anxiously backstage. To his surprise, he wrote, he heard "those very words which in her opinion were so confusing, and which she had just begged to have left out, being pronounced with such force and control that by them more than anything else she captured the audience."[67] The climax of the performance was in fact the difficult monologue, and more than one spectator left his impressions of it. "The public's enthusiasm was boundless, and no less so was the passionate hatred of tyranny which carried away the young actress' soul."[68] And Iur'ev wrote to Ermolova:

> It was easily apparent that you were imbued with that feeling which tore Laurencia's soul to shreds and raised to that point of natural force which the popular masses cannot resist, and which can animate a soul of stone. That feeling was transmitted to us, the audience, and was so strong that it seemed capable of choking us.[69]

A large part of the audience was made up of Moscow students, who, after endless curtain calls and applause and hardly knowing "how best to express their delight, offered the young actress gifts, humble, as far as one can recall: a watch, an album, a copy of Shakespeare's complete works."[70] "After the performance the students hurried to gather at the stage entrance, and stopping the carriage in which Ermolova was going home, unhitched the horses and themselves pulled her carriage to her house and carried the actress to her apartment in their arms."[71]

The Moscow newspapers were as enthusiastic about Ermolova's artistic performance as her student audience had been. Little was said of the play itself or its social aspects and political overtones; indeed, considering the remarkable success of the play with the public, it received far fewer press notices than might normally have been expected. All were agreed, however, that Ermolova's performance was flawless. The reactionary *Moskovskie vedomosti,* "The Moscow News," obliquely suggested that the play itself had little to do with the reaction of the audience, giving as the only "obvious reason for such animation and applause Madame Ermolova's acting, which is to such a degree artistically beautiful that it naturally affects even the most indifferent viewer."[72] The more liberal *Sovremennye Izvestiia,* "Contemporary News," went so far as to mention the "hurricane of applause which greeted the scene calling the entire village to revolt against the Commander."[73]

After seeing the opening performance, Moscow's Chief of Police, Ivan L'vovich, expressed the opinion that "the play should be banned. We have enough of our own nihilism already, without having it translated. It is a direct call to revolt."[74] At the second performance, he took the precaution of stationing police around the theater,[75] for the students had gone on their way the evening before, "singing revolutionary songs like, 'Sten'ka Razin.' "[76]

In addition to the revolutionary aspects of the play and the background of increasing peasant uprisings due to economic depression, instances of Russian landowners raping peasant women were far from rare in the countryside; and *Fuente Ovejuna* could hardly fail to remind the public of these outrages.[77] Dostoevskii's father met his death at the hands of his peasants for this reason, and Saltykov-Shchedrin described on numerous occasions how the peasants massacred masters who had violated their women.[78] During the second performance, the actor Timofeev relates, "the theater was overflowing with *alguaziles.*"[79]

Given the structure of the czarist state, and the uneasiness of the Moscow authorities concerning the performance of this work, it seems remarkable that the censors passed it, even in a period of comparative liberalism, and that the authorities permitted it to run beyond the opening night. It is known that Iur'ev had friends who were influential with the censors; for on January 14, 1876, the writer Pisemskii wrote to the censor A. N. Maikov and asked his help in pushing through the Iur'ev translation of Lope.[80] Three days later the censors, who may well have regarded the play as pro-monarchic in the light of its ending, passed *Fuente Ovejuna* for production.[81] In spite of its popularity, however, the play was removed from the Moscow repertoire. Very few of the subsequent performances were reviewed by the press; it was performed sixteen times during two seasons,[82] and ran for eight performances during its first season.[83] According to the Soviet historian V. A. Filippov, the play was never officially banned. That it was not performed with regularity he attributes to the fact that the actor Shumskii died and the less experienced O. A. Pravdin was not qualified to handle the role of the *alcalde* Esteban.[84]

An excellent example of the contrast between St. Petersburg and Moscow at this time can be seen in the reviews of *Fuente Ovejuna* at the Pavlovsk Summer Theater near St. Petersburg in June of 1878. "Yesterday I performed in *Fuente Ovejuna* for the first time in Pavlovsk,"[85] Ermolova wrote her sister. "The local public did not like the play and laughed at every moving scene. I was accepted very well, which I did not expect after the first act. . . . But everyone reproached me for choosing such a play."[86] Petersburg society and bureaucratic circles did not appreciate the work, and inadequate staging contributed to its failure. One reviewer wrote, "The actors tried to perform well, but the audience often laughed at what they said."[87] Another stated, "While this drama was performed several times in Moscow very successfully, it was not successful here due to the extremely scanty staging of the mass scenes, which, instead of producing an effective impression, because of its pitiful comic effect, produced a general reaction of laughter."[88]

Although Iur'ev translated and produced other Spanish Golden Age plays, *Fuente Ovejuna* best reflected his own concept of the role of the people in a state. He believed that a people should be free and educated, and that they were justified in using force to correct injustice. He was far from agreeing with Leo Tolstoy on the matter of non-resistance. At one of their Saturday evening literary gatherings, Iur'ev, recalling Laurencia, asked Tolstoy what he would do if someone attempted to rape his daughter. Would he not use force to defend her? Tolstoy replied that he would appeal to the man's conscience, but Iur'ev could in no way agree with Tolstoy's argument.[89] He had certainly not produced *Fuente Ovejuna* to show that one should appeal to the conscience of a rapist. For their universality, social messages, and philosophical and idealistic content, the Spanish Golden Age plays were meaningful for Iur'ev's own time.

Following the successful performances of *Fuente Ovejuna,* the Maly Theater group produced three more Golden Age plays during Iur'ev's lifetime, two of which were notable failures.

On September 20, 1876, the Maly Theater, in a benefit performance for the actor Alexandrov, offered Lope's *Los melindres de Belisa,* "Prichudnitsa," to the Moscow public. Despite the good performances of Ermolova and other leading actors of the group, the play was poorly received. For the most part, the critics felt that the work was not sufficiently realistic, that the staging was particularly poor. Costumes were taken from the Italian wardrobe and Spanish color and atmosphere were lacking, especially in portraying the nobles.[90] The acting drew favorable comment; Ermolova as the beautiful slave girl Celia in semi-Moorish garb presented a picture "so colorful that it asked to be painted by an artist."[91] The rest of the cast performed their roles with animation and variety and conveyed some of the essential wit and humor of the play. Nevertheless, the play failed.

Particularly unfortunate was the translation, which the critics said was unbelievably bad. Lacking any other, the group had used Piatnitskii's.[92] Some critics believed that the play was useless and silly; others suggested that the work was too Spanish to be understood by Russians.[93] One critic accused Iur'ev and Piatnitskii of trying to Hispanize the Russian theater and inquired how long it would be before Iur'ev transformed himself into a Spaniard entirely.[94]

Further, because of possible censorship pressure, the press ignored the theme of social protest in Lope's play, therefore discouraging the public from attending.

The performance of Calderón's *El alcalde de sí mismo* on November 7, 1876, so successful in its 1866 production, was also a failure. Recalling the earlier performance, the reviewer from *Moskovskie vedomosti* commented on the difference, contrasting Maksheev's performance with that of Sadovskii. "Maksheev failed to penetrate the personality of Benito, merely depicting a dumb, kindly, and comic peasant through buffonery. Trying too hard to be funny, he created laughter only through gesture and voice, without conveying Benito's true personality."[95]

For the second benefit performance of Ermolova the Maly group was also forced to resort to the indifferent talents of Piatnitskii as a translator. In 1866 Iur'ev had translated Lope's *El mejor alcalde, el rey,* but this work had been rejected by the Board of Censors.[96] The Piatnitskii translation of 1876 had been approved after the censors removed the passages dealing with sexual violence, and such words as "rape" and "fornication."[97]

At Ermolova's second benefit performance, on April 10, 1877, Lope's *El mejor alcalde, el rey* failed to measure up to the expectations of the Moscow audience, many of whom had seen *Fuente Ovejuna* the year before.[98] Although Ermolova herself was highly acclaimed by audience and critic alike for her flawless performance,[99] the internal structure of the play, the tendency to glorify the monarch, and the lesser importance of the people's role combined to disappoint the expectations of Moscow's liberals.[100] The play's closing line, "Long live the King," could evoke nothing like the tumultuous ovation which had followed the final curtain of *Fuente Ovejuna.*

Iur'ev never lost sight of the enormous social force of art, its ideological content, and the civic role of art in the theater; but he was far from being a social revolutionary. In his introduction to his translation of *Fuente Ovejuna,* he refers to the sanctity of government, whose function he felt was to personify the wishes of the people and to protect their well-being. He believed in the king as the ultimate judge of his country's problems and advocated harmony between government and people.[101] Lope's image of the king who punishes the evil-doer and offers paternal protection to his people was precisely the image of monarchy which Iur'ev sought to preserve, and best explains his choice of *Fuente Ovejuna, El mejor alcalde, el rey,* and the changes he made in *La Estrella de Sevilla,* the last Spanish Golden Age play produced in his lifetime.

Two critics of opposite opinions reviewed *El mejor alcalde, el rey.* The reviewer for the newspaper *Golos,* "The Voice," praised Lope for his respect for the monarchy, and pointed out that the concept of the king as father of his people and the object of their love and eternal loyalty was a national virtue shared by both the Russian and Spanish people.[102]

Alexander N. Ostrovskii, the playwright, took exception to Lope's play on moral grounds. In his review he gave a detailed analysis of the play, its historical background, and the ways in which it differs from other of Lope's plays. The concept of honor in this play, he felt, contrasted sharply with that in *Fuente Ovejuna* and made the work difficult if not impossible for the Russian audience to understand. Ostrovskii, who had sprung from the merchant classes who peopled many of his own plays, drew a sharp distinction between nobility of the blood and nobility through virtue: virtuous conduct and moral values, not escutcheons, were the coat-of-arms of nobility. His chief complaint against *El mejor alcalde, el rey* lay in the fact that the character Nuño was less concerned that his daughter had suffered rape than that his own honor as a nobleman had been violated.[103]

A friend and colleague of Iur'ev, Ostrovskii was Russia's most important living playwright. He was greatly interested in the popular element in literature, which Pushkin had defined as *narodnost'*.[104] In his youth he traveled extensively through the Volga region, collecting information about the populace with the idea of writing plays.[105] A member of Pogodin's Slavophile group, he shared their ardent love of folkways, their interest in the observation and study of folkloric poetry, custom, and ritual.[106] Ostrovskii was particularly interested in Russia's popular theaters and sought to establish a broader base for public entertainment.

A clear distinction must be made between popular theaters and the Imperial stage. Like other aspects of life in czarist Russia, the world of entertainment was also based on class and privilege. Private theaters, when these came into existence, and theaters frequented by the aristocracy and *razhochintsy* were out of reach for the masses. The price of admission alone excluded the vast majority of Russia's peasantry and urban laboring class; and police surveillance kept out those who did not appear to belong among the audience. It was not until the beginning of the present century that theaters for the Russian masses began to function with any degree of success and regularity. Those which operated in the nineteenth century were subject to a more stringent control; plays which could be seen on the Imperial stage in Russia's capitals were seldom allowed in the popular theaters. "The majority of the people do not have access to the theater,"[107] Ostrovskii once complained in a letter to the Czar; but his efforts to raise the level of entertainment in the popular theater met with little success.

During the summer of 1872, a theater for the masses was constructed on the fair grounds of the All-Russian Polytechnical Exhibition. The Ministry of Internal Affairs was designated by Alexander II to select the plays. Ostrovskii recommended Calderón's *El alcalde de sí mismo* on this occasion, but the work was not given.[108] Two years later he made a similar recommendation, adding the Iur'ev translations of *A secreto agravio, secreta venganza* and *El médico de su honra,* but without success.[109]

Like his friend Iur'ev, Ostrovskii was widely read in Spanish Golden Age drama. His artistic aim was to create a truly Russian theater, as he felt the Spanish Golden Age dramatists had created for Spain, convinced as he was that "the only plays which have survived the centuries are those which were truly national to their own homeland."[110] And this he succeeded in doing. "In the world tradition of the theater," the Soviet critic Danilov writes, "the closest dramatic expression to Ostrovskii was the theater of Lope de Vega."[111]

Ostrovskii translated all of Cervantes' *Entremeses* into Russian, four of which appeared in print during his lifetime, published by the editor Peter I.

Veinberg in his *Iziashchnaia literatura,* "Journal of Fine Literature."[112] The correspondence between the two men leading up to the publication of the *Entremeses* illustrates the interest of the Russian intellectual in foreign classics. On December 25, 1882, the editor wrote:

> I repeat my most earnest request. If it is at all possible, if your health and time permit it, send me some translation of yours, even if it is only a small one. V. A. Krylov[113] told me that you have already thought of translating Cervantes' *Entremeses.* For my journal it would be a treasure, especially since it is the aim of my journal to publish classical works of foreign literature.[114]

A year later, Veinberg again wrote to Ostrovskii, pleading for "at least one scene from Cervantes."[115] Veinberg published *El juez de los divorcios,* "Sud'ia po brakorazvodnym delam," (1883) and *La guarda cuidadosa,* "Bditel'nyi strazh," (1887), and wrote again to Ostrovskii, asking for a third translation and reminding him that "the subscribers insistently request Cervantes."[116] *El retablo de las maravillas,* "Teatr chudes," was the last published by Veinberg in 1884, though the playwright translated them all before his death in 1886. The remainder appeared posthumously the year of his death. Veinberg wrote Ostrovskii of his hope that all the *Entremeses* would be published.[117] In a letter to Veinberg, Ostrovskii explained his delay:

> All is now ready, but I am conscientious and afraid to appear before the public until I am certain of two things: that my translation is completely faithful to the original work, and that all the words and phrases in the Russian language selected by me to express all Cervantes' shades of meaning leave nothing else to be done.[118]

In November, 1886, shortly after Ostrovskii became the head of the Maly Theater Repertoire Division,[119] *La Estrella de Sevilla,* translated as *Zvezda Sevilli,* was presented as a benefit performance for Ermolova. Iur'ev had translated this play in 1876 and had suggested it to the well-known actor and writer, A. I. Iuzhin-Sumbatov for his benefit performance early in 1886, but it was decided upon for Ermolova. Rehearsals for *La Estrella de Sevilla* were conducted throughout the fall of 1886, under the watchful eye of Iur'ev. A. I. Iuzhin-Sumbatov wrote in his *Memoirs,* "Iur'ev himself directed the rehearsals . . . he argued with us and corrected us; if he made a mistake he was the first to recognize it, but when he felt he was right, on no condition could he be moved."[120]

Owing to several important developments, the performance of *La Estrella de Sevilla* was different from any of the other Spanish plays given at the Maly Theater. First and foremost, historical accuracy in setting and costumes was achieved. During the past decade Russian painters—Bocharov, Shishkov, and others—had started a new trend in historical accuracy in painting; archaeology and historicity demanded a stricter sense of evidence in interpreting the past; these trends were reflected in the theater by theatrical designers and architects who sought more and more to advance stage techniques.[121] Moreover, the Meningen players had visited Russia.[122] Their performance in 1885 made Ostrovskii and Iur'ev painfully aware of the shortcomings of the Moscow Maly Theater. The German troup of Duke Georg Meningen left nothing undone to reproduce historically authentic plays. Twenty-eight carloads were necessary to transport their stage effects, wardrobe, settings, and decorations to Russia.[123] As Iur'ev wrote at the time, "After the Meningen players, one cannot present a play just any way, with just any kind of decoration."[124]

Two of Russia's outstanding stage designers, Anatolii Fedorovich Gel'tser (1852-1918) and F. L. Sollogub, were commissioned to design the sets and wardrobe. Both men did extensive research into Spanish history and culture to produce authentic effects which would blend artistically and accurately with the text of *La Estrella de Sevilla*.[125] One of Gel'tser's important sources for plastic material on Seville was a printed collection of colored sketches of Spain's architectural masterpieces, a work published by Prince A. V. Meshcherskii as a result of his travels to Spain.[126] The prince had become interested in Spain when he met the Viardot's during their stay in St. Petersburg in 1843. He made several trips to Spain, and in 1867 published his sketches and an account of his travels.[127] Gel'tser's attention to the details of Moorish style re-created the delicate columns, fluted arches, and decorative ceilings of the Alcazar.[128]

Sollogub too was a happy choice for Iur'ev. Not only scrupulously conscientious, Sollogub brought to his task a love for Spain from his early youth. He had written poems in the sixties on Seville, the Inquisition, and Spanish passion. He loved the guitar and castanettes, and his image of Golden Age Spain included the plumed hat, flowing cape, Toledo blades, and the secret rendezvous.[129] For his work on *La Estrella de Sevilla,* Sollogub consulted the works of Karl Keller and carefully searched the text of the play for the slightest indication of dress. "I have tried to stay faithful to historical accuracy, closely following the style of the time," he told Iur'ev in a letter. "It is affirmed that in thirteenth century Spain they wore clothes woven from oriental cloth, but adopted the French style of dress."[130]

The combined efforts of the set directors were crowned with success. The play was well received by the audience and critics of Moscow, who paid tribute to the authentic settings and costumes as well as the artistic and aesthetic quality of the performance. One critic wrote: "In this performance, our dramatic stage gave proof that the Meningen players did not pass unnoticed. . . . The mass scene, in the last act, so beautifully presented, produced a deep and lasting impression."[131] Elsewhere, the adjectives "magnificent," "grandiose," and "overwhelming" were used to describe the effect of the settings. Speaking again of Gel'tser's contribution, another critic wrote, "His magnificent settings of a courtyard and garden, a room in the Moorish style, a dungeon, and the Palace square paid tribute to the artist's abilities and techniques and vastly impressed the audience."[132]

The performers received the most lavish praise from Moscow's most influential critics. The *Teatr i zhizn'* critic discussed the internal structure of the play, its spiritual beauty and its meaning for contemporary audiences.

> The play serves as a perfect example of Spanish knightly ideals. The elevated thoughts and feelings, the knightly concept of honor and duty, the idealizing cult for the monarchy, the knight-king, eternal deeds of self-denial and sacrifice—all that is vastly and ideally pure, by which all humanity lived, and still lives, in its best and most unique expression—all these qualities, although remote from our present generation, cannot but be felt by it. He who is searching for high aesthetic pleasure, he whose feeling for poetry has not yet died, should see and enjoy *La Estrella de Sevilla*. . . . The play was a colossal success. The eminent Iur'ev, who was responsible for the production, was the object of the most thunderous applause that could express unlimited enthusiasm.[133]

Considering Iur'ev's fidelity to the letter as well as the spirit of the laws of art, the changes he made in *La Estrella de Sevilla* are particularly interesting. It is true that the reign of Alexander III (1882-1894) brought a swift return to extremely reactionary rule, under which Russian creative and intellectual freedom, limited though it had been, soon found itself back in the stifling atmosphere of Nicholas I's reign.[134] Censorship controls were tightened and theatrical freedom was severely curbed. But the changes Iur'ev made in the play do not appear to be those which censorship would have necessarily required. In the scene of the Spanish original, the king confesses his crime to a group of his nobles in his private chambers.[135] Iur'ev altered this scene by moving the king to the public square and having him confess his crime to the people of Seville. In addition, he adds a scene in which he has the king promise the populace that he will govern more justly, that he will give more concern to the problems of the people, and, most significantly, that he will govern through a group of the city's representatives.[136]

Critics have been divided in interpreting these changes,[137] despite the reasons given by Iur'ev himself at the time:

> They do not alter the intention of Lope* but tend to emphasize it. Lope loved to introduce scenes in which the king communed with a people full of faith and love for royalty, which, for the Spaniard of that time, was the personification of truth. Please recall *Fuente Ovejuna's* final scene. On this basis, wishing to remain faithful to Lope's *Weltanschauung,* in the scenes changed and introduced by us, we had the king address not the judges or the grandees and nobility, but rather the whole population of Seville, and changed the scene of action to the square.[138]

Iur'ev thus offers other evidence of Lope's fondness for kings in communion with their people, in *El villano en su rincón* and *Los Tellos de Meneses.*

Critics of the time regarded *La Estrella de Sevilla* as "a victory of the spirit, of the king over himself, which is the true guarantee of harmony between a king and his people . . . an apotheosis of the monarch purified by the love of his people and a unity with them, which is the only ideal situation."[139]

Iur'ev sought wherever possible to stress harmony between king and people, and the alterations he made in *La Estrella de Sevilla* reflect this harmony. Alexander II on the very day of his assassination had approved a project which would have included in the tsarist government a representative group from among the populace.[140] It could have been no small disappointment to a man of Iur'ev's sentiments that Alexander's project was abandoned at once by the new czar. Nor could the play's reference to just such a representative body in the king's court have failed to remind Moscow's liberals of Alexander II's promise of a parliament.[141] As the critic Zograf pointed out: "Doubtless the theatrical historian who saw revolutionary characteristics in the play is

* The present investigation is not concerned with the authorship of *La Estrella de Sevilla.* At the time, Russian as well as Western Hispanists believed it to be the work of Lope.

mistaken. But at a time when autocracy was attempting to become more and more powerful, the play did have an oppositional undertone."[142]

The production of Spanish Golden Age drama on the Russian stage of the nineteenth century was brought about, despite the many difficulties of tsarist rule and primitive techniques, by the efforts of many of Russia's most accomplished individuals: her scholars, historians, and writers, as well as a group of performers who were not merely actors but gifted men and women who had a great faith in their art and in the social role of the theater. For these people, Spain's great dramatists fulfilled their artistic and aesthetic yearnings and, above all, expressed their idealism. The actor Iuzhin-Sumbatov wrote:

> For Lope, along with Shakespeare and Schiller, calls to the higher freedom of humanity. They are the deifiers of truth and human dignity. Their belief in the future kingdom of truth and its triumph, their hatred for oppression, force, for the debasement of the human conscience over truth, reason, and the will of nations and individuals, inspired us as deeply and sincerely as the artistic power and creative genius of the great writers.[143]

With the exception of Calderón's *El alcalde de sí mismo* all the Spanish Golden Age plays which the Maly Theater presented from 1866 to 1886 have one important similarity: man's loathing for oppression and his desire to extirpate arbitrariness and injustice.

La gran cisma de Inglaterra, although it does not have the theme of the people in a struggle against tyranny, does present the problem of a lascivious and repulsive despot. For the Spaniard, Henry VIII is even more odious because of his break with the Roman Catholic Church. The Russian public, on the other hand, was not interested in Henry VIII as a schismatic; what attracted the Maly Theater to the play was the figure of the English king as a bad and cruel monarch. Lope's *Los melindres de Belisa* for both the Spaniard and Russian had a common message—man has no right to enslave and exploit his fellow man. And this message did not fail to find its mark in both Madrid and Moscow.

Lope's *Fuente Ovejuna* and Calderón's *El alcalde de Zalamea* differ not so much in theme, as in the concept and portrayal of the protagonists. In Lope the protagonist is the entire village of Fuente Ovejuna, which acts as a single dynamic force and symbolizes a national spirit. Pedro Crespo, the hero of *El alcalde de Zalamea,* is a single person who represents the collective spirit of his countrymen. Thus in Lope the group acts as an individual, while in

Calderón the individual acts as a group. For the Spaniard these two plays were monarchistic. They depict the king as a superior man who supports the masses in their struggle against the nobility. The king is a paternal figure exclusively and no other interpretation is possible.

In Russia, however, these plays have two possible interpretations. For the vast majority of nineteenth-century Russians, the Spanish interpretation would seem absolutely legitimate, and it is possible that this is why the tsarist government permitted the play. Still, for a limited number of Iur'ev's contemporaries and for recent Soviet critics, *Fuente Ovejuna* was a call to revolt against the system in general. Those who believed this interpretation wanted to see things that perhaps never existed.

La Estrella de Sevilla depicts the king as a human being with all his weaknesses. For the Spaniard this presentation of the monarch was an anomaly, for rarely did a Spanish playwright portray a Spanish king as less than a person superior in every way to his subjects. Iur'ev's version did not alter this image of the king until the play's end. Iur'ev only emphasized a greater desired link between king and people. And except for the Russian ending, the play had the same importance and meaning—the king is a human being who confesses his sins—to both the Spaniard and Russian.

The productions of Calderón and Lope on the Maly Theater stage between 1866 and 1886 are a high point in the history of the Spanish Golden Age Theater in Russia, and were only possible because of a temporary freedom in literary and theatrical expression. After Alexander II's assassination, only Iur'ev's monarchistic ending permitted the presentation of *La Estrella de Sevilla*. In general the Maly Theater's repertoire reflects Russia's strong interest in realistic literature with the theme of civic responsibility, while staging techniques show an attraction for historical authenticity. At the same time, however, and in contrast to the reigns of Alexander I and Nicholas I, relatively little criticism on the Spanish *comedia* appears in the writings of Russia's intellectuals—a state of affairs which changes during the last years of the nineteenth century.

Notes

1. *Moskovsii Maly Teatr 1824-1924* (Moscow, 1924), pp. 11-12.
2. Vissarion Grigor'evich Belinskii, "O russkoi povesti i povestiakh g. Gogolia," *Polnoe sobranie sochinenii* (Moscow, 1953-1959), I, 259-308.
3. Sergei S. Danilov, *Ocherki po istorii russkogo dramaticheskogo teatra* (Moscow, 1947), p. 223.
4. Nikolai V. Drizen, *Materialy k istorii russkago teatra* (Moscow, 1913), p. 231.

5. Nikolai V. Drizen, *Dramaticheskaia tsenzura dvukh epokh (1825-1811)* (St. Petersburg, 1917), pp. 150-151.
6. Ibid., p. 156.
7. Marc Slonim, *Russian Theater From the Empire to the Soviets* (New York, 1961), p. 60.
8. *Moskovskii Maly Theatr 1824-1924,* p. 40.
9. Ibid., p. 41.
10. Ibid., p. 66.
11. Ibid., p. 137.
12. Ibid., p. 138.
13. Ibid., pp. 66, 138.
14. Nikolai G. Zograf, *Maly Teatr vtoroi poloviny XIX veka* (Moscow, 1961), p. 17.
15. I. A. Svin'in, *Vospominaniia studenta 60-ykh godov, za 1862-1865* (Moscow, 1890), p. 86.
16. *Russkii biograficheskii slovar' Brokgauza i Efrona,* II, 404-405.
17. *Ezhegodnik imperatorskikh teatrov (1920-1903),* Kniga III, Prilozhenie (1-9), 6.
18. *Sto let Malomu Teatru* (Moscow, 1924), p. 54.
19. Alexander N. Bazhenov, *Sochineniia i perevody* (Moscow, 1869), I, iv.
20. Ibid., vi.
21. *Russkii biograficheskii slovar' Brokgauza i Efrona,* II, 404-405.
22. *Ezhegodnik imperatorskikh teatrov (1902-1903),* Kniga III, Prilozhenie (1-9), 7.
23. Bazhenov, II, 478.
24. Ibid., II, 479.
25. I shall discuss Sergei Andreevich Iur'ev's role in the Spanish Golden Age Theater at the Maly Theater in Moscow later in this chapter.
26. Bazhenov, II, 699.
27. Ibid., II, 695.
28. Ibid., II, 699-700.
29. *Russkii biograficheskii slovar' Brokgauza i Efrona,* II, 405.
30. Ibid. Flora Syrkina, *Russkoe teatral'noe iskusstvo vtoroi poloviny XIX veka* (Moscow, 1956), p. 146.
31. Slonim, p. 95.
32. Georg Goian, *Glikeriia Fedotova* (Moscow, 1940), p. 307.
33. A. A. Glumov, *Muzyka v russkom dramaticheskom teatre* (Moscow, 1955), p. 196. The result of their conversation was two songs, the first sung by Jane Seymour in the second act, the second by Margaret Paul, to console the queen in the third act. The songs were performed during the four performances of the play. Glumov, p. 198.
34. P. A. Stepanov, "Glinka i Dargomyzhskii," *Russkaia starina,* XIV (1875), 502.
35. *Bol'shaia Sovetskaia Entsiklopediia,* XIII (1952), 381.
36. Bazhenov, II, 707-708.
37. Ibid., II, 708-709.
38. Ibid., 723-724.
39. Ibid., 724-725.
40. I have not been able to find any information on the translator S. Kostarev.

41. Bazhenov, II, 724-725.
42. Ibid., 727-728.
43. Vladimir Alekseevich Giliarovskii, *Izbrannoe v trekh tomakh* (Moscow, 1960), II, 202.
44. L. M. Lopatin, "Sergei Andreevich Iur'ev kak myslitel'," *V pamiat' S. A. Iur'eva* (Moscow, 1891), p. 198.
45. Ibid., p. 212.
46. *Russkii biograficheskii slovar' Brokgauza i Efrona,* XXIV, 343.
47. Lopatin, p. 212.
48. Sergei Andreevich Iur'ev, "Znachenie teatra, ego upadok i neobkhodimost' shkoly stsenicheskogo iskusstva," *Russkaia mysl',* Book VIII (August, 1883), 171-172.
49. N. P. Iliarov-Platonov, "Vozrozhdenie obshchestva liubitelei Rossiiskoi slovesnosti v 1858," *Sbornik obshchestva liubitelei Rossiiskoi slovesnosti* (Moscow, 1891), p. 156.
50. Sergei A. Iur'ev, "Neskol'ko myslei o stsenicheskom iskusstve," *Russkaia mysl'* (February, 1888), 52.
51. Aleksei Veselovskii, "Iz vospominanii o starom druge," *V pamiat' S. A. Iur'eva,* pp. 143-144.
52. Glama Meshcherskaia, *Vospominaniia* (Moscow, 1937), p. 62.
53. S. A. Iur'ev's Spanish edition for Lope de Vega's works are *Biblioteca de Autores Españoles* and *Colección de las obras sueltas de Frey Lope de Vega Carpio (1776).* See Iur'ev's *Ispanskii teatr tsvetuchchago perioda XVI i XVII vekov* (Moscow, 1877). This work contains several of Iur'ev's essays on the Spanish Golden Age Theater and translations of *El castigo sin venganza* and *Fuente Ovejuna.* The editor of the theatrical journal *Artist* planned to publish all of Iur'ev's translations which included ten Spanish plays. See "K portretu S. A. Iur'eva," *Artist,* N. 4 (1889), 51.
54. Iur'ev wrote an essay on Tirso de Molina based on Western sources that was directed at the general Russian reading public and not for the specialist. See *Teatral'naia biblioteka,* N. 3 (November 1879), 1-13. Among Iur'ev's unpublished studies is "Lektsii ob ispanskom poete Lope de Vega," "Lectures on the Spanish Poet Lope de Vega." See *Tsentral'nyi gosudarstvennyi arkhiv literatury i iskusstva SSSR, Putevoditel'* (Moscow, 1963), 531-532. Fond 636, opis' I, edinitsa khraneniia 52.
55. *Besedy v Obshchestve liubitelei rossiiskoi slovestnosti pri imperatorskom Moskovskom universitete* (Moscow, 1871), 87-135.
56. Ibid., 85-86.
57. *Lope de Vega, Bibliografiia russkikh perevodov i kriticheskoi literatury na russkom iazyke: 1735-1961,* comp. Zakharii I. Plavskin (Moscow, 1961), p. 11.
58. Luis Vélez de Guevara, *El diablo cojuelo,* ed. A. Bonilla y San Martín (Madrid, 1910), xiii-xv.
59. *Vsemirnaia illiustratsiia* No. 333 (May 17, 1875), p. 395.
60. *Golos,* No. 298 (1875), p. 2.
61. *Moskovskii Maly Teatr 1824-1924,* pp. 64-65.
62. *Mariia Nikolaevna Ermolova* (Moscow, 1905), p. iv.
63. Ibid. An anonymous composer wrote music in the Spanish style for these performances of *Fuente Ovejuna.* Glumov, p. 460.
64. Mariia Nikolaevna Ermolova, *Pis'ma* (Moscow, 1939), p. 36.

65. *Mariia Nikolaevna Ermolova* (Moscow, 1905), p. 79.
66. The commander of the order of Calatrava and his men have carried off and abused Laurencia. When she escapes and returns to the village of Fuente Ovejuna she delivers her monologue in which she incites the villagers to riot.
67. Iurii M. Iur'ev, *Zapiski* (Leningrad, 1963), I, 117.
68. *Ermolova* (Moscow, 1943), p. 11.
69. Ibid.
70. Ibid, p. 79.
71. Tatiana Shchepkina-Kupernik, *O M. N. Ermolove* (Leningrad ,1940), p. 68.
72. *Moskovskie vedomosti,* No. 62 (March 10, 1876), p. 4.
73. *Sovremennye izvestiia,* No. 67 (March 10, 1876), p. 1.
74. Vladimir Alekseevich Giliarovskii, *Liudi teatra* (Moscow, 1941), p. 166.
75. A. Iablochkina, *Zhizn' v teatre* (Moscow, 1953), p. 92.
76. S. N. Durylin, *Mariia Nikolaevna Ermolova* (Moscow, 1951), p. 140.
77. George Tanquary Robinson, *Rural Russia Under the Old Regime* (New York, 1949), p. 49.
78. Nikander Strelsky, *Saltykov and the Russian Squire* (New York, 1940), p. 22.
79. *Mariia Nikolaevna Ermolova* (Moscow, 1925), p. 97.
80. A. F. Pisemskii, *Literaturny arkhiv, materialy i issledovaniia, Pis'ma* (Moscow, 1936), p. 339.
81. Ibid., p. 739. Iur'ev had completed the translation of *Fuente Ovejuna* by September 18, 1875. Ibid., p. 321.
82. Iurii M. Iur'ev, *Zapiski,* I, 576. *Fuente Ovejuna* was removed from the Maly Theater stage after its final performance on September 29, 1876. Ibid.
83. Zograf, p. 369.
84. V. A. Filippov, "Lope de Vega na stsene moskovskogo Malogo teatra," Unpublished essay kept in the Vserossiiskoe teatral'noe obshchestvo in Moscow, p. 12. The composer and critic Cesar Cui planned to write an opera on *Fuente Ovejuna.* Cesar Cui, *Izbrannye Pis'ma* (Moscow, 1955), p. 88.
85. Ermolova, *Pis'ma,* p. 38.
86. Ibid.
87. *Sankt Petersburgskie vedomosti,* No. 171 (June 24, 1878), p. 2.
88. *Peterburgskaia gazeta,* No. 123 (June 25, 1878), p. 3.
89. Iur'ev, *Zapiski,* I, 120-121.
90. Zograf, p. 369.
91. *Moskovskie vedomosti,* No. 243 (September 24, 1876), p. 5.
92. Plavskin, p. 13. Another critic complained that the actors could not perform well because they "were not accustomed to performing a play in which the plot becomes so complicated." Filippov, p. 14.

However, the other performances were good:

Madame Nikulina playing the role of Belisa, was able to transmit the role with vivacity, variety and animation. Madame Medvedeva as Lizarda combined the nobleness of a Madrid aristocratic lady with the passion of a woman not completely nunlike. Reshimov performed the role of Eliso with his typical liveliness. The same could be said about Lenskii who performed the role of Juan. *Moskovskie vedomosti,* No. 243 (September 24, 1876), p. 5. See Lope de Vega, *Los melindres de Belisa,* ed. Henriette Catharine Barrau (Amsterdam, 1933), pp. 67-75.

93. *Russkie vedomosti,* No. 243 (September 26, 1876), p. 4.

94. *Novoe vremia,* No. 221 (October 9, 1876), p. 2.

95. *Moskovskie vedomosti,* No. 286 (November 8, 1876), p. 3.

96. Sergei Iur'ev's translation of *El alcalde de Zalamea* was not passed by the state censor. Leningrad State Theatrical Library (hereafter referred to as LGTB), MS. 29707, May 11, 1866.

97. LGTB, MS. 67601, March 27, 1876.

98. Plavskin, p. 14.

99. Zograf, p. 370.

100. *Golos,* No. 144 (July 5, 1877), p. 2.

101. S. A. Iur'ev, *Ispanskii Teatr,* p. 210.

102. *Golos,* No. 144 (July 5, 1877), p. 2.

103. Alexander N. Ostrovskii, *Polnoe sobranie sochinenii* (Moscow, 1952), XIII, 161.

104. A. I. Dukinskaia, *A. N. Ostrovskii* (Moscow, 1951), pp. 18, 90. L. Lotman, *A. N. Ostrovskii i russkaia dramaturgiia ego vremeni* (Moscow, 1961), p. 63.

105. Boris V. Varneke, *History of the Russian Theatre,* trans. Boris Brasol (New York, 1951), p. 323.

106. Ibid., p. 321.

107. Ivan Shcheglov, *Narodnyi Teatr* (St. Petersburg, 1898), p. 124.

108. *Teatral'noe nasledstvo* (Moscow, 1956), I, 361.

109. Ostrovskii, *Neizdannye pis'ma k A. N. Ostrovskomu* (Moscow, 1932), p. 605.

110. Dubinskaia, p. 18.

111. Danilov, p. 334. Ostrovskii's library contained many Spanish plays and histories of Spanish literature. See *Biblioteka Alexandra Ostrovskogo* (Moscow, 1965), passim. In his unpublished papers there is a translation of Calderón's *La devoción de la cruz* written in the 1880's and an unfinished essay entitled, "Vot shto govoriat samy ispantsy ob *Intermediakh* Servantesa," "This Is What the Spaniards Themselves Say About Cervantes' *Entremeses.*" (1886). Tsentral'nyi gosudarstvennyi arkhiv literatury i iskusstva, *Putevoditel',* pp. 338-339.

112. Ostrovskii, *Polnoe sobranie sochinenii,* XI, 379. For the publication dates of the other Cervantes *Entremeses* see *Migel' de Servantes, Bibliografiia russkikh perevodov i kriticheskoi literatury na russkom iazyke: 1763-1957,* comp. A. D. Umikian (Moscow, 1959), pp. 70-72. The text for the Ostrovskii translation was *Los entremeses de Miguel de Cervantes Saavedra,* ed. Gaspar y. Roig (Madrid, 1868). Ostrovskii, *Polnoe sobranie sochinenii,* XI, 379.

In the introduction to his translation Ostrovskii says, "In these portraits written with a light stroke, Cervantes' genius is truly in its element. Here there continuously flows an unending stream of his inimitable humor. In the portrayal of personalities, enthusiastic, marvelous and funny Cervantes has no equal." Ibid., 378-380.

Ostrovskii was probably prompted to translate Cervantes' *El juez de los divorcios* because between 1843 and 1845 he was employed at a divorce court. See Danilov, p. 351.

113. V. A. Krylov, a director of the Alexandrinskii Theater in St. Petersburg was also interested in the Spanish Golden Age Theatre. I will discuss Krylov in Chapter IV.

The composer Cui had also considered writing an opera based on Calderón's *El alcalde de Zalamea.* On July 11, 1884, his friend the music and art critic Stasov wrote, "Dear Cesar, after returning home from your place last night, I read both Spanish plays. As far as Calderón's *L'Alcade de Zalamea* is concerned, I find it not adaptable for an opera which would be good. Therefore I shall not say one word about it." However in the same letter Stasov suggest he write an opera based on Ruiz de Alarcón's *El tejedor de Segovia,* Cui, p. 508.

114. Ostrovskii, *Neizdannye pis'ma,* p. 49.

115. Ibid., p. 51.

116. Ibid., p. 55.

117. Ibid., p. 56.

118. Ostrovskii, *Polnoe sobranie sochinenii,* XIII, 380.

119. The repertoire division was composed of S. A. Iur'ev, Storozhenko, and the painter and art historian Fedor Ivanovich Sollgub. Zograf, p. 407. Storozhenko lectured on Calderón and Lope at the Theatrical Institute which Iur'ev established in 1888 to prepare actors and actresses for the Maly Theater. See E. T. Kirova, *40 let v teatre* (Moscow, 1931), p. 18.

120. A. I. Sumbatov, "Otnosheniia Sergeia Andreevicha Iur'eva k stsene za poslednie tri goda ego zhizni," *V pamiat' S. A. Iur'eva,* p. 189.

121. Slonim, p. 95.

122. Varneke, p. 348.

123. Dmitrii Koroviakov, *Vokrug teatra* (St. Petersburg, 1894), p. 3.

124. *Peterburgskii dnevnik teatrala,* No. 9 (1904), 3.

125. "Anatoli Gel'tser, *Artist,* No. 33 (1894), 83-86.

126. Zograf, p. 503.

127. A copy of Meshcherskii's *Ispaniia-Al'bom* (1867) is housed at the Library of Congress. In his memoires Meshcherskii later wrote, "I later read his [Louis Viardot's] famous work, *Description of the Madrid Gallery,* which I could see for myself when I was in Spain. The Madrid Gallery ought to be considered one of the principal picture galleries in Europe for its wealth and the unusually good condition and freshness of the paintings." A. V. Meshcherskii, "Vospominaniia kniazia A. V. Meshcherskago." *Russkii arkhiv,* I (1901), 496.

In 1850 Meshcherskii traveled to Western Europe and Spain because of a respiratory illness. He mentions a book on his travels to Spain, but I have never seen any reference to it. Ibid., 500.

128. Zograf, p. 509. The setting for Hugo's *Ernani* which the Maly Theater presented in 1889 was originally used for *La Estrella de Sevilla.*

129. N. V. Davydov, *Iz proshlago* (Moscow, 1913), pp. 177-178.

130. Zograf, p. 503.

131. *Teatr i zhizn'* No. 196 (December 14, 1886), pp. 1-2.

132. *Russkie vedomosti,* No. 343 (December 14, 1886), p. 3.

133. *Teatr i zhizn',* No. 196 (December 14, 1886), pp. 1-2.

134. James Billington, *The Icon and the Ax* (New York, 1966), p. 435.

135. *Diez comedias del siglo de oro,* Hymen Alpern and José Martel (New York, 1939), p. 231.

136. *Russkie vedomosti* No. 346 (December 17, 1886), p. 5.

137. The critic from *Russkie vedomosti,* S. Vasil'ev, attacked Iur'ev for the changes because they altered the Spanish playwright's artistic purpose and called Iur'ev's adaptation "A Russian fantasy on a Spanish theme." *Russkie vedomosti,* No. 353 (December 22, 1886), p. 5.
138. *Russkie vedomosti,* No. 13 (January 14, 1887), pp. 2-3.
139. *Sovremennye izvestiia* No. 22 (December 15, 1886), p. 1.
140. James H. Billington, p. 385.
141. Ibid.
142. Zograf, p. 502.
143. Iuzhin-Submatov, p. 604.

IV: From Realism to Symbolism (1886-1910)

The period from 1886 to 1910 is one of transition between the age of realism and symbolism; and although the Spanish plays performed during this time were relatively unexciting comedies of manners, from them Russian symbolists became interested in Tirso de Molina's *El burlador de Sevilla* and Calderón's more serious religious themes. *La devoción de la cruz,* produced in 1910 by Vsevelod Meierkhol'd, marks the first performance of a Spanish Golden Age play by a modernist group.

Two currents in literary thought emerge during this period. Nonacademic or subjective criticism comes from the Russian symbolist movement, from writers such as Dmitrii Sergeevich Merezhkovskii (1865-1941) and Konstantin Dmitrievich Bal'mont (1867-1943); while original scholarship on the Spanish classical theater in Russia first appears in the writings of the learned jurist, Maksim Maksimovich Kovalevskii (1851-1916) and the Hispanist Dmitrii Konstantinovich Petrov (1872-1925).

Conditions in the country at large, and uninspired leadership in the theater after the death of such men as Iur'ev and Ostrovskii, brought about a general decline in the artistic and intellectual levels of theatrical performances in Russia after 1886. Nicholas II, who ascended the throne in 1895, was weak-willed and unimaginative. Dominated by his superstitious German wife and surrounded by reactionary advisors, he lived remote from the realities of his time. While it would be wrong to believe that Russia had made no social or political progress during the previous half century, the throne that Nicholas inherited from his father rested on a complex, routinized, and bureaucratic police state. Peasant unrest, defeat in the war with Japan, a series of strikes and riotous demonstrations in the major cities, culminating in the Revolution of 1905, characterize the Russian social scene of these years. These factors explain the unexciting role of the Spanish Golden Age plays in the Russian theater during this period. The role of the theater itself, in fact, was implicitly laid down by Nicholas' director of the theatrical division of the Board of Censors, Nikolai Shakhovskoi, when he said: "I consider the theater to be an ally of the government in distracting the minds of the people from heated political questions."[1]

At a time when serious Russian scholarship was making steady progress in virtually all fields, when an experimental avant-garde was beginning to focus on symbolic meaning in imaginative literature, on the Russian stage classical repertoire was giving way to farce, light melodrama, and comedies of manners. As the century drew to a close, Spanish Golden Age plays, though more frequently given than in previous years, followed the same trend. *La Estrella de Sevilla* was given only once in Moscow, at the Maly Theater in 1890;[2] and in the city of Iaroslav in 1894.[3] In 1905 it was rejected by the censors.[4] At a time when liberal men of the zemstvo, "local government," were demanding of Nicholas a regular popular representation in a separate elective body,[5] a group of Moscow's players applied for permission to produce the Iur'ev translation in the Narodyni Theater, one of the popular theaters accessible to the general public. Unfortunately, the massacre of the Russian citizenry known in history as Bloody Sunday occurred at this time. The people massed in the square before the Winter Palace, imploring the tsar for better conditions and a voice in the government, bore too striking a resemblance to the Iur'ev ending of *La Estrella de Sevilla.* The censor, Mikhail Tolstoi, made no secret of his reason for declaring the play unsuitable for performance, six days after Bloody Sunday:

> Because the king makes a public confession and promises to give the people an opportunity to express their opinions about the government through a council representing them. . . . In view of such an ending, I suggest that the play not be allowed to be performed on the People's [Narodnyi] nor any other stage.[6]

Lope's *Fuente Ovejuna,* Shakespeare's *Coriolanus,* and Schiller's *Die Jungfrau von Orleans* were likewise banned.[7]

After the removal of the Imperial theater monopoly in 1882, a number of private theaters waxed and waned. These groups played to a more select audience, were smaller and more intimate, and their repertoire often differed from that of the Imperial stage, but they were subject to the same rigid censorship controls.[8] Plays like *Marta la piadosa, El perro del hortelano, El anzuelo de Fenisa,* and others characterized as comedies of manners made up the Spanish repertoire presented by the Imperial and private stages of Moscow and St. Petersburg.[9] These plays were devoid of any religious content or political overtones.

The two Imperial dramatic theaters in St. Petersburg, the Alexandrinskii and the Mikhailovskii, catered to the court, the upper bureaucracy, and the diplomatic corps. In addition to censorship controls, the character of the audience determined the theatrical fare of St. Petersburg. The Mikhailovskii was the home of the ballet, the opera, and of plays given in the French language.[10]

The Alexandrinskii confined its repertoire to melodramas, light comedies, and the pseudo-psychological plays then coming into vogue. Most of these were pedestrian works of contemporary French and Russian playwrights who are completely forgotten today.[11] Between 1871 and 1890, only four performances of Shakespeare were seen on the Alexandrinskii stage, two of Molière, and one of Goldoni.[12] Turgenev, Ostrovskii, and Chekhov were given, but Ostrovskii's serious works were not performed very often;[13] Chekhov's *Ivanov,* a portrait of the "superfluous man" which the author considered typical of his epoch, received scant notice, while Gorky's works were never performed at all on the Imperial stage.[14]

The privilege the beneficiary had of selecting his own play from time to time had served to enrich the Maly Theater repertoire for Moscow's audiences during Iur'ev's lifetime. In St. Petersburg it served to maintain the status quo, since the beneficiary naturally chose plays calculated to suit the tastes and understanding of his audience. A commission headed by Ostrovskii tried to improve the general program of the Alexandrinskii Theater, but their efforts met with little success, and after his death in 1886, the repertoire continued to be dominated by plays dealing with light and silly love triangles and family situations—trite pieces which never outlived their authors.[15]

Another serious factor in the decline of the Russian theater at this time was the management.[16] Government-appointed managers and directors owed their positions more often to political influence than to managerial competence or artistic ability. Several were abysmally ignorant. Pchel'nikov, who directed the Imperial theaters between 1882 and 1898, reported that Tolstoy's *Power of Darkness* completely lacked any literary or artistic qualities because it failed to bring in money. Half the plays in the repertoire of the Maly Theater during the years of Pchel'nikov's administration were put on because he knew their untalented authors. A. A. Maikov, another manager of the Imperial theaters in Moscow, was equally unenlightened. When given a memo to the effect that the musicians of the orchestra needed music stands for the second violins, Maikov replied, "The Imperial Theater is rich enough to have only first violins." When the celebrated Samarin died, Maikov named an actor to fill his role of Famusov in Griboedov's *Wit Works Woe,* because he was the same height and weight as Samarin and the old costumes would fit him.[17]

Many members of the management were themselves would-be playwrights, and were able to exert pressure on the actors to have their own mediocre pieces given during the benefit performances. In this way more than one director of the Alexandrinskii Theater repertoire section gathered to himself a fleeting fame as a playwright and a part of the proceeds of the box office.[18] Deep differences were thus created between the administration and the troupe,[19] and the actors themselves spent a great deal of their time fighting with one another, one seeking to advance at the expense of the other.[20]

That such a situation existed at all was unfortunate, but it was particularly lamentable during the latter part of the nineteenth century, when the Alexandrinskii Theater could boast of Savina, Davydov, and several others who were among Russia's most outstanding and gifted actors. Many of these men and women made serious efforts to improve the general repertoire;[21] several were particularly interested in western classics. Vladimir N. Davydov (1849-1925) fought with the management of the Alexandrinskii for years in his efforts to include Lope, Molière, and Shakespeare in the repertoire. He refused to act in a play he considered inferior and left the Alexandrinskii stage for two years when the management refused to include the more serious dramatic works in the repertoire.[22]

Iurii Mikhailovich Iur'ev (1872-1948), Sergei's nephew, became a member of the Alexandrinskii troupe. Accustomed from his boyhood to readings of Shakespearian and Spanish drama, many of which he had seen performed at the Maly Theater under his uncle's direction, he brought with him the traditions he had inherited from his youth and his uncle's love for the Spanish Golden Age Theater.[23] Despite the efforts of men like him and Davydov to uplift the artistic and intellectual levels of the repertoire, farce, light melodrama, and comedies of manners prevailed.

The four Spanish plays given by the Russian stage toward the end of the nineteenth century were Tirso's *Marta la piadosa,* "Blagochestivaia Marta," Lope's *El perro del hortelano,* "Sobaka sadovnika," and *El anzuelo de Fenisa,* "Seti Fenizy," and Moreto's *El desdén con el desdén,* translated in Russian as one of the following: "Spes' za spes'," "Chem ushibsia tem i lechis'," "Prezrenie za prezrenie," or "Donna Diana."

Marta la piadosa was offered first by private theaters in Moscow and St. Petersburg. On October 17, 1889, the Goreva Theater, established by the actress Elizaveta Nikolaevna Goreva (1869-1917),[24] offered *Marta la piadosa* as one of the first selections for its Moscow audience. Presented with the conscientious preparation of the group, in the lavish atmosphere of the Goreva stage, the play was well received. The age-old theme of arranged and loveless marriages was one which was well known to the Russians. The tragedy of such a custom in their own social structure had long been dealt with by some of their greatest writers. While Tirso's play is a comedy which ends on a happy note, the social message of the work and the emphasis placed on the individual's right to happiness were heartily endorsed by the Goreva audience. The journal *Budil'nik,* which praised the brilliant scenery and luxurious costumes and settings, recommended the play very highly and inquired why the Moscow Maly Theater had never produced the work.[25]

The journal *Artist* provided its readers with a detailed portrait of Tirso, calling him "the most Spanish of all the Spanish,"[26] and pointed out that Tirso's ability to depict character and personality distinguished him from his fellow playwrights of the Spanish Golden Age. The critic complained that the "poetic halo of all-powerful love with which Tirso surrounded his heroine disappeared in Madame Annenkova-Bernar's performance,"[27] and provided his readers with a character sketch of Tirso's Marta. While *Artist* was mildly critical of individual portrayals, it hailed the performance as a whole and lamented that Spanish Golden Age plays had for so long been abandoned, pointing particularly to the great influence Tirso had on other western dramatists.[28]

Three months later, in January, 1890, *Marta la piadosa* was again performed, this time in a private theater in St. Petersburg, the Nemetti Theater. Established by the actress Vera Linskaia-Nemetti in 1887, the Nemetti presented chiefly light comedy and catered to the aristocracy.[29] In this performance Madame Svobodina-Perfileva played the role of Marta rather convincingly, but the group as a whole was uninspired and received poor reviews.[30]

In addition to these two groups, the Alexandrinskii group presented *Marta la piadosa* in the fall of 1898. This group occasionally gave matinees at the Mikhailovskii Theater, and it was on this stage that they presented *Marta la piadosa* on five separate dates during September and October.[31] The reviewer for *Teatr i iskusstvo* pointed to the inability of the actress, Madame Michurina-Samoilova, to portray the true image of Marta. He also complained of poor acting and a lack of cohesion among the troupe, and suggested that the play be removed from the repertoire.[32] Despite the faults complained of by the critic, however, the fact that *Marta la piadosa* was given five times during one season attested to its popularity with the St. Petersburg audience.

El perro del hortelano was offered on the Russian stage for the first time in February, 1891, when the actress Maria Gavrilovna Savina (1854-1915) chose it for her benefit performance.[33] This play went on to establish a record for the Alexandrinskii Theater, being presented twenty-five times in three years.[34] Alexander Nikolaevich Bezhetskii (1878-1913), whose pseudonym was Maslov, translated the play at Savina's request. Bezhetskii had traveled to Spain in the eighties and published his impressions of the country in 1884.[35] A minor novelist and playwright, he had written a piece on the Don Juan theme, *Sevil'skii Obol'stitel',* "The Tempter of Seville," which had been performed on the Imperial Stage in 1890.[36] His known translations from the Spanish consist of three Lope plays, all of which were performed on the Russian stage: *El perro del hortelano,* 1891; *El anzuelo de Fenisa,* 1893; *La boba para los otros y discreta para sí,* 1909.[37]

Maria Gavrilovna Savina had been interested in the Spanish theater since her earliest years on the stage. In 1873 she had chosen for her benefit performance Lope's *Los melindres de Belisa,* but the company had been unable to produce it.[38] Savina occupied the same place in the Alexandrinskii company as that occupied by Ermolova in the Maly.[39] A polished actress, Savina was well aware that her talents did not extend to the heroic repertoire that her Moscow counterpart had mastered. She too liked western drama; but she chose roles that fitted her talents and avoided the more serious plays.[40] For her benefit performances, Savina strove to please her audience in the roles of "society lady" and in the lighter comedies, which she did so well.[41] She often asked Viktor Alexandrovich Krylov (1836-1906) and Modest Il'ich Chaikovskii (1850-1918), the composer's brother, to provide plays that would suit her talents.[42] Krylov, who wrote under the pseudonym of Alexandrov, translated and adapted Moreto's *El desdén con el desdén,* which was performed in 1893.[43] In the opinion of the critics, the Spanish plays chosen by Savina for the Alexandrinskii repertoire were those which best suited her tastes and acting ability, and they constituted an improvement in the company's repertoire.[44]

The choice of *El perro del hortelano* was a likely one for Savina. A friend of Turgenev, she was well known for her portrayal of Natalia in his *Mesiat v derevnii,* "A Month in the Country,"[45] a play which has essentially the same theme: the rivalry in love between a mature woman and a young girl. The role of Diana Belflor, parallel to that of Natalia in the Turgenev play, was admirably suited to Savina's artistic temperament, and to her intuitive understanding of such a role may be credited the play's success. "These roles are her true genre," the critic from *Artist* wrote, commenting on her ability to portray a whimsical and capricious Spanish lady.[46]

A critic from *Novoe vremia* praised the production and offered his readers a comment on the Spaniard's passionate nature: "Probably no other nation is so dedicated to love and to fighting. . . . Spanish poets have been especially successful in depicting love and jealousy, and the portraits of enamoured women are painted with extreme sensitivity and elegance."[47]

In Moscow, the Maly Theater performed *El perro del hortelano* on August 30th and September 1, 1893. This production met with scant success.[48] The Moscow critics felt that the play itself was frivolous and childish, and that on the basis of it Lope could hardly be considered a serious playwright.[49] The St. Petersburg audience of the next decade took an opposite view.

On October 28, 1903, *El perro del hortelano,* in the Bezhetskii translation used by Savina, was given at the St. Petersburg Maly Theater, also known as the Suvorin Theater.[50] In the opinion of the critics, the play was a resounding hit. The critics praised it not only because of the performance but because of the contrast it made with the standard repertoire of the Suvorin.[51] Apparently the audience as well as the critics had had a surfeit of psychological problems on the stage. For the Russian intellectual portrayed in drama insanity had become the escape from reality which suicide had provided for the romantic hero of the early nineteenth century.[52] By the end of the century, insanity had become virtually an obsession for the stage.[53] The freshness of Lope's three hundred-year-old play gladdened the hearts of the critics. "On the stage healthy people cried, had healthy worries, healthy joys, healthy love and jealousy. They are intelligent, stupid, clever, good, or evil, but they are all sane. Among them are neither degenerates, crazy people, nor those under psychiatric care."[54] After the second act of Lope's play, an elderly doctor in the audience shouted, "Glory to Thee, Lord, not one madman."[55] The humour and elegance of Madame Mironova's portrayal of Diana Belflor drew favorable praise from the critic, as did that of Mikhailov, who played Tristán, "a prototype for Figaro. . . ."[56]

In 1893, Savina chose another Lope play for her benefit performance, which Bezhetskii translated for her: *El anzuelo de Fenisa,* "Seti Fenizy." The play created a considerable difference of opinion among the reviewers. *Niva* was highly pleased at the new addition to the Alexandrinskii repertoire, finding "the personalities marvelously well defined, the lines so witty and interesting that at times one forgets the work is more than two hundred and fifty years old."[57] The reviewer for *Russkaia zhizn'* admired Lope's skill in portraying the female personality and found the play's raciness reminiscent of a Boccaccio *novella,*[58] while *Artist* praised it for its Spanish costumes. In contrast to the success of her Diana in *El perro del hortelano,* however, Savina's performance as Fenisa was described as "monotonous." Dalmatov in the role of Lucindo "looked more like a Russian merchant than a Spaniard." Only Davydov, as Tristán, the servant, was well received.[59]

Writing in another vein, the reviewer for *Petersburgskii listok* sharply condemned the work itself, branding it as pornographic material only fit for the brothel. Observing a delicacy of language which precluded the word "brothel," the reviewer employed a euphemism coined by the novelist Saltykov-Shchedrin, "finishing schools devoid of classical languages." He complained that the play "caused grown men to blush and women to depart with their young daughters after the first act,"[60] and demanded its immediate removal from the Imperial stage.

On the other hand, Aleksei Sergeevich Suvorin (1834-1912), the editor of *Novoe vremia,* was delighted with the Lope work and hailed it as a welcome change from those courtesans "who are automatically reborn by love."[61] He felt that transformations such as those seen in Dumas' Marguerite Gauthier, for example, were neither typical nor convincing. In his opinion, women of easy virtue tended to remain so. Lope's Fenisa, who continues to ply her trade as a prostitute despite her love for Juan de Lara, he found much more realistic.[62]

Suvorin's opinion was greeted with a storm of protest among Russian society, and the critic writing in *Teatral'noi mirok* undertook to defend his fellow publicist. He agreed that Suvorin was entitled to be skeptical of loose women who are supposedly reborn by love, and offered his own judgment in the matter: "One can sincerely believe in people, and in good, and at the same time doubt or at least be skeptical of the sudden transformation of a courtesan into an honest woman."[63] The more conservative viewpoints apparently won out, for *El anzuelo de Fenisa* was never again performed in tsarist Russia.

In the Fall of 1893, Moreto's *El desdén con el desdén,* "Chem ushibsia, tem i lechis'," translated by Krylov, with a musical score by N. S. Korotkov, was produced by the Alexandrinskii Theater.[64] Krylov's translation was in reality an adaptation of the Russian text used for the 1834 performance of this play.[65] The production was well received, and the role of Diana, played by Michurin-Samoilova, who had played the role of Marcela in *El perro del hortelano,* was particularly well presented. Critics wrote that they were happy to see "still another beautiful play taken from oblivion,"[66] and pointed out that the Spanish classics were but little known in comparison with the French plays which had for so long been based upon them.[67]

The Krylov translation of *El desdén con el desdén* was again performed, in 1895, at the Korsh Theater,[68] another of Moscow's private theaters; and on October 14, 1899, at the Novy Theater.[69] The Novy had been opened the year before in Moscow as a branch of the Maly and Bolshoi theaters. Neither performance appears to have been commented upon anywhere in the press.[70]

In December of 1909, Lope's *La boba para los otros y discreta para sí* "Gertsoginiia Pastushka," translated by Bezhetskii, was presented at the Mikhailovskii Theater by students of the Alexandrinskii Theatrical Institute.[71] Historical accuracy was emphasized and Italian Renaissance music accompanied the performance.[72] Owing to the inexperience of the actors, however, the production did not impress the critics; this did little to dampen the response of the audience, composed mainly of young persons, who "answered the play with animated, infectious laughter, and youthful enthusiasm."[73]

By the end of the nineteenth century Spanish Golden Age drama had taken its place beside that of classic Greek and western drama in Russia. Many impressions and recollections of it were recorded by Russian travelers, writers, scholars, and musicians. Peter Il'ich Chaikovskii (1840-1893) was very interested in Spanish music and greatly admired Glinka's ability to combine and harmonize Spanish themes, as he did in "A Night in Madrid."[74] In Chaikovskii's own music, "Danse Espagnole" in *Swan Lake* and "Serenade of Don Juan" in his *Six Romances* are examples of Spanish themes.[75]

Accompanied by his brother Modest, Chaikovskii paid a visit to Iurii Iur'ev following the 1893 performance of *El desdén con el desdén*. The composer had been very favorably impressed with the play, and after complimenting the actor on his portrayal of Don Luis, informed Iur'ev that he intended to use the Moreto work for an opera.[76] Unfortunately, Chaikovskii died a few months later, without finishing the operatic score. His brother Modest and the composer Sergei Ivanovich Taneev (1856-1946), did attempt to finish it.[77] The librettist, A. A. Benkstern, made a new translation of the Moreto play from the French,[78] and from this Taneev and Modest Chaikovskii worked out the scenario in August of 1895. Here again, the music was never composed, but the sketches for a three-act opera in six scenes remain in the unpublished documents of Taneev. His library contained both Russian translations of the Moreto play, as well as a copy of *Fuente Ovejuna* in Russian,[79] and he too intended to write an operatic work based upon a Spanish Golden Age play. In 1884, he had written to Peter Il'ich Chaikovskii: "I have come upon a theme for my next opera. It is Lope de Vega's drama, *Fuente Ovejuna,* a marvelous play from the time of Ferdinand and Isabella, which contains many marvelous things for the operatic stage."[80] This work was never completed, but the unpublished libretto can be found in Taneev's archives.[81]

The first original Russian study on the drama of Lope was written in 1889 by Maksim Kovalevskii. An outstanding jurist and professor of law, in 1886 he published a study on Russian slaves in Medieval Spain. In preparation for this he had examined documents in Gerona, Barcelona, Palma de Mallorca, and Valencia.[82] As a memorial to his late friend, Sergei Iur'ev, in 1889 Kovalevskii wrote an essay entitled "Narod v drama Lope de Vegy, *Ovechii Istochnik*," "The people in Lope de Vega's Drama, *Fuente Ovejuna*."[83]

Kovalevskii analyzes this play with the legalist's mind, observing that Lope's technique lays before the audience an accurate portrait of the political and social structure of Spain in the late fifteenth century. In a relatively brief but well-documented history of Spain, Kovalevskii points out that various articles of the Spanish legal code had, by the end of the fifteenth century, prohibited the free movement of the peasantry, a liberty they had enjoyed before the feudal system curtailed their freedom of movement and of land use. With feudalism firmly established, the Spanish peasantry were no longer able to leave the land to which they were attached.[84] As the country moved from a feudal structure to absolutism, the sufferings of the peasantry, in Kovalevskii's argument, are the direct result of dissention and factionalism among the ruling classes and the military orders.[85] On the basis of this argument Kovalevskii analyzes Lope's *Fuente Ovejuna,* citing many passages which support his thesis, as he unfolds the action and plot of the play for his readers.

Kovalevskii concludes that only when a people is faced with the certain knowledge that it has no other recourse against repression does the idea of rebellion take root in its mind.[86] In showing the gradual awareness of Lope's people, faced with such a knowledge, Kovalevskii points to the genius of the playwright in having endowed his characters with a great dignity and sense of honor, a characteristic of Spanish drama which had so impressed Herzen and Iur'ev. Kovalevskii's documentation provides an interesting insight on the wide range of Spanish material available to the Russian scholar of his day, apart from the value of his work as the first original study on Lope as a social historian. This same theme was considerably enlarged upon a few years later by the Hispanist, Dmitrii Konstanovich Petrov, professor of philology at St. Petersburg University, who was the first Russian to write a doctoral thesis on the Spanish theater.

As a student, Petrov was encouraged in his choice by the comparatist, Alexander Nikolaevich Veselovskii (1838-1906), who helped him obtain a travel grant to study abroad.[87] Petrov studied Spanish literature in France, under Morel-Fatio and Gaston Paris, and under Menéndez Pelayo in Spain. To these men he acknowledges his indebtedness for their encouragement and assistance.[88] In 1899, while still a graduate student, Petrov translated and wrote important commentaries on several of the Calderón works.[89] For his master's essay, he chose to examine the theater of Lope, setting forth the premise that his theater of manners was a true reflection of Lope's own time. He regarded it as important not only for its moral and aesthetic qualities, but for its social reflections as well.

Published in 1902, and entitled *Ocherki bytovogo teatra Lope de Vegy,* "Studies on Lope de Vega's Comedies of Manners," his master's essay examines scores of plays written during the first two decades of the seventeenth century and dealing with Lope's Spain.[90] Petrov divided his work into three sections: "The Family in the Love Comedies of Lope de Vega," "Dramas of Honor," and "Virtuous Women." He examines these aspects of Lope's plays for their sociological content, comparing and correlating them with numerous other sources, mainly memoirs of Spaniards and foreign travelers to Spain during Lope's time. These documents further confirmed Petrov in his opinions on how closely Lope's plays reflected the realities of his own social structure; he concluded that they could, in fact, be regarded as social chronicles.[91]

Beginning with an analysis of the family structure, Petrov studied the inferior position of the Spanish women, constantly subjected to the watchful eye of their male relatives. He sees honor as the driving force of Lope's comedies of manners, a concept directly related to the matter of chastity in the maiden and fidelity in the wife. Until a girl is married, her father, brother, or other kinsman is charged with the responsibility of guarding her chastity, a responsibility which passes on to her husband thereafter.[92] Petrov notes too the blood-letting involved where a woman has been dishonored in any way that violates her sexual purity: the spilling of her blood to satisfy the outward forms demanded by the Spanish seventeenth century honor code. In particular, he examined this aspect of Spanish reality in *Los milagros del desprecio* and *El maestro de danzar.*

The question of the husband as a many-eyed Argus is again taken up in the next section when Petrov examines the honor theme in husband-wife relationships in Lope's plays. Citing among others, *La vitoria de la honra* and *El sufrimiento del honor,* Petrov concludes that the Spaniard was by no means surprised to see a man kill his wife, on the stage or off, if he merely suspected her of infidelity.[93] Dedicating his closing remarks to plays about the virtuous women of Spain, Petrov points out that Lope sought to show that there were indeed virtuous wives; and that they remained so despite long absences of their husbands and repeated efforts by other men to seduce them.[94] Lope also depicts women who were virtuous despite their husbands' faithlessness,[95] and women who choose to marry poor but good men instead of rich and evil suitors.[96] Among the plays studied for this aspect of Lope's theater, Petrov points in particular to *La bella mal maridada, Los hidalgos de la aldea,* and *La viuda, casada y doncella.*

Petrov's essay is a very carefully documented work and ranks among the most erudite studies ever done on the Spanish Golden Age theater. It was one of the first known works, as the American Hispanist George Irving Dale has suggested, to study the honor code in Lope and its relations to Spanish life.[97]

In 1907 Petrov published his doctoral dissertation, entitled "Zametki po staroi ispanskoi komedii," "Comments on the Spanish Classical Comedy." The dissertation consists of the previously unpublished Lope play, *Lo que pasa en una tarde,*[98] from the manuscript in the Biblioteca Nacional in Madrid, and Petrov's analysis and critical commentaries on this and other works. His dissertation reveals a knowledge of Spain and her culture which few scholars of his age possessed, as he deals with the multiple and complex components of Spanish life as seen in this play. Spain's holidays, the amusements of her people, the position of the hidalgo in society,[99] and the important role of Seville and Madrid in her cultural and historical development are also assessed by Petrov with remarkable acuity. Two complete chapters of the dissertation are devoted to a thoroughly documented history of the Golden Age theater, from the early sixteenth century until the death of Lope.

Elaborating on Lope's own life and love affairs, as he felt them to be mirrored in the dramatic works, and analyzing Lope's technique as a playwright, Petrov arrives at certain broad conclusions concerning Lope's art. For him, Lope's plays constituted his *Ars Amandi;*[100] he considered Lope's heroes to be passionate and jealous, his heroines haughty and disdainful, and felt that his ability to portray women far excelled his ability to depict men, his heroines being far more dynamic and viable than his heroes. Petrov concluded that Lope was, in fact, the world's greatest portrayer of women.[101] He regarded love as the most driving force in Lope's work, and pointed to the playwright's masterful understanding of all the shades of emotion that may be experienced in love,[102] ranging from jealous rages to complete indifference, from tenderness to disdain. He concluded that the two most salient features of love in Lope are that his lovers usually consummate their love physically in marriage, and that they never do so before.

Petrov's contribution to Spanish scholarship in Russia was a great one. He brought to his work that dispassionate judgment and critical analysis which are the hallmarks of the careful scholar. He was as well a man caught up in the personal joys and intellectual fascination of teaching and research; his thoroughness and enthusiasm in both became legendary in Russia. Petrov's love for the Spanish theater was communicated to his students; and one of them, a poet, Vladimir Piast, subsequently became the translator of many Spanish plays.[103]

Another current in literary thought in Russia at this time sprung from the symbolist movement in literature. In the closing years of the nineteenth century, caught up to some extent in the personal malaise which accompanied the Russian intellectual of the times and the social malaise which the times surely justified, quite a number of Russian writers sought escape in the literature of the western symbolists, especially from France.

Many of the symbolists had as their basis "art for art's sake,"[104] and the movement came at a period in Russia when civic instincts had been stifled by government repression. Aestheticism was substituting beauty for duty, and individualism emancipated man from all social obligations.[105] Many of the Russian symbolists were men of the highest intellectual level, very much influenced by writers such as Dostoevskii, Nietsche, and Vladimir Solov'ev (1853-1900).[106] The symbolist movement in Russia produced a renaissance of poetry second only to the age of Pushkin, and a period of prodigious research into the plastic arts, the theater, music, and the ballet.[107] Art historians studied the great painters of the west, and symbolist poets and writers were drawn to religiosity. In much the same manner as the Spanish mystics had grown in number and intensity as a reaction against early Protestantism, many Russians reacted against the positivism of the age in a vigorous renewal of religious affirmation.

Calderón had a message for these men. His view of earthly existence in *La vida es sueño,* or the portrayal of the self-willed individual who subjugated himself only to God in *La devoción de la cruz,* were views that found ready acceptance among many Russian symbolists. These same ideas were expressed by A. L. Volynskii (1865-1926), who wrote under the name of Akim Flekser. In 1896 he published an article entitled "Religiia i sovremennaia literatura," "Religion and Contemporary Literature," in which he said:

> Religion brings into our view a mysterious law, inexplicable by any instrument of human knowledge. No discovery of science, no idea of any kind casts light on the mystery of human existence. Our life is a dream which only death will awaken. Individualism, in essence, consists of the destruction of the terrestrial and the subjugation of the individual to a Godly force, from which individuality comes, and to which it returns.[108]

The extremities of individualism, as seen in Eusebio in *La devoción de la cruz,* or Tirso's Don Juan, amount to what Flekser called "demonism." In his view, demonism freed the human mind from its restraints and aroused the desire to declare war on the world's basic virtues. Conversely, he believed that no matter to what lengths a man may carry individualism in his attempt to impose his own will, he must eventually submit himself to God's will.[109]

These tenets of symbolism were basic to the thought of Dmitrii Merezhkovskii, who was strongly drawn to the religious aspects of life. As the contemporary Russian religious historian, Nicholas Zernov, states:

> Merezhkovskii was the first critic to treat Tolstoy and Dostoevski as preëminently religious teachers, a side of their work which had been overlooked by the Russian intelligentsia. His articles provoked heated controversies and marked a turning point in the evolution of Russian culture. It closed a period of persistent anti-Christian bias which had characterized the mentality of the left-wing intellectuals.[110]

In his youth Merezhkovskii had found in Calderón, Cervantes,[111] and the Spanish mystic poets an expression in literature for his philosophic and religious convictions.[112] He too believed that man is helpless in the presence of God, and that although as an individualist he can assault the basic laws of society, the freedom embodied in such lawlessness can ultimately produce happiness only in communion with God. A short poem he published in 1890 manifests this conviction:

> I need not happiness, my Lord!
> I came here to breathe
> The life-giving coolness of your forest
> And hearken to your rustling leaves.
>
> Only in your bosom
> Am I cleaner and kinder in my heart.[113]

Between 1886 and 1887 Merezhkovskii wrote a play in which he employed the basic theme of Calderón's *La vida es sueño.* Zinaida Gippius, the poetess, relates that before her marriage to Merezhkovskii, he was writing "a long poem from Spanish life called *Silvio ili vozvrashchenie k prirode,* 'Silvio, or The Return of Nature,' based on Calderón's *La vida es sueño.*"[114] In the introduction to this work, however, Merezhkovskii states:

> The basic theme of this drama is the same as Calderón's famous play, *Zhizn'-tol'ko son,* "La vida es sueño." But aside from the similarity of the external plot, this work is completely foreign to the work of the Spanish playwright and is completely independent of it.[115]

Merezhkovskii's work contains the idea that earthly life is a dream, and his hero Silvio shares Segismundo's desire for freedom. Silvio too has been imprisoned by his father, Bazilio, an astronomer king who has read in the stars that his son will misuse his power to rule. Both of Calderón's drugging scenes are repeated in the Merezhkovskii work, as Silvio is brought to the palace in order to test the prediction of the stars made at his birth. He behaves badly, mistreating the women and killing a courtier in a fit of temper, is drugged and returned to his forest prison. A revolt of the people subsequently recalls him to the throne.

Departing from the essentials of the Calderón work, Merezhkovskii's Silvio is skeptical about God—a fact that does not figure in the Calderón play at all; in fact, he doubts that God exists at all. At the same time, Silvio is earnestly seeking to learn the mystery of human existence. His father, Bazilio, tells him that the secret of life lies in the study of science; while his tutor Klotaldo insists that it rests with God, and a knowledge of God will make men free. Klotaldo instructs Silvio to seek God through nature, for it is here that He is most manifest.

The enigmatic nature of life and the universe almost drive Silvio to suicide, however. After he is restored to his rightful throne, he must decide upon the fate of his now imprisoned enemies. He is on the verge of casting himself into the sea when Estrella, a sister of one of his prisoners, appears and begs for her brother's life. She pleads with Silvio for mercy, compassion, and justice. Having grown up with the animals of the forest, such qualities are alien to Silvio; and he grants freedom to his prisoners out of mere indifference. Silvio continues to deny the existence of God, but as Segismundo is brought to a new awareness of God through Rosaura, Estrella insists that his freeing of the prisoners constitutes an act of mercy, which in itself is a recognition of the existence of God.

In a sudden agony of spiritual conversion, Silvio recognizes the presence of God in the light of the sun, His messenger. He acknowledges for the first time in his life that God does exist, that He is the source of harmony in a world of anguish and despair, that man is insignificant and helpless without God's presence. Only in the belief in God can man find his answers for his own suffering. For the secrets of life, of the universe, only God is real. He ends by singing a hymn of glory to the sun, who shows us the way by shedding His light.[116]

Silvio is a compendium of Merezhkovskii's thought concerning God and man's necessity of finding Him. Although his first poems dealt with social protest, as early as 1883 his poems have a religious orientation which characterizes the majority of his works.[117] His poems depict a man who is searching for a God he is not even sure exists. Merezhkovskii's God is ubiquitous, omniscient, and omnipotent, but he cannot find Him. Many of Merezhkovskii's early poems deal with the life-is-a-dream motif. In several of these poems death is represented as preferable to life because man is a slave and life is a torment. Man can never be free, and consequently must surrender to the forces of nature, which are God. Related to Merezhkovskii's interest in *La vida es sueño* is his interest in the legend of Buddha's life, which was also a major source for Calderón's play.

In *Silvio,* in contrast to *La vida es sueño,* there is no satisfying love relationship between man and woman. Merezhkovskii cannot love because in his opinion love between man and woman is a conflict and struggle. This attitude towards love explains its absence from *Silvio.* If love between man and woman is not harmonious, then man seeks his love in God, the source of all harmony. In this belief, Merezhkovskii resembles the Spanish mystic poets such as Fray Luis de León, Santa Teresa de Jesús, and San Juan de la Cruz (about whom Merezhkovskii wrote several essays).

In 1891, four years after *Silvio,* Merezhkovskii published an essay entitled "Kalderon v svoei drame, *Poklonenie krestu,*" "Calderón in His Drama, *La devoción de la cruz.*"[118] The essay consists of three parts: Calderón as a mirror of the Spanish people, the plot summary of the play, and the symbols in *La devoción de la cruz.* This essay is not only a sequel to *Silvio,* but emphasizes one of symbolism's most important aspects, i.e., the adoration of the self-willed man and his power and desire to impose this will upon others. This interest in Calderón among the Russian symbolists differs radically from that of the previous generation. The reader will recall that Iur'ev and his circle were essentially interested in the Spanish masses and in collective elements as seen in *Fuente Ovejuna* and Iur'ev's adaptation of *La Estrella de Sevilla.* The symbolists, however, desire to emphasize the individual. True, one could find collective elements in Calderón *(El alcalde de Zalamea),* but the emphasis in Calderón is placed on the individual's struggle against the elements of nature, himself, and God *(El médico de su honra, La vida es sueño,* and *La devoción de la cruz).*

In the first part of his essay Merezhkovskii describes Calderón as the most representative of dramatists and as a man who did not resemble the rationalistic man of nineteenth-century Europe. What most characterizes Calderón's heroes is their strong will and passion, traits which Merezhkovskii also saw in a portrait of Calderón attached to one of Calderón's earliest editions. In Merezhkovskii's opinion, Calderón had the bravery and strong will of a warrior, the meditation of a poet, and the abstinence of a monk.[119] The playwright also combined the warmth of a Spanish evening with the zeal of the Inquisition, the lofty ideals of honor and chivalry with harshness and fanaticism. And as a monk and warrior he believed unquestionably in the dogma of the Roman Catholic Church. Calderón, the spokesman for the Spanish people, best depicted their favorite ideals, the love of woman and honor. The Spaniard, according to Merezhkovskii, used his iron will to achieve the two loves.[120]

Part three is the heart of the essay. In it Merezhkovskii defends Calderón against an attack by the German philosopher Mauritz Karriere, who said Calderón's intention was to show that even the most horrible crime should be pardoned in the eyes of God if the criminal truly loved God. The German objected to Eusebio's salvation despite his crimes.[121]

Answering this criticism, Merezhkovskii stated that Calderón's play is not based on a fetish for the cross, but rather on the essence of Christianity, i.e., that faith in God means a love for God and that without faith there can be no love for God. It is this power of love for God which saves Eusebio and Julia. Since they are of a dual nature (good and evil), they are typical of man in general. They are torn between sin and virtue, and between complete liberty and complete submission. They cannot be saved through their nature, which is partly evil, but through their will.[122] Eusebio and Julia are saved only through their love for God, who is represented symbolically by the cross; their love for God is far greater than their sins. Merezhkovskii believes that man must love God first and above all other things. Then comes man's love for man.

Merezhkovskii asks his contemporaries to cast aside their prejudices against things Catholic and to appreciate those works of art which Catholicism inspired. His essay is a call for intellectuals to reevaluate Calderón, to try to understand and appreciate him as a great literary giant and a man representative of his native culture and time.[123]

Konstantin D. Bal'mont (1867-1943), the critic, poet, and translator, was also interested in Spain's classical theater and supplemented this interest with trips to the Iberian peninsula early in his career.[124]

His first undertaking in the field of Spanish theater was the publication in 1900 and 1912 of a three-volume edition of several Calderón plays with essays and notes.[125] Bal'mont gives the following reason for choosing as his first translation Calderón's *El purgatorio de San Patricio:*

> I chose for the first translation *El purgatorio de San Patricio* not only because this drama immediately gives an image of Calderón's literary style, but because of its motif of repentance which links Russian and Spanish literature. As strange as it may seem, Dostoevskii and Lev Tolstoi are the northern brothers of Tirso, the author of *El condenado por desconfiado,* and of Calderón, the author of *El purgatorio de San Patricio* and *La devoción de la cruz.* No one has ever used the psychological theme of repentance like the Russian and the Spaniard. Only, with the Spaniard the approach is limited to Roman Catholicism, while in the Russian the approach is universal.[126]

In the extensive introduction to *El purgatorio de San Patricio* (iii-cxiii), using Western sources, Bal'mont presents a well-documented essay on Calderón, Cervantes, and Lope. Like the romantics, Bal'mont considered Lope inferior to Calderón,[127] and in his analysis of *El médico de su honra,* he traces parallels between Don Gutierre and Othello. In his essay on *La vida es sueño,* a play he had seen in Madrid, Bal'mont says:

> The greatest creation of Calderón's imagination is his amazing drama entitled *La vida es sueño.* In this philosophical drama, which like a mirror focuses all of light's rays, we see the complete symbolization of all that is earthly. The hero, the Polish prince Segismundo, is the artistic symbol of the human being with all his passions and spiritual contradictions. The only consolation for man's woes is embodied in the play's title.[128]

The translations have abundant notes and explanations. There is also an excellent bibliographic section dedicated to the Spanish theater, Calderón in general, and to many of his plays in particular. Bal'mont says he used for the translation *Biblioteca de autores españoles*.[129]

In 1904 Bal'mont published a book of essays entitled *Gornye Vershiny,* "Mountain Tops," which included two essays on the Spanish Golden Age theater, Francisco Goya, and translations of Spanish folk songs based on Rodríguez Marín's *Cantos populares españoles*.[130] These essays were originally delivered as lectures at Oxford, The Moscow Historical Museum, and The Free Russian University in Paris.[131] In the two essays on the Spanish theater Bal'mont discusses basic Spanish elements: honor, love, death, will, i.e., extreme freedom which borders on demonism.

In his essay, "Chuvstvo lichnosti v poesii," "The Presence of the Personality in Poetry," Bal'mont raises several questions: Is it better to be the object of someone's will or to be the projector of that will? Is it better to be the vanquisher or the vanquished? Is it better to be the master or the slave? Is it better to have one's freedom held in check or to be absolutely free?[132] Bal'mont revered those men "who rule their own destinies, and are not afraid to take destiny by the throat, for they are their own rulers."[133] Bal'mont felt a great attraction for Spain's greatest writers precisely because they were men of strong will, which is reflected in their literary creations.[134] Among these writers Bal'mont included Cervantes, Tirso, Calderón, Lope, and Mira de Amescua.[135]

In the second of these essays, "Tip don Khuana v mirovoi literature," "Don Juan in World Literature," Bal'mont states that Don Juan has captured the imagination of more writers than any other literary character because of his indomitable will to achieve his amorous aims. Tirso's Don Juan "will stop at nothing to achieve his aim."[136] Don Juan in Bal'mont's opinion, "defies the elements and has no fear of Judgment Day."[137] Thus it is Don Juan's demonic individualism and fearlessness which drew the Russian symbolists to Tirso's masterpiece.

The performances of Spanish Golden Age plays between 1886 and 1910 are relatively unexciting, but do reflect the general repertoire of the Russian stage during a period of severe theatrical censorship. Consequently, innocuous and apolitical comedies of manners by Lope, Tirso, and Moreto are the standard bill of fare.

On the other hand, this period gives rise to Russia's first original comedia scholarship, which reflects a realistic approach to Spain's classic theater. At the same time several Russian symbolists with a more subjective approach to literature study Spain's playwrights for their religious themes. It is this fortuitous combination of approaches that gives birth to the comedia as it appears on the Russian symbolist stage of Meierkhol'd, Evreinov, and Tairov.

NOTES

1. Sergei S. Danilov, *Ocherki po istorii russkogo dramaticheskogo teatra* (Moscow, 1948), pp. 421-422. Like his grandfather, Alexander III disliked plays dealing with social protest. Alexander M. Brianskii, *V. N. Davydov, Zhizn' i tvorchestvo (1849-1925)* (Moscow, 1939), p. 37.

2. *Ezhegodnik imperatorskikh teatrov* (1890-1891), p. 8.

3. *Lope de Vega, Bibliografiia russkikh perevodov i kriticheskoi literatury na russkom iazyke: 1735-1961,* comp. Z. I. Plavskin (Moscow, 1962), p. 22.

4. For the 1909-1910 season, the actor of the Maly Theater, A. P. Lenskii, proposed *La Estrella de Sevilla.* However, the administration of the Maly Theater did not accept his proposal. Nikolai G. Zograf, *Maly Teatr v kontse XIX-nachale XX veka* (Moscow, 1966), p. 354.

5. Nicholas V. Riasanovsky, *A History of Russia* (New York, 1963), p. 354.

6. *Teatral'noe nasledstvo* (Moscow, 1956), I, 394.

7. S. N. Durylin, *Mariia Nikolaevna Ermolova* (Moscow, 1953), p. 160.

8. *Sto let Alexandrinskomu Teatru* (Moscow, 1932), p. 206.

An exception to the official censorship policy was a performance of Calderón's *El alcalde de Zalamea.* The visiting German actor Ernst Possart and his troupe presented this play at the Paradiz Theater in Moscow twice between February 1 and April 13, 1891. *Artist* No. 135 (April, 1891), 156. See *Teatral'naia entsiklopediia,* IV, 449.

George Paradiz (1846-1901), a German actor and entrepreneur, built his theater in 1886 and presented the finest Western actors and playwrights. The fact that actors performed the play in German, and would reach only the educated elite, accounts for this production of *El alcalde de Zalamea.* Iurii M. Iur'ev, *Zapiski* (Moscow, 1963), I, 603.

9. Zograf, *Maly Teatr vtoroi poloviny XIX veka* (Moscow, 1960), p. 425.

10. *Sto let Alexandrinskomu Teatru,* p. 206.

11. Ibid., p. 210.

12. Durylin, p. 287.

13. For example, Ostrovskii's *Temnoe tsarstvo,* "The Kingdom of Darkness," a play about Moscow's narrow-minded merchant class. Brianskii, p. 38.

14. Danilov, p. 482.

15. Zograf, Maly *Teatr vtoroi poloviny XIX veka,* p. 425. See *Ezhegodnik imperatorskikh teatrov, Prilozhenie* (1905-1906), pp. 41 and 43. Danilov, pp. 425-426.

16. Nikolai A. Gorchakov, *The Theater in Soviet Russia,* trans. Edgar Lehrman (New York, 1957), p. 14.

17. Ibid.

18. Brianskii, p. 56 and Iur'ev, *Zapiski* (Moscow, 1948), p. 252.

19. Brianskii, pp. 34, 87, 136.

20. The actress V. A. Michurina-Samoilova (1866-1948) recorded an especially

illuminating incident in her memoirs. During rehearsal for *Marta la piadosa,* she and the actor Dal'skii had worked out a technique whereby the effect of a resounding slap in the face was achieved: Dal'skii, turning slightly away from the audience, was to lift his hand unnoticed to protect his face as Samoilova struck him. During the performance, however, he forgot to do so, and the actress struck him a stinging slap in the face; whereupon Dal'skii grabbed her hand and squeezed it with all his strength. Despite her whispered pleas and protests of pain, he maintained his painful grip on Samoilova's hand until the end of the scene. V. A. Michurina-Samoilova, *Polveka na Aleksandrinskoi stsene* (Moscow, 1935), p. 68.

One critic reviewing *Marta la piadosa,* in fact, remarked that the actress gave the general impression of having "hurried through" some of the scenes. *Teatr i iskusstvo,* No. 36 (1898), pp. 932-933.

21. A. P. Lenskii, "Prichina upadka teatral'nago dela," *Teatr i iskusstvo,* No. 11 (1897), pp. 202-204.

22. Brianskii, p. 45. Davydov's interest in the classical repertoire of Lope and Calderón began when as a young man he saw their plays performed on the Maly Theater in Moscow stage. V. N. Davydov, *Rasskaz o proshlom* (Moscow, 1962), p. 52.

23. Iur'ev, *Zapiski* (Moscow, 1948), p. 165.

24. *Teatral'naia entsiklopediia,* II, 17. *Artist* No. 3 (1889), p. 112. The Goreva Theater's attempt to have lavish and authentic settings for its productions was a result of the Meiningin players' performances in Moscow. Evgenii Alexandrovich Znosko-Borovskii, *Russkii teatr nachala 20 veka* (Prague, 1925), pp. 98-99.

25. *Budil'nik,* No. 42 (1889), p. 5.

26. *Artist,* No. 3 (1889), p. 113.

27. Ibid., p. 115.

28. Ibid., p. 113.

29. *Entsiklopedicheskii slovar' Brokgauza i Efrona,* XXXIV (1896), 714.

30. *Birzhevye vedomosti,* No. 25 (January 25, 1890), p. 4.

31. Performed in August 30, September 1, 6, 10, and October 18. *Ezhegodnik imperatorskikh teatrov* (1898-1899), p. 43.

32. *Teatr i iskusstvo,* No. 36 (1898), pp. 932-933. Scenes from these performances are found on p. 927. There also exists in the Leningrad State Theatrical Library an unpublished album of photographs taken at these performances.

33. Plavskin, p. 19.

34. Ibid., p. 20.

35. Aleksei Nikolaevich Bezhetskii, *Putevye nabroski* (St. Petersburg, 1884).

36. Bezhetskii, *Sevil'skii Obol'stitel'* (St. Petersburg, 1896).

37. Plavskin, pp. 46, 42, 43.

38. M. V. Karneev, *Dvadtstat' let na imperatorskoi stsene* (St. Petersburg, 1894), pp. 59-60.

39. I. Shneiderman, *M. G. Savina* (Leningrad, 1956), p. 163.

40. Savina's conservative nature deterred her from performing roles such as Laurencia in *Fuente Ovejuna.* Danilov, p. 432.

41. *Sto let Aleksandrinskomu Teatru,* p. 322.

42. Danilov, p. 426.

43. Almost twenty of Alexandrov's plays were performed at the Alexandrinskii

Theater. *Sto let Aleksandrinskomu Teatru,* p. 210. See V. A. Krylov, "Vospominaniia," *Istoricheskii vestnik,* IV (1906), 501.

44. *Sto let Alexandrinskomu Teatru,* p. 224.

45. Danilov, p. 431.

46. *Artist,* No. 14 (1891), 142-143.

47. *Novoe vremia,* No. 5383 (February 22, 1891), p. 3.

A photograph of Savina in the role of Diana is in *Ezhegodnik imperatorskikh teatrov* (1890-1891), 197. Translated by D. D. Koroviakov, Calderón's *La dama duende,* "Nevidimka," was scheduled for performance by the Imperial theaters, but was never performed. Ibid. (1891-1892), p. 269.

48. Performed fourteen times. Zograf, *Maly Teatr v kontse XIX-v nachale XX veka,* p. 540.

49. *Russkie vedomosti,* No. 240 (1893), p. 3. Photographs of the play are in *Ezhegodnik imperatorskikh teatrov (1893-1894),* pp. 275-279.

50. Photographs of the performances are in *Birzhevye vedomosti,* No. 523 (October 22, 1903), p. 3.

51. From 1895-1900, A. S. Suvorin's theater called Teatr literaturno-khudozhestvennago obshchestva produced plays dealing mainly with psychological problems. Danilov, p. 476.

52. James H. Billington, *The Icon and the Ax* (New York, 1966), p. 403.

53. Ivan Ivanovich Ivanov, "O sovremennoi nevrastenii i starom geroizme, *Teatr i iskusstvo,* No. 47 (1899), 827.

54. *Novoe vremia,* No. 9936 (November 1, 1903), p. 4.

55. Ibid.

56. Ibid.

57. *Niva,* No. 3 (1893), p. 73.

58. *Russkaia zhizn',* No. 2 (January 3, 1893), p. 3. The translator, Vladimir Petrovich Begichev (1828-1891), was once director of the Maly Theater in Moscow and inspector of the Imperial theater repertoire. *Ezhegodnik imperatorskikh teatrov* (1891-1892), 474.

59. *Artist,* No. 30 (1893), 176.

60. *Peterburgskii listok,* No. 2 (January 3, 1893), p. 4.

61. *Novoe vremia,* No. 6092 (January 8, 1893), p. 4.

62. Ibid.

63. *Teatral'nyi mirok,* No. 2 (1893), pp. 8-9.

64. The Alexandrinskii Theater performed the play thirteen times. *Ezhegodnik imperatorskikh teatrov (1893-1894),* pp. 128-129. It was also performed at the Paradiz Theater in 1886. *Teatr i zhizn',* No. 123 (1886), p. 2.

65. *Artist,* No. 31 (1893), 169.

66. *Novoe vremia,* No. 6297 (September 19, 1893), p. 3.

67. Ibid. Moreto's *El desdén con el desdén* appealed very much to the late nineteenth-century Russian aristocracy for the same reason that it appealed to a decadent seventeenth-century Spanish aristocracy; the frivolous theme and atmosphere so distant from the harshness of reality. Moreto's play resembles the theater of the eighteenth-century French playwright Marivaux more than it resembles the plays of Moreto's contemporaries.

68. S. Vasil'ev, *Teatral'naia Khronika, Sezon 1895-1896* (Moscow, 1896), p. 92.

69. *Russkie vedomosti,* No. 283 (October 13, 1899), p. 3. The Novy Theater

performed *Donna Diana* thirteen times. Zograf, *Maly Teatr v kontse XIX-nachale XX veka,* p. 554.

70. *Teatral'naia Entsiklopediia,* IV, 84. Nikolai Khodotov (1878-1932), played the role of Perrin (Polilla) at an Alexandrinskii Theater Institute performance in September, 1891. On November 8, 1897 he played the role of the servant Roberto at the Institute's performance of *El alcaide de sí mismo.* Nikolai Khodotov, *Blizkoe y dalekoe* (Moscow, 1962), pp. 279, 281.

71. Performed seven times between December 4, 1908 and January 27, 1909. *Ezhegodnik imperatorskikh teatrov (1909),* vypusk 6-7, pp. 80-82.

72. *Rech',* No. 335 (December 6, 1909), pp. 6-7.

73. Ibid.

74. *Perepiska M. A. Balakireva s P. I. Chaikovskim* (St. Petersburg, 1912), p. 30.

75. B. Jurgenson, *Table Thematique des oeuvres de P. Tschaikovsky* (Moscow, 1897), pp. 107, 32.

76. Iur'ev, *Zapiski* (Moscow, 1963), I, 407.

77. *Pamiati Sergeia Ivanovicha Taneeva (1856-1946),* ed. Vladimir Protopovov (Moscow, 1947), p. 48.

78. *S. I. Taneev, Lichnost', tvorchestvo i dokumenty ego zhizni,* ed. K. A. Kuznetsov (Moscow, 1925), p. 177.

79. Ibid., p. 203.

80. *P. I. Chaikovskii, S. I. Taneev, Pis'ma,* ed. V. A. Zhdanov (Moscow, 1951), p. 108.

81. Kuznetsov, p. 176.

82. M. M. Kovalevskii, "O russkikh i drugikh pravolavnikh rabakh v Ispanii," *Iuridicheskii vestnik,* XXI, Kniga 2 (1886), 238-252.

83. Kovalevskii, "Narod v drame Lope de Vega, *Ovechii Istochnik,*" *V pamiat' S. A. Iur'eva* (Moscow, 1891), pp. 97-130.

84. Ibid., p. 106.

85. Ibid., pp. 98-99.

86. Ibid., p. 107.

87. Alexander Nikolaevich Veselovskii, one of tsarist Russia's greatest literary and folklore scholars, was in Spain in 1859-1860. After finishing Moscow University he became family tutor for Prince M. A. Golytsin, Russia's ambassador to Spain (1856-1859). In his *Diary,* Veselovskii speaks of visiting Madrid University. Much of Veselovskii's interest in Spanish literature stems from his days in Madrid. Alexander Nikolaevich Veselovskii, "Diarum Russici cujusdam magistri, quum in Hispania docuit, scriptum," *Pamiati Akademika Alexandra Nikolaevicha Veselovskogo* (Petrograd, 1921), p. 50. See *Nauchnyi Biulleten' Leningradskogo gosudarstvennogo ordena Lenina Universiteta,* No. 14-15 (1947), pp. 64-66.

Alexander's brother Alexei (1843-1918), one of Russia's greatest comparatists and friend of S. A. Iur'ev, wrote about the pre-Lope stage in his *Starinnyi Teatr v Evrope* (Moscow, 1870), p. 144.

88. D. K. Petrov, *Ocherki bytogogo teatra Lope de Vegy* (St. Petersburg, 1902), iii-v. The appendix to Petrov's master's thesis is a rare Lope de Vega play, *El sufrimiento del honor,* first published in Zaragoza (1641), Ibid., pp. 15-16.

89. D. K. Petrov, "Odin iz ideal'nykh geroev," "One of The Ideal Heroes," *Zhurnal ministerstva narodnago prosveshcheniia* (July-August, 1899), 251-263.

In this study Petrov advances the thesis that Fernando, the hero of Calderón's *El príncipe constante,* has the same heroic qualities established by the writers of Greek and Hindu drama: compassion and the ability to suffer.

Petrov translated Calderón's *La vida es sueño* (St. Petersburg, 1898) and made a complete translation of *La Estrella de Sevilla.* See Leningrad State Theatrical Library MS. 1/12/7/23/ 75492. In 1901 Petrov published a study entitled "O tragediakh Kal'derona," a survey of the most important studies on Calderón by Western scholars. *Zhurnal ministerstva narodnago prosveshcheniia* (January-February, 1901), 39-76.

90. Petrov, *Ocherki,* p. 11.

91. Ibid., pp. 441, 21-26.

92. Ibid., p. 31.

93. Ibid., pp. 220-221.

94. Ibid., p. 318.

95. Ibid., p. 292.

96. Ibid., p. 323.

97. *Hispania,* XI (May, 1928), 291. See Carlos Clavería, "El amor, sus principios y dialéctica en el teatro de Lope de Vega," *Escorial,* No. 47 (1944), 19-41.

98. Petrov, *Zametki po staroi ispanskoi komedii* (St. Petersburg, 1907), Appendix, 1-115.

99. Ibid., p. 23.

100. Ibid., p. 55.

101. Ibid., p. 173.

102. Ibid., p. 14.

103. Vladimir Piast, *Vstrechi* (Moscow, 1929), pp. 163-165.

104. *Istoriia russkoi literatury,* ed. D. N. Ovsianiko-Kulikovskii (Moscow, 1923), V, 93.

105. D. S. Mirskii, *A History of Russian Literature From Its Beginning to 1900* (New York, 1949), p. 407.

106. Ibid., p. 409.

107. Ibid., p. 410. An article on the nineteenth-century Spanish composer and musicologist Felipe Pedrell entitled, "Dva inostrannykh kompozitora," "Two Foreign Composers," appeared in *Artist,* No. 33 (1894), 49-57.

108. Akim Flekser, "Religiia i sovremennaia literatura," *Severnyi vestnik,* No. 10 (October, 1896), 243-244.

109. D. N. Ovsianiko-Kulikovskii, *Istoriia Russkoi Literatury XIX v.* (Moscow, 1910), V, 95-96. Georgette Donchin in her book on Russian symbolism says, "Echoes of Western glorification of Evil in all its forms, from demonism to sexual vice, can found in almost all the Russian symbolists." Georgette Donchin, *The Influence of French Symbolism on Russian Poetry* (Gravenhage, 1958), p. 140. See also Renato Poggioli, *Poets of Russia 1890-1930* (Cambridge, Mass., 1960), p. 127.

110. Nikolai Zernov, *The Russian Religious Renaissance of the Twentieth Century* (New York, 1963), p. 87.

111. Dmitrii S. Merezhkovskii, "Alonso Dobry," "Alonso the Good," *Russkaia mysl',* VII (1884), 70-72. "Don Kikhot i Sancho Panza," an essay in *Severnyi vestnik,* No. 8 (August, 1889), 1-19 and No. 9 (September, 1889), 21-41.

112. Zinaida Gippius, *Dmitrii Merezhkovskii* (Paris, 1951), p. 61.

113. From early youth Merezhkovskii was obsessed by mysticism and his search for God. Ovsianiko-Kulikovskii, V, 100.
114. Gippius, p. 21.
115. D. S. Merezhkovskii, "Silvio ili vozvrashchenie k prirode," *Severnyi vestnik*, No. 2 (February, 1890), 69-90, No. 3 (March, 1890), 63-81, No. 4 (April, 1890), No. 5 (May, 1890), 57-75. For this study I am using "Silvio" from Merezhkovskii's book *Simvoly* (St. Petersburg, 1891).
116. Merezhkovskii, *Simvoly*, p. 344.
117. Mirskii, p. 412.
118. Merezhkovskii, "Kal'deron v svoei drame *Poklonenie Krestu*," *Trud*, XIII (December, 1891), 650-670.
119. Ibid., p. 651.
120. Ibid., p. 652.
121. Ibid., p. 669.
122. Ibid., p. 665.
123. Ibid., p. 669.
124. *Russkaia literatura 1890-1910*, ed. Semon V. Vengerov (Moscow, 1914-1918), I, 60.
125. Bal'mont's plans for translations of Spanish plays included Calderón's comedies of manners, dramas of jealousy and honor, and fantastic plays; plays of demonism by Tirso, Mira de Amescua, and Belmonte; the peasant dramas of Lope, Tirso, and Francisco de Rojas Zorrilla. Konstantin Bal'mont, *Sochineniia Kal'derona* (Moscow, 1904), back cover. See Ludmilla Buketoff Turkevich, *Spanish Literature in Russia and in The Soviet Union: 1735-1964* (Metuchen, New Jersey, 1967), pp. 21-22.

Petrov believed Bal'mont never finished the translations because his interest changed to other areas of literature. D. K. Petrov, "K. D. Bal'mont i ego perevody s ispanskogo," *Zapiski neo-filologicheskago obshchestva pri imperatorskom S. Peterburgskom Universitete*, Vypusk VII (1914), p. 30. Like Merezhkovskii, Bal'mont admired and read the Spanish mystic poets Santa Teresa and San Juan de la Cruz. Bal'mont, *Morskoe svechenie* (Moscow, 1908), p. 47.
126. Bal'mont, *Sochineniia*, I, iv.
127. Ibid., xv.
128. Bal'mont's translation of *El príncipe constante* is the first in Russian. N. F. Arbenin only published an excerpt in *Artist*.
129. Bal'mont, *Sochineniia*, II, 765.
130. Bal'mont wrote a sonnet entitled, "Kal'derón"

La vida es sueño. Life is a dream
There is no other truth so great.

Bal'mont, *Sonety* (Moscow, 1917), p. 221.
131. Bal'mont, *Gornye vershiny* (Moscow, 1904), pp. 11-25. See *Pravitel'stvenny vestnik*, No. 75 (April 4, 1889), p. 3, and No. 77 (April 7, 1899), p. 3.
132. Bal'mont, *Gornye*, p. 11.
133. Ibid., p. 10.
134. Ibid., p. 16.
135. Ibid., p. 14.
136. Ibid., p. 175.
137. Ibid., p. 178.

V: New Directions on the Stage (1910-1917)

The preceding chapter discussed the growth of Russian symbolism, beginning with the late 1880's, and showed that several Spanish playwrights satisfied the ideals and aspirations of the Russian symbolists. Although few in number, the performances of Spanish Golden Age plays in the Russian symbolist theater between 1910 and the Bolshevik Revolution were the realization and fulfillment of the theories established by earlier symbolists, both Russian and Western European. Like their predecessors, this second generation of symbolists was essentially apolitical and sought to free art from political and social association.[1] They were influenced, as were their Western counterparts, by religion and mysticism. But in contrast to S. A. Iur'ev's generation, they were more attracted by plays like Calderón's *La devoción de la cruz* and *El purgatorio de San Patricio* than by Lope's *Fuente Ovejuna.*

No clear insight into the twentieth-century Russian theater is possible without an understanding of the Moscow Art Theater, established in the summer of 1897 by the actor Konstantin Stanislavskii and the playwright and critic Vladimir Nemirovich-Danchenko. This group's influence on the theatrical innovators Vsevolod E. Meierkhol'd, Nikolai N. Evreinov, and Alexander Tairov was substantial. Stanislavskii and Nemirovich-Danchenko founded the Moscow Art Theater as a protest against the oppressive atmosphere, clichés, and unprofessional and unrealistic performances of the Russian stage. They could not accept the theatrical dilettantism and lack of cultural and educational background, so characteristic of many actors, about which the critic Bazhenov had complained in the 1860's.

Stanislavskii and Nemirovich-Danchenko were preoccupied with historical accuracy, in which they were influenced by the Duke of Saxe-Meiningen's company during its tours of Russia. In Russia, until Stanislavskii, comparatively few performances reflected the quest for historical authenticity which the Russian audience saw in S. A. Iur'ev's production of *La Estrella de Sevilla.* Stanislavskii wanted to recreate the historical and spiritual atmosphere in which a play was set. He wanted every prop on the stage to be as authentic as possible. In short, the production must be true to life. To produce *Othello,* Stanislavskii traveled to Venice; and for his production of Aleksei Konstantinovich Tolstoy's *Tsar Feodor Ivanovich:*

> Instead of simplified stereotypes for boyars, the Russia of 1600 came to life on the stage, reproduced with loving thoroughness and truthful-

ness, the Arkhangelsk Cathedral, the customs, costumes, ornaments, and furnishing—all were genuine, unprecedented, and unmistakably truthful.[2]

Unlike those of other Russian troupes, the productions of the Moscow Art Theater were well planned. Every object on the stage had to have a reason for being there. Sound effects imitated nature in order to create a given atmosphere or mood; music and color were also used. The actors spent many hours in preparation for a performance, and Stanislavskii never permitted a play to be performed until it was completely ready.

In the Moscow Art Theater, the actors, from the leads to the extras, were the center of all attention, for the Moscow Art Theater was an actor's theater. The actor was even more important than the director, and Stanislavskii trained him to live the part he was playing and to fit it in with the entire production. He created an atmosphere of harmony, and each part was to the entire performance what a detail is to a painting.

The actor had to know the character he was playing and had to imagine and create the character's "prehistory and post-history," i.e., what happened to the character before and after the play. This technique was called psychological realism. So absorbed in his role was the actor that he had to forget there was an audience watching him. The large and realistic three-dimensional stage helped to augment this feeling of separation between actor and audience as well as to heighten the air of realism. To establish the concept of separation and distance:

> Stanislavsky created the convention of the fourth wall; [the back of] a mirror on the stage was turned toward the public and considered a wall. Corners, projections from rooms, and furnishings did not face the audience in the worn-out manner of the old theater but were arranged in realistic patterns. Frequently the furniture faced away from the front, and this curbed the actor's compulsion to face the audience.[3]

Stanislavskii's theater was also a theater of political protest. Consequently it performed some of Maxim Gorkii's most important plays on socialistic themes.[4]

Although realism was the basic aim of the Moscow Art Theater, it also gave some works in the stylized and symbolist manner. Among such performances were Andreev's *The Life of a Man* (1907), and *Hamlet,* directed by the English theatrical innovator Gordon Craig (1911).[5] It was at the

Moscow Art Theater that Anton Chekhov achieved his greatest fame, and the Theater's unofficial name is the House of Chekhov.[6]

The theater in Russia between 1905 and 1917 was characterized by a sharp duality of attitudes: realism, as espoused by the Moscow Art Theater, and symbolism with its attempts at theatrical innovation by Vsevolod E. Meierkhol'd, Nikolai N. Evreinov, and Alexander Tairov. The number of symbolist playwrights was comparatively small and the repertoire was greatly supplemented by Western plays reconstructed on symbolist lines.[7] Among these were plays by Golden Age playwrights such as Calderón, Cervantes, Lope de Vega, and Tirso de Molina.

As the Moscow Art Theater combated the weaknesses and inadequacies of the late nineteenth-century Russian theater, the innovators of symbolist theater rebelled against Stanislavskii, despite the fact that many of them were influenced by him and benefited in many ways from his techniques.[8] In general, the symbolists rejected Stanislavskii's obsession with authenticity and realism. Many of them looked upon the theater as a temple and felt that the theatrical spectacle, as it had been in ancient Greece and medieval Europe, was essentially a religious experience.[9] They felt that the audience was to the actor what the communicants were to the priest; for in Christianity the Mass is an excellent example of audience participation in a symbolic presentation. The future Soviet Minister of Education, Anatolii Lunacharskii, early in the twentieth century hoped, "The temples will become theaters and the theaters will become temples."[10]

Whereas Stanislavskii had sought to separate the actor from the audience as much as possible, the symbolist theater sought to engage the audience as participants. "Its staging gives the theater-goer an opportunity to use his imagination in inferring whatever is implied on the stage."[11] Only those furnishings and properties were used that were absolutely necessary for the course of the action.[12] In many cases the stage was converted into a runway which jutted out into the seating area. Stanislavskii's realistic three-dimensional stage was reduced as much as possible to two dimensions, thus reducing even more the distance between the actor and his public.

The first important innovator of the Russian symbolist theater to recognize the eternally universal qualities of the Spanish Golden Age Theater was Vsevolod Emelevich Meierkhol'd (1874-1941). Meierkhol'd's interest in the classical theater of Spain was twofold. In accordance with the mystical and religious tendencies of the symbolists, he felt a great attraction for Calderón's plays on religious themes and produced *La devoción de la cruz,* and *El príncipe constante.* On the other hand, he was enamoured of the Spanish folk theater and on several occasions directed Cervantes' *Interludes.* In Meierkhol'd's opinion a playwright was neither a neo-classicist, nor a romantic, but whatever a producer wanted him to be. The producer had free rein to interpret the play as he saw fit, and the text was "merely a pretext for an impressionistic and symbolic composition."[13]

In contrast to Stanislavskii, Meierkhol'd believed in the theater of the director, a theater in which the actor loses much of his own personality. The actor "was subordinated to a clear-cut pattern of movement and intonation arising from the director's fancy. The pattern was symbolical, stylized, and abstract."[14] The actor was nothing more than a puppet (as two dimensional as possible) of the director's whims and fantasy. The two dimensional effect arose from Meierkhol'd's attempt to give him a bas-relief, panel-like effect.[15] So obsessed was Meierkhol'd by the importance of the director that he called his the triangular theater; the actor and audience formed the base while the director stood at the triangle's apex. Thus it was the director who controlled the audience by means of the actor.[16] Meierkhol'd introduced the two-dimensional stage to the Russian theater,[17] because like many other symbolists, he felt that the performance was a religious experience, and he therefore reduced the distance between the actor and his audience. Meierkhol'd believed that the actor should be conscious of the fact that he was performing for an audience and that the theater-viewer must never forget he was watching a play.[18]

Meierkhol'd's props were symbolic and simple. A tree replaced a forest; two chairs piled on top of one another represented a mountain. On some occasions, however, he did utilize authenticity in the decorations and settings. This idea Meierkhol'd shared with Stanislavskii. But in Meierkhol'd's case his aim was not historical authenticity in reconstructing the past, but complete freedom for his fantasy. As the Russian theater historian Nikolai A. Gorchakov stated:

> He wanted to create a feeling for the period through symbols and stylization. He decided, for example, to do *Schluch und Jau* [Gerhart Hauptmann] in a stylized "age of powder." Court ladies were seated in bowers along the footlights; they were using outsized needles to embroider a ribbon en masse. The queen's chamber had a bed that was ornate and grandiose—including an extraordinary canopy—to the point of being ridiculous.[19]

Meierkhol'd loved the classic painters and often molded his presentations so that the audience felt as if it were seeing a painting acted out. Meierkhol'd gave great emphasis to the role of the stage designer and painter. He invited artists such as Benois, Sapunov, and Sudeikin, whose talent enhanced the success of many of his productions.[20] Meierkhol'd felt that in general the Russian repertoire had little to offer and was not adaptable to the symbolist theater, and he therefore turned to other theaters: Greece, Spain, Molière, and the commedia dell'arte.

Meierkhol'd's interest in the theater, music, and painting stems from his mother's encouragement.[21] His fascination for the folk theater can be traced to his childhood memories of itinerant carnival show-box theaters[22] in the provincial city of Penza.[23] Meierkhol'd's acting career began in his teens when he gave up the study of law at Moscow University (1895-1896), and from 1898 to 1902 he was one of Stanislavskii's best performers. Eventually their ideological differences caused their relations to deteriorate to such a point that Meierkhol'd left the Moscow Art Theater to tour the provinces. Nevertheless Stanislavskii was aware of his ability, both as a director and innovator and in 1905 he invited Meierkhol'd to direct the Moscow Art Theater's Stage Laboratory, the Studio. Even here Meierkhol'd's innovations were too extreme and soon Stanislavskii asked him to leave.[24]

In 1906 the actress Vera Kommissarzhevskaia invited Meierkhol'd to become chief director at her theater, which she had formed to combat the academic atmosphere of the Imperial Theaters. But here again Meierkhol'd's ideas proved even too extreme for her and she asked him to leave. During his stay at the Kommissarzhevskaia Theater, Meierkhol'd developed techniques in creating mood through the use of color, lighting, painting, and music. He later applied the results of these experiments to the Alexandrinskii Theater and other groups.[25]

It was at this point that Meierkhol'd also began working on the concept of the two dimensional stage which he called the "scenic platform." He reduced the number of props to a basic minimum and used flat canvasses which gave the two dimensional effect. In addition, the iconography, entrusted to his designers, reflected the mood and the tone of the play.[26] Among the plays which he produced at the Kommissarzhevskaia Theater were Ibsen's *Hedda Gabler* (November 10, 1906) and Maeterlinck's *Soeur Béatrice* (November 22, 1906).[27]

An eye-witness report describes the *Hedda Gabler* production:

> The stage seemed enshrouded in a haze that was a mixture of blue, green, and silver. The back drop was blue. At the right an enormous French window extended the entire height of the stage. Through the window, one could see the greenish-indigo sky with its twinkling stars (in the final act). To the left of the curtain, an indigo tapestry showed a gold-and-silver lace. On the floor was a greenish-blue carpet. The furniture was white. The piano was white. The vases were a greenish white and contained white chrysanthemums. There were white furs on the strangely shaped divan. And, like sea water, like the scales of a sea serpent, was Hedda Gabler's dress.[28]

Meierkhol'd's presentation of Maeterlinck's *Soeur Béatrice* synthesized his symbolist technique with a religious theme. This play, whose story is very similar to the Spanish legend called "Margarita la tornera," was one of several plays on Spanish themes which Meierkhol'd produced. In the production, writes Gorchakov:

> Meyerhold created a chorus of nuns that seemed to have stepped out of the bas-reliefs in a medieval cathedral. The groupings in the scene showing Béatrice's death used as their point of departure old paintings. In order not to destroy the similarity to the ancient iconography, Meyerhold clothed the chorus in a single kind of gray garment, and he made it move constantly in half turns, endowing it with gestures, that were few and monotonous.
>
> Despite this harsh effort to make the actor two-dimensional, Meyerhold succeeded in transmitting a most religious feeling. He was aided by the settings, which were reminiscent of primitive miniatures. The production soared high above the trivia of everyday life. His version of *Soeur Béatrice* clearly showed both that the theater arts had potentialities beyond realism and that the Russian theater had not known about them.[29]

In September, 1908, V. A. Teliakovskii, Director of the Imperial Theaters, invited Meierkhol'd to be a director at the Alexandrinskii Theater, where he remained until the 1917 Revolution. At first he was not allowed to experiment on the Imperial Stage, but later was able to do so.[30]

What attracted Meierkhol'd to the Spanish Golden Age Theater?[31] From a technical point of view, the Spanish popular stage (not the more sophisticated ones at the Buen Retiro and the Palacio Real) resembled Meierkhol'd's concept of the ideal "scenic platform." This small stage helped bring the actor and public closer and made the performance more intimate. It was constructed with great simplicity; a few planks formed a narrow and shallow stage with no stage machinery and little scenery. For the most part props were almost non-existent, as Cervantes says in his description of Spanish itinerant stage, in the times of Lope de Rueda.[32]

The décor made the Spanish audience participate in the action and imagine the changes which were implicit rather than explicit. "The public had to imagine a change of scene though none was visible on the stage. Decoration in the modern sense of the word was unknown."[33] As the American Hispanist Hugo Rennert stated:

> The painting of scenery according to the rules of perspective, so that the stage should have some appearance of reality, was wholly unknown. A few houses painted on paste board did duty for a street or a forest, while the simplest curtain in the background or the sides remained unchanged. . . . If it was necessary to hide, one hid behind the curtain. If one had to cover the stage with grass one simply stretched out a carpet on the stage. If one had to leave, one exited through the audience.[34]

The nature of the Spanish Golden Age repertoire also interested Meierkhol'd. One of his few comments on this matter appeared in a letter dated July, 1911, to the English specialist on the Russian theater, George Calderon. Meierkhol'd speaks of the Spanish theater as containing a feeling of national force, a religious undercurrent, and, oddly enough, an aspiration to free the individual from Medieval scholasticism. Concerning its dramatic forms, he points out the quickly developed action concentrated in the plot and, "In addition the Spanish Theater is not afraid to break the harmony of the highest level of tragic pathos introducing the comic grotesque which reaches a clear and unique caricature."[35]

Meierkhol'd began to direct when significant contributions to the field of Spanish studies had been made by Russian scholars, such as Merezhkovskii, Bal'mont, and D. K. Petrov. One of the most influential contributors to Meierkhol'd's understanding the technical and spiritual aspects of the Spanish theater was the poet Vladimir Piast, a student of D. K. Petrov and the translator of several Tirso plays. In his memoirs Piast relates that while he was working on a paper at the Imperial Library on the versification in *El Cid,*

Meierkhol'd studied the history of the Spanish theater. Piast sat next to him and answered whatever questions Meierkhol'd had.[36]

Calderón's *La devoción de la cruz* was Meierkhol'd's first production of a Spanish Golden Age play. He directed the work at the apartment of the eminent Russian symbolist theoretician and mystic, Viacheslav Ivanov. Because the apartment was located in a tower in an apartment building, it was called the Bashennyi Teatr, "The Tower Theater."[37] Those who visited the Ivanov circle were among Russia's intellectual elite and included figures such as Merezhkovskii, Bal'mont, and the poets Valerii Briusov and Alexander Blok. One of the group's aims was to make the apartment into a center for religious drama. Alexander Blok's wife Liubov Dmitrievna hoped to convert the Bashennyi Teatr into a theater with a low plank stage for mystery plays, and Ivanov himself planned to make his apartment into a second Oberammergau.[38] Therefore Meierkhol'd's choice of Calderón's *La devoción de la cruz* for the Bashennyi Teatr was a most appropriate one. Merezhkovskii had praised the work because of its powerful religious message and Bal'mont had translated it in 1902. On April 9, 1910, Meierkhol'd directed the first performance in Russian of a Spanish play on a religious theme, in an atmosphere which was more like a religious service than a play.[39]

For the performance Meierkhol'd incorporated many of his techniques, including a small and simple stage very much like that of the Spanish popular theater and striking colors and costumes which created a specific mood.

Because of the limited space, the maximum number of actors on this stage at any one time was four. The Russian theater historian Evgenii Znosko-Borovskii, who saw the performance,[40] stressed the simplicity of the stage and props and praised the magnificent contribution Meierkhol'd made in reproducing the primitive Spanish stage. "Immediately upon entering we saw an authentic Spanish theater, an itinerant theater. The actors left the stage through the audience. It had no decoration—only some cloth."[41]

The space behind the back curtain served as the *lo alto del teatro,* of Madrid's seventeenth-century popular theaters.[42] Julia (played by N. P. Krasnova) stood in this space on the back of some chairs as she looked out of her convent window and spoke to the guitar-strumming Eusebio.[43] The contribution made by the stage decorator, S. I. Sudeikin, cannot be overemphasized. Utilizing yards of red and black cloth to cover the back of the stage, he produced an illusion of depth and bas-relief on this very shallow stage.[44] From the same cloth he made a curtain divided into two parts, each of which was opened and closed by two little blackamoors, the cork-blackened children of the apartment building's doorman.[45] Sudeikin designed the Spanish costumes as well.[46]

In words that recall Rennert's comments on the Spanish stage, Znosko-Borovskii praised the group's perfection in the use of symbolic and imaginative props: "If it was necessary to hide, they hid behind a curtain, if it was necessary to sprinkle grass and branches on the stage, they simply stretched out a rug. If an actor had to exit, he simply left through the audience."[47]

There is sufficient evidence to believe that the Bashennyi Teatr group planned to produce several other Spanish Golden Age plays. Immediately after Meierkhol'd presented *La devoción de la cruz,* he visited Western Europe—Sweden, Germany, France, Greece, and Italy. The Bashennyi Teatr group send Meierkhol'd a letter dated May 21, 1910, entitled "Nashemu Rekhidoru," "To Our Regidor," in which the members indicated that they were studying Cervantes' *El teatro de las maravillas,* one of his most charming Interludes:

> We have been reading
> Cervantes now,
> Our imaginations are alive
> With the *Theater of the Marvels.*[48]

Apparently the group planned to perform Tirso de Molina's *El condenado por desconfiado,* because on May 23, 1911, Vladimir Piast, who had played the role of Ricardo the bandit in *La devoción de la cruz,* read his translation of the Tirso play to members of the Bashennyi Teatr.[49]

During the summer of 1912 Meierkhol'd again directed Calderón's *La devoción de la cruz* as well as three Cervantes Interludes in the Ostrovskii translation:[50] *Dos habladores, La cueva de Salamanca,* and *El viejo celoso.*[51] These plays belonged to Meierkhol'd's two favorite categories: religious drama and the folk tradition. The actors belonged to the hastily formed Tovarishchestvo akterov, pisatelei, khudozhnikov, i muzykantov, "The society of actors, writers, artists, and musicians," a group established to commemorate the death of August Strindberg who died on May 1, 1912.

The group, which also consisted of Russia's intellectual elite, was financed with an inheritance recently received by Liubov Blok. The Bloks rented a large country home and extensive grounds near the village of Terioka, close to the Finnish border.[52] Madame Blok's choice of the Calderón play is related to her concept of the theater as a religious experience, a concept associated with the Bashennyi Teatr group. She also took this opportunity to do some acting, a hobby which she liked very much.[53]

The Terioka Theater opened on June 9, 1912, and among the plays for the first evening's performance were *Vliublennye,* "The Lovers," a pantomine by Meierkhol'd, and *Boltuna,* "Dos habladores,"[54] an Interlude often attributed to Cervantes. In a letter to his mother (June 10, 1912), Blok expressed pleasure with the performance: "They performed Cervantes' beautiful and motley farce marvelously." About his wife's performance the poet wrote, "Liuba performed. She was relaxed on the stage. She had on a pretty costume and makeup, but sometimes she overacted, perhaps out of nervousness."[55]

On June 29, 1912, the group performed Calderón's *La devoción de la cruz* and Cervantes' Interludes, *La cueva de Salamanca,* and *El viejo celoso.*[56] Calderón's *La devoción de la cruz* was presented very much as it had been performed at the Bashennyi Teatr. There were, however, a number of changes in the decorations and settings, which were the work of Iu. M. Bondi, an illustrator of many works by Alexander Pushkin.[57]

The group had first planned to use gloomy, exaggerated colors and ardent tones, with fiery yellow rear lighting which was supposed to radiate through a curtain slit in many places. Meierkhol'd rejected this proposal because he felt it would not create the mood necessary to the play. Consequently the entire production was given under bright lighting, with an unusually white tone which was to heighten the strict Catholic fanaticism which permeates the play.[58]

Meierkhol'd chose as a basic setting an enormous white tent on whose ceiling could be seen part of a starry sky. Above the front curtain were the Spanish words, "La devozion [sic] de la cruz." At the back of the stage was a curtain sliced into narrow vertical strips through which the actors entered and exited. Above this rear curtain was drawn a line of blue crosses which was higher on the sides and gradually lowered toward the center of the stage. On each side of the stage stood a high white lamp, which did not burn, but was symbolic light. The actual lighting came from hanging lamps.[59]

In the second act, high triptych-like screens with sketches of a convent were transported onto the stage by two youths at the sound of an offstage bell each time it was necessary to show the convent's walls. There were also three screens on which were painted a number of Catholic monks. The abovementioned blue crosses and the one carried on stage by a black-clothed youth and placed in Eusebio's path, were symbolic of the leitmotif, self-limitation, and symbolized both the unbearable weight of the cross and the thirst for life and earthly delights and joys of love.[60] There were no footlights and the stage was almost level with the floor.[61]

Meierkhol'd, whose comments reveal his interest in the Spanish Golden Age theater, said of the production:

> Generally the strictness, gloominess, and simplicity were obtained by the white color; the sketches on the tent and on the screens (very simple and strict) were done by contours of blue paint. The viewer should have clearly seen that here no decoration would have served any purpose, here only the actors performed. The setting is only a page on which the text is written. Therefore, all that was related to the setting was transmitted symbolically. Actors were not tied to trees because there were none. They were simply tied to two columns of the theater at the front of the stage. The rope on their wrist could not bind them because the loop was not drawn. The peasant Gil who was supposed to hide in the bushes simply rolled himself up in the curtains.[62]

Alexander Avelevich Mgebrov, who performed the role of Eusebio, felt that Meierkhol'd "outdid himself in producing *La devoción de la Cruz*"[63] and that Meierkhol'd was interested in Calderón less as a Catholic than as a great and forceful artist.[64] Thus Merezhkovskii's plea to his countrymen to disregard Calderón's religious fanaticism and to accept the Spaniard as a great artist found a reception in the dramatic art of Meierkhol'd.

The two Cervantes Interludes directed by Vladimir N. Solov'ev[65] were presented in the tradition of the carnival show booth given by itinerant actors using the barest and simplest props.[66] The background for these Interludes was formed by a number of portable screens painted differently for each Interlude. For *La cueva de Salamanca* they were painted a brownish red with crossbows and other weapons sketched on them, while the actors performed in a geometric figure with the main character in the center.[67] After 1912 Meierkhol'd experimented with what the theater historian Nikolai Gorchakov calls "the sculptured aspects in acting":

> He taught the actors how to make the most use of the acting platform. He believed that the form and pattern of the actor's motions and gestures should embrace the basic value of the stage. He taught the actors how to live in the form of a design, how to move in a circle, a square, or a rectangle in a room or in an open spot.[68]

This new interest in geometric figures explains Meierkhol'd's innovations in Cervantes' two Interludes.

Meierkhol'd's productions at Terioka received little attention by the press, with the exception of an article which appeared in *Novaia Studiia,* "New Studio," and a short notice in *Teatr i iskusstvo, "Theater and Art."* The latter spoke of the performances as a protest against naturalism on the stage.[69] This limited description on behalf of *Teatr i iskusstvo* is understandable because the journal's editor, A. P. Kugel, was violently opposed to Meierkhol'd's ideas.[70]

On November 17, 1914, Meierkhol'd's Studio again performed Cervantes' *La cueva de Salamanca,* again under the direction of Solov'ev, with decorations by A. V. Rykov.[71] Among the subjects studied at his Studio was the itinerant theater of the commedia dell'arte and the theater of Lope de Rueda. The Studio's curriculum included music, stage directing, settings, and the history of the theater.[72]

The decorations for *La cueva de Salamanca* were based on a system of triptych-like screens with alternating greens, blues, reds, and yellows. On the stage stood two barrels used either as stools or as the base for a high table covered with a table cloth. All the actors were in their work clothes—a technique which Meierkhol'd later used for productions during the Soviet period. The colors for the men were dark strawberry with pinks and blues, with an orange belt and *molletières.* The women wore dark pink with a dark strawberry belt and carried ribbons in their hands.[73] The auditorium was arranged in the following manner: the chairs were placed in a semicircle in front of the stage with a center aisle and aisles on both the left and right sides. The stage was actually a low platform over which hung a white silk curtain with a mask drawn on it. The proscenium was the floor of the auditorium, and was covered with a blue cloth.[74]

Meierkhol'd's next production of a Spanish Golden Age play was Calderón's *El príncipe constante,* "Stoikii Prints," which was presented at the Alexandrinskii Theater on April 23, 1915. The occasion was the farewell jubilee benefit performance of Iu. E. Ozarovskii, who played the role of the Moroccan king Tarudante.[75]

Alexander Iakovlev Golovin (1862-1930), who was interested in things Spanish,[76] designed the settings.[77] He had designed sketches for Massenet's *Don Quichotte*[78] and for Meierkhol'd's revolutionary production at the Alexandrinskii Theater (1910) of Molière's *Don Juan.* Meierkhol'd's production of *Don Juan* contained many elements which he had incorporated the previous spring at the Bashennyi Teatr's presentation of *La devoción de la cruz.*

V. G. Karatygin, the composer and critic, composed the stage music for *El príncipe constante.*[79]

It seems probable that Meierkhol'd chose this Calderón play because of its religious theme,[80] its Moorish setting, and the fact that Bal'mont had already translated it. In May, 1910, while in Munich, Meierkhol'd was very highly impressed by an exhibit he saw there of Moorish art.[81] The stage for the Terioka production of *La devoción de la cruz* was very reminiscent of the Moorish custom of designing the ceilings of palaces as a representation of the stars in the heavens, as found, for example, in the Alcazar in Seville.

The sets used for *El príncipe constante* were essentially the same ones used for the Golovin-Meierkhol'd presentation at the Alexandrinskii Theater of Molière's *Don Juan* (1910),[82] the second act of which was also on the evening's program. In order to coordinate the locale of both plays, the setting for the Calderón work was the interior of a luxurious Spanish residence of the seventeenth century and therefore did not represent scenes from the fifteenth century, the time the action takes place. To show that the play takes place in Tangiers, some additional canvasses and screens were used.[83]

The critic V. Solov'ev, writing in *Apollon,* said of the settings:

> Meierkhol'd and Golovin offered *El príncipe constante* to the public's attention as a continuation of the stage techniques of the Symbolist theater which the public saw for the first time in Molière's *Don Juan.* This continuation consisted first in the fact that for *El príncipe constante* Meierkhol'd and Golovin had used a scene setting which depicted the chambers of a luxurious home in which the performance of the play takes place. Other elements of the Molière play remained. However, there were several features created for the Calderón play. A rear canvas depicted the fortress walls of Tangiers. Blackamoors carried canvas screens across the stage that depicted the sands of the African seashore and the blue of the African skies.
>
> As in Molière's *Don Juan,* the proscenium was extended far into the audience and the prompter's booth was removed. The entire style of the props was reminiscent of the seventeenth century, the time when Calderón lived and not when the events in his play really took place.[84]

The artistic principle of the play was expressed in the review by the literary historian V. M. Zhirmunskii, published in *Liubov' k trem apel'sinam,* "Love for Three Oranges:"

> The aim of the director and the stage designer was not the external verisimilitude of details from real life. They wanted to recreate the historical surroundings in which the action took place, creating an image of old Spain, in such a way however as to avoid the temptation of producing only historical authenticity on the stage. The artistically sensitive viewer should have contemplated the setting as if it were a painting or the music of a symphony. He should have viewed the performance like a theatrical spectacle embodying the internal meaning of the dramatic work. The performance created an abstract frame which created the basic mood of the work.[85]

In an attempt to manifest the lyrical flow of *El príncipe constante,* Meierkhol'd undertook a new technique. He gave the main role not to an actor, but to an actress (N. G. Kovalenskaia). Zhirmunskii offered a clear explanation why Meierkhol'd made such a decision:

> Fernando's faith is a passive one, a faith of love and tolerance, a faith of prayer and hope, a faith of non-resistance, a feminine faith. Usually the essence of a Calderón drama is related to his many masculine figures who personify the strength of honor, the importance of the king, the imposition of their personality and will, and the conquering faith. In contrast, the faith of Fernando is quiet, although no less fiery, but more profound, more dependent upon intimate feelings than the action itself. This image of passive will is what related it to the concept of feminity and gives expression to this feeling. Kovalenskaia was successful in creating the noble saintliness that personifies the prince.[86]

The influence Meierkhol'd had on the Soviet Theater does not fall within the scope of this study. Nevertheless one should be aware that many of his innovations, so important in the development of the Soviet Theater, did originate in his study of the Spanish Golden Age Theater. As the Russian theater historian Nikolai Gorchakov states, "None of Meyerhol'd's pre-Revolutionary innovations had such a great influence on the Soviet theater as those devices that he had discovered by reviving the acting techniques of the commedia dell'arte and other national theaters of the past."[87]

The second Russian theatrical innovator interested in Spain's Golden Age Theater was Nikolai Nikolaevich Evreinov (1879-1953). Born in Moscow of well-to-do parents, Evreinov studied composition with Nikolai Rimskii-Korsakov at the St. Petersburg Conservatory and law at the St. Petersburg Imperial Law Institute.[88] His broad interest in many subjects led him to become a playwright, director, theatrical historian and theoretician, and anthropologist.

As a student of the theater he believed that realism in the nineteenth century had caused the theater's downfall, and like Meierkhol'd, he abhorred the realism of Stanislavskii's productions.[89] Evreinov once wrote: "When I see Chekhovian plays portrayed by the Stanislavsky school of acting, I invariably want to scream at them for their nightmarish presentation of life."[90] Nevertheless, Stanislavskii influenced Evreinov because of the importance the former gave to the actor's role and to historical authenticity on the stage.

Evreinov could not agree with Meierkhol'd's suppression of the actor to convert him into an instrument for fulfilling the director's whim and fancy, thus destroying the actor's spontaneity. In the words of Nikolai Gorchakov, Evreinov and his followers "did not seek to submerge the actor in the concepts of the director. Instead of trying to turn the actor into bas-reliefs, circles, and cubes, they considered him the prime foundation of the theater . . . the player was again the sovereign of the theatrical world."[91] On the other hand, Evreinov agreed with Meierkhol'd that the audience had to be made a participant in the action and that symbolic imagery and props would facilitate this.[92]

Both believed that the contemporary theater had little to offer in technique and repertoire. A revival of the theater in the twentieth century was possible only by bringing back what Evreinov also considered to be the highest levels in the history of the theater: the Greek, Medieval, commedia dell'arte, the Spanish Golden Age Theater, as well as several other national theaters.[93]

Meierkhol'd paid little attention to the role of the actor in his reconstruction of the physical stages of the past and consequently he was less interested in authentically resuscitating the acting techniques of the past. (Znovsko-Borovski pointed out this fact in his review of the Bashennyi Teatr's performance of Calderón's *La devoción de la cruz.*)[94] Evreinov, on the other hand, "began to fight for a revival of the theater by asserting the need to bring to the Russian stage the productional techniques and acting styles in use during the most theatrical periods of the past."[95]

Evreinov's theories about the role of the theater and its importance in our daily lives are among his most significant contributions. A theater, in his opinion, must be neither a temple, nor a mirror of society, nor a source of social protest, nor a peepshow. The theater must and can be only a theater.[96]

He explained his approach to the theater in his book *Teatralizatsiia zhizni,* "Making Life a Theater." According to Evreinov, when a viewer goes to see a performance he cares little about the philosophical content, the aesthetic pleasure, or the social message of the play. The theater mainly appeals to and satisfies what Evreinov terms *Teatral'nost,'* "theatricality." *Teatral'nost'* is a theatrical instinct inherent in all living creatures, savages or civilized. *Teatral'-nost'* therefore brings the theater into daily life.[97] It is a means by which man or an audience can transform themselves into whatever or whomever they want to be. *Teatral'nost'* applies as well to the actor who would really like to be the character which he is portraying on the stage.[98]

Because of *teatral'nost'* both man and animal live a life of spontaneous and daily theater. The cat and mouse act out a little play before the former devours the latter.[99] Children use their theatrical imagination in playing games.[100] Savage man wears the skins of animals and the feathers of birds in his theatrically religious rituals because he wants to acquire the traits of these creatures.[101] Evreinov points out how civilized man's social obligations and ceremonies are another form of *teatral'nost.'* When we have a social event to attend which we do not necessarily want to attend, we are forced to act as if we really did want to be there.[102]

Evreinov concluded that each period in man's history had its own theatrical characteristics which allowed him to participate in and experience vicariously the spectacle before him. Seventeenth-century Spain was one such period:

> She set at that epoch an exceptionally high example of historic stage management: Inquisition-tribunal with masked judges and hellish stage-craft of torture, huge autos-da-fé, where executioner and martyr rivalled each other in the strict adherence of their parts, the brilliance of sinister costumes—all was harmonized and stylized. There was the duelling ritual which enabled masters of fencing to glory in the part of gallant gentlemen who, even dying from wounds, never failed to drop some complimentary remark about their beloved ones. The vulgar butchery was transformed then into the refined spectacle of the bull-fight, and the affected speech of Góngora with its tempting unnaturalness supplanted the natural idiom of the nation.
>
> Add to this, endless and purely operatic processions of various kinds, religious, royal, military, criminal ("walking" the criminals through the streets), wedding and carnival (the processions of Tarask [sic]). The theatrical "filling" penetrated into every part of the "pie of life" baked by the ecclesiastics with thin, acrid oil, and it became impossible

> to distinguish the "filling" from the "crust," the religious form of a ceremony from its theatrical contents. The best actors gave up the stage and entered the monasteries, while the most ascetic monks left their cells and entered the actors' guilds. The greatest playwrights of the seventeenth century were the monks Lope de Vega, Carplo [sic] and Calderón, while the most sainted nun (at whose death, legend has it, the church-bells began of themselves to toll her passing) was the actress Baltasara. It is possible that renunciation of the world by a monk is also dictated to him by the instinct of transformation, which is nothing but theatricality in disguise? The history of the ultra-theatrical Spain furnished sufficient ground for such an assumption.[103]

Before 1917 Evreinov had directed at numerous theaters. In 1908 he replaced Vsevolod Meierkhol'd at the Kommissarzhevskaia Theater, where he produced, among other plays, Oscar Wilde's *Salome*.[104] In 1912 he became the principal director at the Krivoe Zerkalo Theater, "The Crooked Mirror Theater," at which he produced satirical parodies and grotesque caricatures. Among these was a take-off on Stanislavskii's interpretation of Gogol's *Inspector General*.[105]

As early as 1905 Evreinov thought about recreating theaters of the past and was aware of the problems involved in such an undertaking:

> The theater does not mean only dramatic literature. In the concept of theater there enters, in addition to the play itself, the complete presentation, the acting, and the audience which if inculcated with the feeling of theatricality, participate, in one way or another, in the performance. To resuscitate an entire theater means to resurrect an entire section of the cultural and social life of a given period. . . . All means to achieve this are good, although one cannot but see the basic difficulty of the task, for the most important part of the spectacle can suffer from archeological exactness. The text of a play alone cannot be the only true and dependable source, but also the construction of the stage, the costumes, the actors' movements, their way of pronouncing their parts, thousands of details from the theatrical life of a given time. All of these factors create possible mistakes and errors because of our lack of complete documentation. On the other hand, the imagination cannot be too irresponsible but should be based on the most scholarly details available, for the task of re-creating the period of past theaters in their aesthetic and social background.

> A successfully completed assignment of this nature will uncover a whole series of truly theatrical techniques, forgotten at present, but which before were alive and full of charm for the viewer and in addition will create a truly theatrical spectacle which is attractive to the contemporary viewer as well.[106]

Just as fate had brought Stanislavskii and Nemirovich-Danchenko together, it joined the lives of Evreinov and Baron Nikolai Vasilievich Drizen. They met by chance on January 5, 1907, at a dinner given in honor of A. P. Kugel, editor of the theatrical journal *Teatr i iskusstvo,* "Theater and Art." Drizen, a director at the Imperial Theaters, editor of the *Ezhegodnik imperatorskikh teatrov,* "The Imperial Theater Yearbook," and theater scholar, was interested in Evreinov's ideas and decided to use his influence and support to carry them out.[107] This is how the Starinnyi Teatr, "The Ancient Theater," was born. This private theatrical group, in the words of the Russian theater historian, Eduard Stark, attempted to convert the stage into "Wells' time machine."[108]

In its quest for authenticity, the Starinnyi Teatr requested help from Russia's foremost historians, musicologists, painters, and theater scholars[109] and in 1907 performed several Western medieval plays:

> *Tri volkhva,* "the Three Magi," an eleventh-century liturgical drama; *Deistvo o Teofile,* "A Play about Theophile," a twelfth-century miracle play; *Igra o Robene i Marione,* "A Play about Robin and Marion," a thirteenth-century work by Adam de la Halle; *Dva brata,* "Two Brothers," a fifteenth-century morality play; and two sixteenth-century farces—*O chane,* "About a Tub," and *O shliape-rogache,* "About the Cuckold's Hat," by Jean Dabondance.[110]

In 1911-1912 the Starinnyi Teatr presented a series of Spanish Golden Age plays by Calderón, Cervantes, Lope, and Tirso.[111] Evreinov and Drizen decided to perform these plays because of their *tealral'nost,'* i.e., because the Spanish public, actors, and playwrights brought the theater into their daily lives. The Spaniard lived the theater that he saw because the theater and his life were so closely related. Evreinov pointed out these elements in his description of seventeenth-century Spain. We have seen that by 1905 much scholarly material, both Russian and Western, was available to the Russian reader, and in 1909 Evreinov had already published an essay on the Spanish actor in the sixteenth and seventeenth centuries.[112]

In order to perform the Spanish plays, extensive research was necessary, and the entire winter of 1910-1911 was dedicated to this task. Russia's finest specialists in Spanish culture were invited to join the group, and members of the group journeyed to Spain and her ex-possession in Italy, Naples. Drizen journeyed to Lourdes to become imbued with Catholicism (AD 85) and Evreinov traveled to Naples to do research on the Spanish theater as it was performed during the Spanish occupation of southern Italy (AD 39).[114]

In addition to Evreinov and Drizen there were other influential members. N. I. Butkovskaia,[113] the publisher, and M. K. Miklashevskii, the actor and commedia dell'arte scholar, joined the troupe and contributed greatly. Miklavshevskii and Drizen journeyed to Spain, where they conferred with leading authorities on Spanish theater, painting, and music, gathered iconography, saw contemporary performances of Spanish Golden Age plays and studied the Spanish dance forms and their role in the Spanish theater (AD 35). Miklashevskii was especially interested in the Spanish dance and took down copious notes on this art form (AD 59). As a result, a Spanish dance group was established at the Starinnyi Teatr in the fall of 1911 under the direction of Presniakov, a dancer of the Imperial State Theater (AD 59). The dances so impressed the ballerina Pavlova that she said she had never seen anything like it anywhere (AD 42).

Among the Russian specialists invited to offer assistance were Pavel Osipovich Morozov (1854-1920), D. K. Petrov, Alexander Konstantinovich Glazunov (1865-1936), Cui, and L. A. Sakketti.[115] Morozov, a theatrical historian and translator of Lope's *El gran duque de Moscovia,* and Petrov gave lectures on Spanish seventeenth-century theater and life during rehearsal periods and performances. The others lectured on Spanish music.

Among the Spaniards who contributed were the musicologist Felipe Pedrell, Fita y Colomer of the Royal Spanish Historical Society, and Don Vera, the archivist of the Toledo Cathedral Library.[116] Pedrell was known to segments of the Russian theatrical world because an extensive article on him appeared in the theatrical journal *Artist* in 1894. Pedrell sent Cui examples of Spanish religious and lay music of the sixteenth and seventeenth centuries (AD 35).

Using materials provided by these musicians, Il'ia Alexandrovich Sats (1875-1912) and Shpis Eshenberg arranged and composed the lay and religious music for these Spanish Golden Age plays (AD 38). Sats had done the music for the group's medieval cycle and was associated for a number of years with the Moscow Art Theater.[117] No information is available on Shpis Eshenberg.

The Starinnyi Teatr also invited the Spanish painter Ignacio Zuloaga to paint the scenery and costumes for the forthcoming performance of Lope's *El gran duque de Moscovia*.[118] When Zuloaga was not available, they decided to ask the Russian painter N. K. Kalmakov to do the work.[119] Zuloaga apparently had been invited because of his friendship and contact with Russian art collectors such as I. A. Morozov, N. Riabushinskii, and S. I. Shchukin,[120] who had been purchasing canvasses from him since the turn of the century.

On September 15, 1911, during the first rehearsal, Drizen explained the group's aims to the participants. He said that if old art had been distorted by the playing of harpsichord compositions on a concert grand, by the retouching and modernizing of old canvasses and frescoes, then the art of performing old plays had also suffered the same fate. Even if the texts themselves had not been altered, the original techniques of performing them had been lost. Consequently the ideal rebirth of the classic stage was possible only if its original techniques were also reborn by the aid of scholarly research into the theater's past.

Drizen stated that the Spanish theater along with the Greek theater and Shakespeare was one of the world's great theaters. It was characterized, in his opinion, by ecstatic religiousness, unusual force of national ideals, a special concept of honor, great mirth, and the Spaniard's love of his dance and music. In addition, the Spanish Golden Age Theater appealed to all levels of seventeenth-century Spanish society.[121]

Miklashevskii spoke on the different stages in use during Lope de Vega's time: the *corral* or municipal stage, the Royal theater in the Buen Retiro, the stage used by itinerant actors, as well as a three-tiered stage used for *Autos Sacramentales*.[122]

Evreinov in his talk attempted to answer questions dealing with the Spanish Golden Age actor. He wanted to know what demands were made on the Spanish actor by the public and by the playwright and which actors could be above the audience's whims and tastes. Evreinov studied the actor's life and the level of development that the Spanish Golden Age theater reached in the sixteenth and seventeenth centuries. Evreinov had the personal assistance of D. K. Petrov, and his scholarly sources included works by Hugo Rennert and the memoirs of Spanish seventeenth-century theater-goers as well as Agutín de Rojas' *El viaje entretenido*.[123]

The rehearsals were long and grueling and for most of the participants there was almost no monetary remuneration. In a conversation in June 1965 during my stay in Leningrad, Victorina Chekan, the troupe's Laurencia in *Fuente Ovejuna,* told me, "It was a labor of love and enthusiasm by artists inspired by the fieriness of the Spanish theater."[124] The rehearsals took place in an apartment acquired for the troupe by Butkovskaia.[125] Great emphasis was given to the physical movement and psychology of the actors and dancers, with the aim of transforming them into the Spaniards who had at one time performed the plays.[126] Instruction was also given in the use of the fan, cape, sword, and tambourine. Gymnastics were taught according to the method of Emile Jacques Dalcroze,[127] who in January, 1911, had given a demonstration of his technique in Moscow.[128]

The audience for these performances was the highest aristocracy.[129] The basic aim of the cycle was esthetic and no political theme existed. Nevertheless Drizen had to use his influence to get *Fuente Ovejuna* past the censors, and even then several lines were removed from the performance.[130] Many of the Spanish diplomatic community in St. Petersburg expressed great interest in the group's undertaking. The Spanish ambassador, the Conde de la Viñaza, thanked Baron Drizen for an invitation to the performances.[131] And according to the press, the Spaniards were impressed and surprised to see a Lope play about Russia *(El gran duque de Moscovia)*.[132]

The Starinnyi Teatr, in St. Petersburg, gave all its performances in an old exhibition hall known as Solianyi Gorodok. The academician and architect Vladimir Alekseevich Shchuko (1878-1919) redid the hall's drab walls, the entire foyer, and the auditorium to look like the home of a wealthy seventeenth-century Spaniard.[133] The imported Spanish furniture came from the private collection of the artist S. A. Galiashkin (AD 52). M. D. Gefter was in charge of the stage lights (AD 35). Evreinov's use of a simulated private home as the setting for the performances was a technique he had used in 1907 for the staging of *A Play About Robin and Marion* for which he "recreated the entire flavor of a presentation at a knight's castle."[134] The reader will recall that Meierkhol'd later staged *Don Juan* and *El príncipe constante* in a similar fashion. Within the Spanish theater this technique dates back to the end of the fifteenth century, when Juan del Encina presented his religious plays at the palace of the Dukes of Alba.

Before each performance D. K. Petrov spoke on Spanish Golden Age Theater, and L. A. Sacchetti and M. K. Miklashevskii spoke on Spanish Golden Age music and stage techniques (AD 46). In contrast to the Spanish plays directed by Meierkhol'd, the Starinnyi Teatr's productions of Spanish Golden Age plays received great coverage by the Russian press. In fact, articles on the group's activities began to appear weeks before the actual performances began.

The Starinnyi Teatr divided its schedule into two parts (AD 36), the fall of 1911 in St. Petersburg and the winter of 1912 in Moscow. On November 18, they presented Lope's *Ovechii Istochnik*, "Fuente Ovejuna," in the Iur'ev translation, and in the Ostrovskii translation, *Dva boltuna,* "Los habladores," an interlude often attributed to Cervantes; on November 25, Lope's *Velikii kniaz' Moskovskii i gonimyi imperator,* "El gran duque de Moscovia," in a translation by Pavel Osipovich Morozov, and Tirso's *Blagochestivaia Marta,* "Marta la piadosa," translated from the French by Tatiana Shchepkina-Kupernik (1874-1952), the future translator of several Lope and Tirso plays; on December 1, Calderón's *El purgatorio de San Patricio* in Bal'mont's translations.

The Starinnyi Teatr's repertoire gave a broad view of the nature of Spain's classical theater. *Fuente Ovejuna* was chosen because of the theme of popular revolt and because many people had either seen or heard of Ermolova's performance in 1876; *Los habladores,* because of the general interest in the stylized folk theater; *El gran duque de Moscovia,* because of the Russian public's curiosity in seeing a Spanish play based on the Boris Godunov theme; *Marta la piadosa,* because it is a fine example of a Spanish comedy of manners; *El purgatorio de San Patricio* because of the symbolists' general interest in the Spanish religious drama.

True, it was Baron Drizen who eased *Fuente Ovejuna* through the censors. But Evreinov could well have chosen the play because it resembled his own first play, *Bolvany i Kumirskie bogi* (1900), "Idols, False Gods," which deals with the Russian schismatic Old Believers and their struggle for religious freedom against Peter the Great and unjust authority.[135] In fact, so unusual was the choice of this play that a critic commented, "*Fuente Ovejuna* is something completely different for the St. Petersburg audience, accustomed to a more temperate contemporary stage" (AD 109).

Before a full house which paid the very high admission charge (AD 132), Evreinov directed *Fuente Ovejuna* and *Los habladores.* N. K. Rerikh designed the setting and V. V. Emme executed it.[136] The setting for the play was unique. A back canvas portrayed a rocky elevation on which was located the commander's castle overlooking the town of Fuente Ovejuna. Shchuko designed a simple plank stage like that used by Spanish itinerant actors, containing very few props. A back curtain on the stage represented the town square (AD 123). The rich and authentic costumes, designed after the sketches of the artist Ivan Iakovlevich Bilibin (1876-1942), were the work of M. F. Zavadskoi and R. S. O'Konnel. The music was by Il'ia Sats (AD 119).

The critics spoke very highly of the spectacle, especially of the dances performed at Laurencia's and Frondoso's interrupted wedding (Act II). These dances, performed by young girls, were, according to one critic, "full of ecstasy bordering on the bacchanalian." The dancers repeated them between the second and third acts. According to another critic, these dances, once prohibited by the Spanish Inquisition, were very sensual because the girls danced with their legs uncovered to the knees and wore very décolleté blouses (AD 123).

Despite the more than sixty rehearsals, these amateur actors did not perform very well, showing a weakness seen in other Spanish Golden Age plays performed at this time (AD 160). On the best performer, the actress Chekan as Laurencia, all a critic could say was, "She has temperament, but her declamation and direction leave much to be desired" (AD 119). Mgebrov performed the role of Esteban, the mayor of Fuente Ovejuna, "ably . . . but who can make out his unclear and hollow diction" (AD 131)? K. V. Kievskii as the commander drew the attention of the audience "with his good diction . . . and noble stage appearance." Alexander Alexandrovich Geirot (1882-1947) as Frondoso had "temperament and awareness of style" (AD 119).

Between Acts I and II of *Fuente Ovejuna* the troupe performed *Los habladores,* a farce about a man (Sarmiento) whose wife Beatriz talks constantly. When a very talkative fugitive from justice (Roldán) appears, Sarmiento invites him to his house hoping that he will make his wife stop talking; hence the title of the Interlude. Again, the critics had very little to say about the actors. One did write, "Outstanding was the talkative wife (Madame A. M. Somova) and the servant girl (Inés)."

Under Miklashevskii the group presented *Marta la piadosa.* Prince Alexander Konstantinovich Shervashidze (1872-?) designed the staging and costumes, which were executed by Smotritskii (AD 151). This setting represented the performance of a Spanish Golden Age play in the courtyard of a Spanish inn. A group of very poor and ragged itinerant actors (una compañía de la legua) enters. To the right is a big brick wall, to the left the wall of a house in front of which the actors construct a makeshift plank stage elevated on barrels. Thus the stage is much like the one used for *Fuente Ovejuna* and *Los habladores.*

Nevertheless a curious twist was added. On the stage watching the performance was an audience dressed like Spanish villagers. From the balcony of the house spectators tossed coins to the actors, who in turn directed little verses to the "Spanish" audience. The performers then mingled with this audience by sitting at their tables. Two men of this audience even began a pre-planned fight over the affections of one of the dancers. The acting in *Marta la piadosa* was very poor, worse than that of the group's debut. However, a critic did like the actress Grabovskaia in the role of Marta, of whom he wrote, "Hers is a talent which has promise" (AD 148).

In a setting which was reminiscent of the Royal Theater in Madrid's El Buen Retiro, Butkovskaia directed Lope's *El gran duque de Moscovia* with music by Sats (AD 151). The costumes, coiffures and settings by Kalmakov were based on numerous Velázquez paintings (AD 157). Kalmakov may have made use of the Spanish painting housed in the Hermitage. The critics praised Butkovskaia's directing and felt that the acting was much better than in previous plays. "The actors were good throughout and were in complete accordance with the basic style of the play, which is imbued with great pathos" (AD 157).

A production under Drizen's direction of Calderón's *El purgatorio de San Patricio* brought the Starinnyi Teatr's fall season to a magnificent close. Shchuko reconstructed Cosme Loti's stage used at the Buen Retiro, which was used during the reign of Philip IV (AD 180). Shchuko's stage, with candles on both sides, was divided into three sections. This allowed for an immediate change of scene by simply walking to another section. The settings were by Evgenii Evgeneevich Lansere (1875-1946), while Bilibin and O'Konnel designed the costumes (AD 160).

In the opinion of many critics Il'ia Sats' music for voice, organ, and orchestra was "powerful, full of mystic charm, detached from the world, and full of submission to the Supreme Will" (AD 161). Baron Drizen later wrote, "Sats, in writing music for the Calderón play, was forced to immerse himself in the spirit of Catholic Spain and was successful in doing so."[137]

Calderón's *El purgatorio de San Patricio* (1630) deals with the conversion of Ireland to Catholicism:

> In the play Saint Patrick is shipwrecked on the Irish coast along with Ludovico Enio, a criminal and Christian sinner, and Filipo, a pirate captain at the service of King Egerio. Egerio rewards Ludovico with a position of honor and brands Patrick as a slave because he is a Christian.

> Ludovico falls in love with Polonia, but soon stabs her to death, for which he is sentenced to die. Meanwhile Patrick has fled to Rome and returns to Ireland, authorized by the Church to convert the country to Catholicism. When Egerio demands that Patrick perform some miracle, the Saint promptly brings Polonia back to life. At Patrick's request an Angel of Good and an Angel of Evil appear. The former announces the existence of a cave in which one can see visions of Purgatory, Hell, and Heaven, and immediately destroys the Angel of Evil.
>
> Patrick says that anyone who has not confessed his sins will die as soon as he enters this cave. The king disregards Patrick's warning and perishes in the flames. On the other hand, a man who has confessed his sins and wants to cleanse himself of them may enter the cave. Ludovico confesses his sins and enters. When he returns he tells of the visions he saw and describes the happiness of Purgatory, the tortures of Hell, and the bliss of Heaven. Ludovico, now a repented sinner, dies and can now hope to go to Heaven.[138]

The critics marvelled at Calderón's power and religious feeling but lamented that the acting did not really reflect the Spaniard's greatness. On the other hand, the critics felt that in this play the actors' role was unimportant since "the protagonists are only part of a religious theme; they are insignificant before the Supreme Will personified in the figure of Patrick" (AD 161). Of all the actors, the critics spoke best of Mgebrov in the role of St. Patrick. "The actor did not have much strength, but his soul burned with a real fire" (AD 174). Viktorov in the role of Egerio "made the audience laugh by his funny intonation" (AD 174).

Within weeks after the fall season, Drizen and Evreinov split and each formed a Starinnyi Teatr (AD 131) and planned to take his troupe on tour to Moscow, Evreinov to the Kupecheskoe Sobranie, "The Merchant's Club" (AD 259); Drizen to S. F. Saburov's Internatsional'nyi Teatr, "The International Theater" (AD 207) for which tickets went on sale on January 15, 1912 (AD 205). Evreinov, who considered himself the founder of the group, claimed that Drizen was too dogmatic, too dictatorial an administrator, and received too much credit for the troupe's success (AD 254). Drizen said that his financial and material support gave him as much or more right to have the final decision on many matters (AD 255) and would not allow the group's wardrobe, sets, and decorations to leave his possession (AD 248). Either there was only one Starinnyi Teatr or there was no Starinnyi Teatr. Evreinov finally gave in to Drizen who took the group to Moscow (AD 244).

The Moscow tour opened on February 13, 1912, with one performance of *Marta la piadosa* and *El gran duque de Moscovia,* not at the Internatsional'nyi Teatr (it was unavailable for that evening) but rather at the Literaturno-Khudozhestvennyi Kruzhok, "The Literary-Artistic Circle."[139] Again the critics lavished praise on the settings but were unimpressed by the actors, who were essentially those who had performed with the group in the fall of 1911 (AD 265). One critic spoke very disparagingly about *El gran duque de Moscovia* because "the author with charming naïveté confused Ivan the Terrible, Feodor, Dmitrii, and Godunov. But despite these historical innaccuracies others were delighted that Lope had written such a play. The theater was filled almost to capacity" (AD 265).

On the following evening at the Internatsional'nyi Teatr, the troupe performed *Fuente Ovejuna* and *Los habladores* before a much smaller audience. In the light of the importance this play had at the Maly Theater (AD 265) in Moscow in 1876, it is difficult to explain why so few people attended. Nevertheless, the audience frequently interrupted the performance with enthusiastic applause, and again it was the settings which inspired the critics. Rerikh's rear canvas, according to one critic, set the somber and grim mood for the play (AD 269). The acting was not good but Chekan did receive some favorable comments. The critics also liked the work of Baron Drizen (AD 261); one stated, "In the artistic ensemble of the entire performance could be seen the hand of an excellent director" (AD 266). And the play itself was judged "a magnificent, deeply touching, and unusually colorful and truthful melodrama" (AD 266). *Los habladores,* performed between Acts I and II, was criticized because of the poor acting. "The actor playing the main role made such a hash out of his lines that one could not even make out one word he said" (AD 265).

On March 4, in a setting like that of the December production, the group performed Calderón's *El purgatorio de San Patricio.*[140] Again the staging was good, the acting generally poor (AD 308). As one critic stated, the acting was poor "because one can re-create the physical stage, but a director cannot resuscitate the Spanish actor of the seventeenth century. . . . the Spanish actor who performed these plays was imbued with the same faith with which the author of *Patrik* was imbued" (AD 309).

One of the most interesting documents found in Drizen's *Al'bom,* "Album," is a letter dated January 14, 1912, from the director of an orphanage called the Obshchestvo Sinego Kresta, "The Blue Cross Society."[141] This man praised Drizen's choice of *El purgatorio de San Patricio* because the play had instilled a great religious fervor in the orphans present at the performance. He quoted to Baron Drizen the words of another director of this orphanage: "Our priests should send their parishes here [to the Starinnyi Teatr] instead of giving their weekly sermons. And it would be advisable to teach the popular theaters [for the masses] how to perform them" (AD).

The third and last of tsarist Russia's innovators of the symbolist theater who were interested in the Spanish classical theater was Alexander Iakovlev Tairov (1885-1950). After abandoning his law studies, he took up a career as an actor and joined the Kommisarzhevskaia Theater (1906-1907), whose main director, Meierkhol'd, had a great influence on him.[142] In 1911-1912 he acted in the Reineke-Nezlobin Theater in Moscow.[143] In August 1913, the director Mardzhanov convinced Tairov to join his group, the Svobodnyi Teatr, "The Free Theater," in Moscow.[144]

Tairov had become most discouraged with the contemporary naturalistic stage and decided to join this group to implement some of his theatrical ideas. Soon, however, the Svobodnyi Teatr came to an end and Tairov, under the influence of Konstantin Aleksandrovich Mardzhanov (1872-1933), established his own group. In October 1914, the moment of Russia's entry into World War I and a period of great hardship and brutality, Tairov managed to establish the Moscow Kamernyi Teatr, "The Chamber Theater," a name chosen for the friendly and intimate atmosphere the word connotes.[145]

He was not a revolutionary bent on breaking away from the traditional theater. He was interested in a synthetic, eclectic theater which fused declamation,[146] song, pantomime, music, art, and dance with acting. All of these elements, in the words of Tairov, "are harmoniously combined to produce a single monolithic theatrical work."[147] Like the actors of the Starinnyi Teatr, Tairov's actors were trained to dance, act, and sing, and underwent strenuous physical exercise as well as dramatic instruction. So much emphasis was given to the physical beauty of the actors that not enough attention was given to their acting ability,[148] a lack which many critics observed in the group's performances.

Tairov's extensive training as an actor and director, in addition to his association with Stanislavskii, Meierkhol'd, Kommisarzhevskaia, and Evreinov, helped him to synthesize their concepts in a continuous development of his own ideas.[149] Tairov rejected the naturalistic theater as did Meierkhol'd and Evreinov, but differed with them on how to implement these antinaturalistic views. He differed from Evreinov because he felt it unnecessary to reconstruct the physical stages of the past but did agree with him and

Stanislavskii that the center of a performance had to be the actor. Meierkhol'd's concept of the puppet-like actor did not appeal to him.

Like Meierkhol'd and Evreinov, Tairov wanted to combine art and music for stage productions, and he employed the services of some of Russia's finest artists and musicians. In contrast to Meierkhol'd, Tairov sought a three-dimensional stage that would be large and spacious enough to act as the actor's "keyboard." This large stage allowed Tairov to permit plays with large numbers of people appearing at the same time.[150]

His repertoire, which was aimed at the selected minorities and not at box-office success, included works by Shakespeare, Calderón, and E. T. A. Hoffman.[151] Tairov attempted to flee the horrors of contemporary reality and believed that the theater was like a myth or a fairy tale.[152] He could not tolerate plays dealing with psychological and realistic themes. He preferred non-realistic plays on religious themes (Judeo-Christian and Oriental) as well as harlequinades.[153] For such themes he turned to Ancient Greece, Hindu India, and Catholic Spain.[154] The group's first presentation (December 12, 1914) was Kalidasa's Hindu religious play, *Sakuntala,* and the third (December 29, 1914) was Calderón's *La vida es sueño,* both in Bal'mont's translations.[155]

Surprisingly, the three reviews available of *La vida es sueño* indicate that Tairov made little use of pantomime, dancing, and singing for this performance. On the contrary, little innovation in the production appeared. The settings were the creation of Kalmakov, the artist who had done the settings for the Starinnyi's performance of Lope's *El gran duque de Moscovia* the season before.[156]

The three reviews of the performance agree that in this production, as in the previous performances of Spanish Golden Age plays of those years, the acting was poor. The reviewer from *Russkaia zhizn',* "Russian Life," speaks of the poor quality of the acting.[157] Iakov L'vov, the reviewer from *Novosti sezona,* "News of the Season," felt that contemporary Russian actors did not know how to perform Calderón's honor-and-sword romanticism, but praised the troupe for its attempt to perform Calderón, "who so brilliantly combines deep philosophical thought, the temperament of the Spaniard, the religious fanaticism of a Catholic, and the effective poses of the Romantic."[158] L'vov complained about the poor quality of the mass scenes, which did not have enough people, and the unimpressive acting of the majority of the performers. Only the actor Shalakhov "performed in the play's style and portrayed its temperament and depth. The remaining actors performed as if they were extras (Madame Stepnaia) or exaggerated so much they looked funny (Mr. Krechetov)."[159]

Act III of *La vida es sueño* contains a mass scene in which the people free Segismundo from his prison with the hope of his taking the rightful throne. Since Tairov liked mass movements on the stage, one may ask why there were so few actors on the stage. The answer to this question lies in the effects of World War I on Tairov's groups. In his *Zapiski,* "Notes," Tairov states:

> In Moscow a million misfortunes awaited me. Frightened by the war, the workers had fled to the country, and the construction of the theater was bogged down in a half-completed and perilous state. The better part of the young men on whom I had placed such high hopes had been drafted. Alice Koonen, who was to play Shakuntala, was stranded abroad. . . . There was not a cent in the box-office, and on top of everything, war, war, war.[160]

Iur'ii Sobolev, the critic from *Rampa i zhizn,'* "Stage and Life," felt that even the fine decorations and staging were boring and suffered from lifeless historical authenticity. His comments on the acting also were generally unfavorable. With the exception of Shakhalov as Segismundo and Sukharev as Basilio, the remaining actors were not up to the roles they played. The critic warned the Kamernyi Teatr to improve the quality of its actors. "Do not forget about the actors. Without actors a good performance is impossible . . . even if you present an eleventh-century tragedy."[161]

Both the director Zonov and the costumes and scenery impressed the critics. "Interesting is Zonov's production which preserves Calderón's interior feeling."[162] Concerning the decorations, L'vov commented, "The decorations and costumes by the artist Kalmakov are interesting. They show the roughness and splendor of the sixteenth century which combines the macabre colors of a prison on which rests the shadow of Catholic fanaticism and the luxury of a royal chamber."[163] The critic from *Russkoe Slovo,* "The Russian Word," felt that the choice of the Calderón play had improved the general repertoire of the Russian theaters and that the Kamernyi Theater should be commended for presenting such an eternally great work of theatrical art.[164]

In addition to the innovations of Meierkhol'd, Evreinov, and Tairov, there were traditional performances of Spanish Golden Age comedies of manners. Between 1910-1917 the Alexandrinskii Theater, in keeping with the tradition established some years before by Kotliarevskii (see Chapter IV), presented two Spanish plays at the Mikhailovskii Theater: Calderón's *El alcaide de sí mismo* and Tirso's *Marta la piadosa.* Meierkhol'd did not direct these performances.[165]

El alcaide de sí mismo was performed seven times between September 15 and November 17, 1911.[166] A review in *Birzhevye vedomosti,* "Stock Market News," spoke favorably of the Alexandrinskii's interest in presenting such plays. The reviewer includes a survey of the play's performance in Russia since the reign of Peter the Great and gives a short plot summary for those who had not read the Iur'ev translation. Prince Shervashidze, who did the setting for the Starinnyi Theater's *Marta la piadosa,* designed the tower room, the scene of Benito's imprisonment. The remaining sets were taken from other plays. During the intermission an ensemble performed compositions by Lully and Rameau to harmonize with the period in which Calderón lived.[167]

A performance in late November, 1915, of *Marta la piadosa* by the Alexandrinskii Theater left much to be desired. In the opinion of the critic from *Apollon,* Vladimir N. Solov'ev, the production suffered mainly from the poor direction of Iur'ii L'vovich Rakitin, which was "too superficial, not well thought out, and did not reflect the spirit of Tirso's play." Rakitin did not adhere to the acting and staging techniques (despite the settings by Shervashidze) of the Spanish Golden Age theater, and his lack of a uniform style and mood affected the actors, who performed poorly. In addition to the inferior direction and acting, the prose translation by Maria Valentinovna Vatson (1853-1932) was also inadequate.[168]

In March, 1912, the Maly Theater in St. Petersburg performed Lope's *El perro del hortelano* in a benefit performance for the actor N. N. Levashev. The *Birzhevye vedomosti* critic praised the actress Valentina Alekseevna Mironova (1873-1919) for her ability in the humorous role of Diana, but he was highly displeased by Neradovskii's performance of Teodoro and recalled how well Dalmatov had performed the same role in 1893 at the Alexandrinskii Theater. The critic praised Gavriil Vladimirovich Glovatskii's (1866-1939) decorations which depicted Naples.[169]

During May, 1916, the Malakhovskoi Summer Theater (established in the small village of Malakhov near Moscow) also performed Lope's *El perro del hortelano.* The group, which catered to the aristocracy and was not politically oriented, invited good actors and directors more to entertain than to teach the audience anything. The critic from *Rampa i zhizn',* Iakov L'vov, received the play well. M. Ia. Muratov, the director, performed the role of Teodoro "with the brilliance of color found in the temperament of the true Spaniard."

The actress Budkevich as Diana performed "with feeling and sparkling style." Manykin-Nevstruev designed the settings and costumes for the production.[170]

In late March, 1914, Ernest Von Possart made his final appearance on the St. Petersburg stage. (His departure from Russia probably resulted from the pending conflict between Russia and Germany.) At the Mikhailovskii Theater Possart and other German-speaking actors performed Moreto's *Donna Diana,* "El desdén con el desdén," in the German translation by Karl August West.

The *Birzhevy vedomosti* critic, M. P--er, began his review of the performance with a survey of the Donna Diana theme in Western theater, referring to Molière and Carlo Gozzi, founder of the modern commedia dell'arte. In contrast to the general level of the acting on the Imperial stage, fine acting characterized this production. Possart, in the role of Perin (Polilla in the Spanish original), overwhelmed the critic with his "expressiveness and inimitable mastery." Madame Von Gagen [Hagen?] in the role of Diana "succeeded in depicting the heartfelt suffering of a proud young woman."[171]

On October 2, 1916, the Alexandrinskii again performed *Marta la piadosa,* the last Spanish Golden Age play performed in tsarist Russia. The reviewer for *Birzhevye vedomosti,* who gave a short outline of the play, spoke very favorably about the production. "The director Rakitin fulfilled his duties well. He always emphasized the humor of Marta's humorous situation. The performances by Miss E. I. Time, Sgudentsov, Leshkov, and Leonid Sergeevich Viven (1887-) were good, as were the settings by Shervashidze."[172]

The seven years which preceded the Bolshevik Revolution mark a high point for the Spanish Golden Age Theater in Russia. For the most part the innovators, Meierkhol'd, Evreinov, and Tairov, solved the problems of the physical reconstruction and decoration of the Spanish stage as well as the costuming of the actor, but neither the modernists nor the Crown theaters were able to re-create the Spanish acting techniques and implement them on the twentieth-century stage. This Russian interest in Spain's classical theater, unique in its scope, depth, and originality, was the flowering of a tradition which began with the birth of romanticism and the rise of Napoleon. The repertoire presented during these seven years is universal because of the wide range of works: the comedy of manners, drama of popular revolt, and religious plays.

Notes

1. Evgenii A. Znosko-Borovskii, *Russkii teatr nachala XX veka* (Prague, 1925), pp. 224-225.
2. Nikolai A. Gorchakov, *The Theater in Soviet Russia,* trans. Edgar Lehrman (New York, 1957), p. 29.
3. Ibid., p. 31.
4. Ibid., p. 47.
5. Ibid., p. 46.
6. Ibid., p. 50.
7. Marc Slonim, *Russian Theater From the Empire to the Soviets* (New York, 1961), p. 188.
8. Znosko-Borovskii, p. 259. The German directors George Fuchs and Max Reinhardt also influenced these Russian innovators.
9. Ibid., pp. 233-234.
10. Ibid., p. 234.
11. Gorchakov, p. 58.
12. Ibid., p. 58.
13. Ibid., pp. 55-56.
14. Ibid., p. 54.
15. Ibid., p. 57.
16. Ibid., p. 59.
17. Ibid., p. 54.
18. Ibid., p. 58.
19. Ibid., p. 54.
20. Ibid., p. 56. Also see Iurii Elagin, *Temnyi Genii* (New York, 1955), p. 97.
21. Nikolai Volkov, *Meierkhol'd* (Moscow, 1929), I, 11.
22. Ibid., I, 14.
23. Ibid., I, 10.
24. Gorchakov, p. 54.
25. Ibid., p. 57.
26. Ibid., p. 56.
27. Ibid., pp. 55, 57.
28. Ibid., p. 56.
29. Ibid., p. 57. "The object of Maeterlinck in his plays is to reveal the inner mysteries of life by making the audience experience them as actual facts. His ambition is to break down the barrier between the stage and the audience and cause the performance to become a kind of religious service in which the individuality of the spectator merges into some sublime vision of the inner world." Alexander Bakshy, *The Modern Russian Stage* (London, 1916), pp. 61-62, 63-65.
30. In 1908, as soon as he arrived at the Alexandrinskii Theater, Meierkhol'd stated that in order to improve the contemporary theater one had to return to Shakespeare and Calderón. Volkov, II, 19.
31. In 1896 Meierkhol'd studied the history of the theater at the Moscow Philharmonic Society. His teacher was Alexander Fedotov, son of the Maly Theater actress, Glikeriia Nikolaevna Fedotova, who in 1866 chose for her benefit performance Calderón's *La gran cisma de Inglaterra.* Fedotov's lectures dealt very much with the Maly Theater repertoire and probably spoke in length about the Lope and Calderón plays performed there. Elagin, p. 59.

32. In the introduction to his *Ocho comedias y ocho entremeses* (1615), Cervantes describes the Spanish popular theater as it was during Lope de Rueda's time:

En el tiempo de este célebre español, todos los aparatos de un autor de comedias se encerraban en un costal y se cifraban en cuatro pellicos blancos guarnecidos de guadamecí dorado y en cuatro barbas y cabelleras y cuatro cayados, poco más o menos. . . . No había figura que saliese o pareciese salir del centro de la tierra por lo hueco del teatro, al cual componían cuatro bancos en cuadro y cuatro o seis tablas encima, con que se levantaban del suelo cuatro. . . . El adorno del teatro ero una manta vieja, tirada con dos cordeles de una parte a otra.

Miguel de Cervantes Saavedra, *Obras Completas* (Madrid, 1965), p. 179. See also Elagin, p. 172.

33. Hugo Rennert, *The Spanish Theater in the Time of Lope de Vega* (New York, 1909), p. 78.

34. Ibid., p. 82.

35. Volkov, II, 187-188.

36. Ibid., II, 180.

37. Znosko-Borovskii, p. 314.

38. Andrei Belyi, *Nachalo veka* (Chicago, Illinois, 1966), p. 315.

39. Another example of a play which combined elements of the folk theater with a religious theme was Alexander Blok's *Balaganchik*, "The Little Peep show" (1908). This work fascinated Meierkhol'd and he produced it. Elagin, p. 120.

40. Evgenii Znosko-Borovskii, "Bashennyi Teatr," *Apollon*, No. 8 (May-June, 1910), 31. The invitation Znosko-Borovskii received read:

Calderón's comedy *Poklonenie krestu* will be performed by the actors of the Bashennyi Theater (25 Tavricheskaia Street), on April 19, 1910. The actors are . . . . The scene takes place in Siena, according to the playwright, in the XIII century. The play will begin at 11:15 in the evening. This program is your ticket.

41. Ibid., 33.

42. Rennert, p. 84.

43. Vladimir Piast, *Vstrechi* (Moscow, 1929), p. 172.

44. Ibid., p. 171.

45. Ibid., p. 173.

46. Ibid., p. 174.

47. Znosko-Borovskii, "Bashennyi Teatr," 35.

48. Volkov, II, 100.

49. Ibid., 180.

50. Ibid., 189.

51. Ibid., 233. 236.

52. Piast, p. 235. For a list of participants see Volkov, II, 232.

53. Piast, p. 235. Also see Bely, p. 336.

54. Alexander Blok, *Sobranie sochinenii* (Moscow, 1963), VII, 486.

55. Ibid., VIII, 392.

56. The group performed Calderón's *La devoción de la cruz* on June 29, 1912. Ibid., VII, 154. On June 27, Blok wrote his mother:

On St. Peter's day I am going to see Calderón's *La devoción de la cruz* (Liubov' is not acting in it). Most likely I shall go with Verkhovskii [Iurii Nikandorovich (1876-1956), a poet and literary scholar and friend of Blok's], whom I shall visit tomorrow, and with Piast. I do not know Calderón, but I think I shall get to know him shortly and later—closely (Ibid., VIII, 395). On September 25, 1912, Blok wrote in his diary that he had to buy a new copy of Bal'mont's second volume of Calderón's plays because "the actors at Terioka had worn the pages through." Ibid., VII, 158.

Curiously enough, in October, 1912, Blok published "Ispanke," "To a Spanish Girl," a poem about a Spanish dancer (Ibid., I, 381). He did the original sketch of the poem during the summer of 1912 (ibid., I, 751). Perhaps he wrote this poem, the only one of his poems on a Spanish theme, as a result of seeing the Cervantes and Calderón plays at Terioka.

57. Alexander Blok, *Zapisnye knizhki, 1901-1920* (Moscow, 1965), p. 214.

58. Volkov, II, 242.

59. Mikhail Babenchikov, *Novaia studiia,* No. 7 (1912), 8.

60. Ibid., 8.

61. Volkov, II, 243.

62. Ibid., II, 244.

63. Alexander Avelevich Mgebrov, *Zhizn' v teatre* (Moscow, 1932), II, 200.

64. Ibid., II, 200. In the fall of 1911 Mgebrov had already performed in Evreinov's Starinnyi Teatr (to be discussed later in this chapter). Mgebrov recalled how the spirit of the Starinnyi Teatr lingered on and said that the opportunity to perform again in a Spanish Golden Age play was very appealing to him (ibid., II, 189).

65. Volkov, II, 235.

66. Ibid.

67. Ibid., 236.

68. Gorchakov, p. 70.

69. *Teatr i iskusstvo,* No. 27 (1910), 524-525.

70. Gorchakov, p. 63.

71. Volkov, II, 367-369 (February 9, March 2 and 29).

72. Ibid., 308. Spanish versification formed part of the curriculum (ibid., 371), Vladimir Piast gave lectures on the Spanish Golden Age Theater (ibid., 315). The group also rehearsed Calderón's *El médico de su honra* and studied his *El príncipe constante* for the coming spring production which Meierkhol'd was to direct at the Alexandrinskii Theater (ibid., 371).

73. Volkov, II, 367-369. See Gorchakov, p. 68, concerning Meierkhol'd's techniques used at the Interlude House.

74. Ibid., II, 368-369.

75. Ibid., 378.

76. Alexander Golovin, *Vstrechi i vpechatleniia* (Leningrad, 1960), p. 41.

77. Volkov, II, 378.

78. E. Gollerbakh, *A. Ia. Golovin, zhizn', i tvorchestvo* (Leningrad, 1928), p. 25. Golovin was also interested in Spanish national and regional types. Ibid., pp. 18-19.

79. Volkov, II, 379.

80. V. Solov'ev, *Apollon* (April, 1915), 28. To the best of my knowledge Meierkhol'd's production of *El príncipe constante* is the first performance in Russian of a Spanish Golden Age play with a religious theme on the Imperial Stage. The Alexandrinskii Theater performed it again on October 3, 1915, with the actor Usachov in the role of Tarudante. In general the critics were not impressed by

the acting which was "not outstanding." *Rampa i zhizn'*, No. 42 (October 18, 1915), p. 11.

81. Volkov, II, 114.
82. *Rampa i zhizn'*, No. 42 (October 18, 1915), p. 11.
83. Solov'ev, p. 27.
84. Ibid.
85. V. M. Zhirmunskii, *Liubov' k trem apel'sinam*, Kniga I (1916), 70-77.
86. Ibid.
87. Gorchakov, p. 67. See *Istoriia sovetskogo teatra. Petrogradskie na poroge oktiabria i v epokhu voennogo kommunizma 1917-1921* (Leningrad, 1933), I, 131.
88. Vasilii Kamenskii, *Kniga ob Evreinove* (Petrograd, 1917), p. 21.
89. Znosko-Borovskii, *Russkii teatr,* p. 333.
90. Nikolai N. Evreinov, *Teatr kak takovoi* (Berlin, 1923), p. 115.
91. Gorchakov, p. 79.
92. Evreinov, *Istoriia russkogo teatra* (New York, 1956), p. 363.
93. Eduard Stark, *Starinnyi Teatr* (Petrograd, 1922), p. 6. Znosko-Borovskii, *Russkii Teatr,* p. 333, and Gorchakov, p. 79.
94. Znosko-Borovskii, "Bashennyi Teatr," p. 33.
95. Gorchakov, p. 77.
96. Ibid., p. 80.
97. Evreinov, *The Theater in Life,* trans. Alexander I. Nazaroff (London, n. d.), pp. 22-24. See Gorchakov, pp. 80-81.
98. Znosko-Borovskii, *Russkii Teatr,* pp. 324-325 and p. 327.
99. Evreinov, *The Theater in Life,* p. 7.
100. Ibid., pp. 42 and 98.
101. Ibid., pp. 26-27.
102. Ibid., p. 108.
103. Ibid., pp. 100-101. An excellent example of audience participation with the performance of a play is found in Cervantes' *El retablo de las maravillas* and in "El retablo de Maese Pedro" in *Don Quijote,* II. Other such examples are the audiences who participate in Seville's Holy Week celebration.
104. Kamenskii, p. 23.
105. Ibid., p. 27.
106. Znosko-Borovskii, *Russkii Teatr,* pp. 333-334.
107. Stark, p. 7.
108. Ibid., p. 10.
109. Ibid., p. 9.
110. Gorchakov, p. 77.

During my studies at the Leningrad Public Library Documents Division, I came across an album compiled by Baron Drizen (Fond 262) which contains clippings and other documents about the Starinnyi Teatr. I shall refer to this album as "A D" plus the number of the clipping or document and place these references in the test. If no number is given I shall indicate this by "A D" with no number.

Unfortunately many of the clippings are without date, page and source reference. Therefore whenever I have been able to find a reference to the Starinnyi Teatr with date, page, and source reference I shall not cite the Drizen document.

111. In an interview before the season began, Drizen told a newspaper reporter about the group's aims and purposes:

You are of course aware that we are not opening a new establishment, but rather, renewing the one that existed four years ago. Now, as in 1907, we are concerned with the same tasks: to restore old forms of the theater as authentically as possible through the use of scholarly research. In the beginning we performed mystery plays, pastorals and farces. . . . This year we are turning to the Renaissance and are attempting to present the Spanish Golden Age Theater (A D 35).

112. Nikolai N. Evreinov, "Ispanskii akter XVI-XVII vekov," *Ezhegodnik imperatorskikh teatrov* (1909), Vypusk 6-7, pp. 20-39. Apparently Evreinov had intended to give a Spanish cycle as early as 1908. In an interview with the press in 1907, Evreinov announced, "The coming season will be dedicated to the Spanish Theater with plays by Lope de Vega, Calderón, and Cervantes. Suggested are Lope de Vega's *Fuente Ovejuna* and Calderón's *La vida es sueño* (A D 11).

113. Mgebrov, II, 44.

114. In a letter to Butkovskaia dated June 30, 1911, Miklashevskii stressed how much he wanted to study the Spanish dance. Gosudarstvennyi Teatral'nyi Muzei Imeni Ostrovskogo, "The Ostrovskii State Theatrical Museum," which will be indicated by the initials GTM. Document Number KP 3433/14/30/VI/1911.

115. GTM, Document Number 5615-29.

116. Ibid.

117. Nikolai Drizen, "Il'ia Sats," *Istoricheskii vestnik* (October, 1913), 215.

118. In a letter dated St. Petersburg, July 26, 1911, Butkovskaia asked Miklashevskii to contract Zuloaga or another Spanish artist for the Starinnyi Teatr. GTM, Document Number KP 3433/20.

119. GTM, Document Number, KP 3433/16/5/VIII/1911.

120. Enrique Lafuente Ferrari, *Ignacio Zuloaga* (Madrid, 1950), p. 111.

121. Nikolai Vasil'evich Drizen, "Predislovie," "Prologue," *Chto takoe Ispanskii Teatr XVI-XVII vekov-vvedenie k spektakliam Starinnago Teatra, 1911-1912,* "What is the Spanish Theater of The Sixteenth and Seventeenth Centuries—An Introduction to the Starinnyi Teatr's Presentations, 1911-1912," (St. Petersburg, 1912), pp. 3-4.

122. Ibid., 11-13.

123. Ibid., 20-39.

124. The actress Chekan told me that when Ermolova saw her performance she said that Chekan was the only actress who could equal her in the role of Laurencia.

125. The apartment was located on the corner of Angliiskii Prospekt (Prospekt Maklina) and Ofitserskaia Ulitsa (Ulitsa Dekabristov), Mgebrov, II, 35.

126. Ibid., 53.

127. Ibid., 60.

128. Volkov, II, 222.

129. Mgebrov, II, 105.

130. Ibid., 49.

131. I am reproducing the letter here in full:

L'AMBASSADEUR D'ESPAGNE
SAINT-PETERSBURG

15/22 Novembre 1911

Monsieur le Baron,

Je vous remercie de votre lettre et je félicite bien sincèrement la société

"Théâtre Ancien" pour les efforts en faveur de l'idéalisation de l'art dramatique.

En même temps je serais très heureux d'assister aux représentations des piéces de notre grand théâtre espagnol ancien and classique traduites dans votre belle et riche langue slave.

Je vous prie, Monsieur le Baron, d'agréer l'expression de toute ma consideration.

El conde de la Viñaza

Ci-joint le montant de trois fauteuils que vous avez bien voulu m'envoyer (AD).

132. *Studiia,* No. 10 (1911), 8.

133. Ibid., 15-16.

134. Gorchakov, p. 78.

135. George Kalbouss, "The Plays of Nikolai Evreinov," (Unpublished Master's Thesis, Columbia University, 1961), p. 16. For the most part the actors and many of the other participants are almost unknown, and very often I can only identify them by their first initial and last name, despite my attempts to track them down during my stay in the Soviet Union.

136. GTM, Document Number KU-7773-92.

137. Drizen, "Il'ia Sats," p. 219.

138. Calderón de la Barca, *Obras Completas* (Madrid, 1966), I, 175-210.

139. *Moskovskie vedomosti,* No. 37 (February 15, 1912), p. 4.

The Literaturno-Khudozhestvennyi Kruzhok, founded in 1899 in Moscow by members of the cultural elite, was a literary circle at which were given lectures on literature and performances of plays. Ermolova and Iuzhin Sumbatov, who had performed in Spanish Golden Age plays, were members. Nikolai D. Teleshov, *Zapiski pisatelia* (Moscow, 1958), pp. 24-26.

140. *Russkoe slovo,* No. 54 (March 6, 1912), p. 7.

141. Most of the unpublished documents in Drizen's *Album* are also letters of praise.

142. Alexander Iakovlev Tairov, *Zapiski rezhissera,* "A Director's Notes," (Moscow, 1921), p. 17.

143. While at the Reineke-Nezlobin Theater Tairov also directed Jacinto de Benavente's *Los intereses creados* translated as "Izgnanku zhizni." Znovsko-Borovskii, *Russkii Teatr,* p. 366.

144. Slonim, p. 217.

145. Tairov, pp. 37-38.

146. Georgii Kryzhitskii, *Rezhisserskie portrety* (Moscow, 1928), p. 8.

147. Alexander Tairov, *Notes of a Director,* trans. and introd., William Kuhlke (Coral Gables: University of Miami Press, 1969), p. 57.

148. Slonim, p. 218.

149. Gorchakov, p. 88.

150. Slonim, p. 219.

151. Konstantin Derzhavin, *Kniga o Kamernom Teatre* (Moscow, 1934), p. 38.

152. Gorchakov, p. 88.

153. Derzhavin, *Kniga,* p. 41.

154. Ibid.

155. Ibid., p. 218.

156. *Novosti sezona,* No. 3016 (December 30, 1914), p. 5.

157. *Russkaia zhizn',* No. 3 (January 4, 1915), p. 6.
158. *Novosti sezona,* No. 3016 (December 30, 1914), p. 5.
159. Ibid.
160. Tairov, p. 33. From the English translation by William Kuhlke.
161. *Rampa i zhizn',* No. 3 (January 4, 1915), p. 7.
162. *Novosti sezona,* No. 3016 (December 30, 1914), p. 5.
163. Ibid.
164. *Russkoe slovo,* No. 299 (December 30, 1914), p. 6.
165. Volkov, II, 204.
166. *Ezhegodnik imperatorskikh teatrov, Sezon 1911-1912, Prilozhenie,* p. 60. September 15, 19, 23, 26, and November 11, 14, 27.
167. *Birzhevye vedomosti,* No. 12534 (September 16, 1911), p. 5.
168. *Apollon,* X (December, 1915), 62-65.
169. *Birzhevye vedomosti,* No. 12842 (March 17, 1912), p. 5. See also *Teatr i iskusstvo,* No. 13 (1912), p. 275.
170. *Rampa i zhizn,* No. 22 (May, 1916), 2.
171. *Birzhevye vedomosti,* No. 14077 (March 29, 1914), pp. 4-5.
172. *Birzhevye vedomosti,* utrennyi vypusk, "Morning edition," No. 15837 (October 2, 1916), p. 6.

VI: Conclusion

This investigation of the role of the Spanish Golden Age Theater in Tsarist Russia from the seventeenth century to the Bolshevik Revolution indicates that Spain's classical theater came eventually to play a significant role in the development of theater in tsarist Russia. Hispano-Russian non-literary contacts, although sporadic until the eighteenth century, can be traced to the Middle Ages. And, as diplomatic and non-literary contacts increased, the popularity and influence in Russia of Spanish literature in general and dramatic literature in particular, increased.

In eighteenth-century Russia there was considerable resistance to Spanish Golden Age Theater, since it did not conform to neo-classic tastes and standards. Furthermore, Spain had an international reputation as a backward and superstitious nation. Consequently, Russia, in her attempts to assimilate western intellectual progress and enlightenment, looked contemptuously upon Spanish culture. Not only were Calderón's works not in the neo-classic style, but his religious plays were also incompatible with the Age of Enlightenment.

Another serious problem in the dissemination of the Spanish Golden Age Theater in Russia was the translations of the plays themselves. At this time these plays appeared in Russia after being translated from the French or German, or in many cases from both. Therefore, the Spanish Golden Age plays which appeared in eighteenth-century Russia differed greatly from the Spanish originals. In addition, the Russians often adapted these plays to Russian surroundings and circumstances. This occurred, for example, with Calderón's *El alcaide de sí mismo* and Catherine the Great's translation of his *El escondido y la tapada* and was common practice throughout the history of Tsarist Russia.

During the reign of Alexander I, two events were responsible for a complete change in attitude toward Spain's literature and culture: the rise of Napoleon and the popularization of German romanticism, the former because it drew Spain and Russia together both spiritually and militarily, the latter because it gave Russian intellectuals a new approach and insight into Spanish literature, with special emphasis on the dramatic art of Calderón de la Barca.

For the educated Russian of this period, both liberal and conservative, Spain in her struggle against Napoleon was a paragon of religious fervor and loyalty to king and country, characteristics which, in 1833, Uvarov incorporated in his credo of Orthodoxy, Autocracy, and Country. The closer Napoleon's armies came to Russia's borders, the greater the number of studies in the Russian press on Spain and her crusade against the trend. When these articles appeared, they stimulated an increased interest among the Russian public in Spanish history and culture. But had it not been for the German romantics, especially the Schlegel brothers, the Spanish Golden Age Theater would not have had the impact it had on Russian culture at that time and much later. One can only speculate how this would have affected the development of the pre-Soviet stage.

In the 1820's, in the wake of this new attitude toward Spain and her Golden Age Theater, many of Russia's intellectuals read, absorbed, and in several instances, were discernibly influenced by Spanish literature and culture. Pushkin, P. V. Kireevskii, Kiukhel'beker, Mikhail Glinka, and Ivan Turgenev are only a few in whose works there can be found indications of influence by and commentaries on Spain's great playwrights.

During the ultraconservative reign of Nicholas I there existed a very strong theatrical censorship. Only plays which were devoid of political and religious controversies, proposed the moral edification of the individual, and strengthened the bonds of loyalty between king and people were allowed to be performed. Spanish Golden Age plays which were presented at this time were allowed production because of the beneficiary system existent in the Russian theater. The most important actors and directors could choose for performance any play which the censor approved. The actors Karatygin and Brianskii, and the director Shakhovskoi, all of the Alexandrinskii Theater in St. Petersburg, chose plays whose themes reflected the intellectual and political atmosphere of Nicholas I's Russia. Still, the censor altered the ending of Karatygin's production of Calderón's *El médico de su honra* by having Gutierre commit suicide. And Brianskii's choice of Calderón's *El postrer duelo de España* was, apparently, a protest against Pushkin's death in a duel. Shakhovskoi's decision to direct Rojas Zorrilla's *Del rey abajo ninguno* was related to his autocratic concepts of loyalty of people toward the monarch. The Alexandrinskii Theater produced Moreto's *El desdén con el desdén* because of its innocuous and non-political theme.

With the reign of Alexander II, Russia entered into a period of social and economic reform, as well as a relaxation of official theatrical censorship. The Russian intellectual of these years who encouraged the existing interest in the Spanish Golden Age Theater used these plays as an instrument to improve Russian society and to raise the general level of the Russian stage. Among these were Bazhenov, the Maly Theater actress Ermolova, S. A. Iur'ev, and the playwright Alexander Ostrovskii.

Soon after the censorship reforms in the early 1860's, Bazhenov realized that the reign of Nicholas I had, for all practical purposes, destroyed the Russian stage. In order to remedy this situation, Bazhenov proposed the production of great Western playwrights and of course included Calderón de la Barca and Lope de Vega. Consequently, in 1866, under Bazhenov's influence, the Maly Theater produced Calderón's *La gran cisma de Inglaterra, El alcaide de sí mismo,* and *El alcalde de Zalamea.*

Not long after Bazhenov's death Iur'ev created even a greater interest in the Spanish Golden Age Theater. Like Bazhenov, Iur'ev influenced members of the Maly Theater troupe, especially Ermolova, to choose Spanish Golden Age plays for their benefit performances. Among the plays performed at the Maly between 1876 and 1886 were Lope's *Fuente Ovejuna, Los melindres de Belisa* and *La Estrella de Sevilla,* the latter being attributed at that time to Lope. The Maly altered this play to create stronger ties between king and people, and produced *Fuente Ovejuna* and *Los melindres de Belisa* as protests against man's inhumanity to man.

Among Iur'ev's and Ermolova's close friends was the playwright Ostrovskii, who translated Cervantes' *Entremeses* and Calderón's *La devoción de la cruz.* Ostrovskii felt a great attraction for the dignity, humor and popular elements found in many Spanish Golden Age plays. These elements possibly constitute an intangible and indirect influence on his works.

The assassination of Alexander II in 1881 had a detrimental effect on the Russian stage, and, thereby, the Spanish Golden Age plays presented. The strict theatrical censorship so characteristic of Nicholas' reign returned, despite the removal of the crown monopoly of the Russian stage. Consequently, the Spanish Golden Age plays performed until 1910 were almost exclusively *comedias de costumbres,* innocuous and nonpolitical in content, such as Moreto's *El desdén con el desdén,* Tirso's *Marta la piadosa,* and Lope's *El perro del hortelano.* These plays also reflect the general Russian repertoire of this period.

Concurrent with the low ebb of the Russian stage was the appearance of Russia's first original scholarship on the Spanish comedia. These works fell into two main categories: the objective or academic written by Kovalevskii and Petrov; the subjective or symbolist by Merezhkovskii and Bal'mont. Kovalevskii's well documented study of *Fuente Ovejuna* attempts to explain from the sociological and historical points-of-view why the villagers revolted rather than seeking another solution. Petrov, in his two erudite and original studies on the theater of Lope de Vega, shows that honor and love are the basis of Lope de Vega's theater and that the murder of unfaithful wives was a common and accepted practice in seventeenth-century Spain. Merezhkovskii and Bal'mont preferred Spanish God-oriented plays which depicted the struggle between good and evil and between the spirit and the flesh. For these neo-romantics, *La vida es sueño* and *El burlador de Sevilla* offered much more than did *Fuente Ovejuna* and *El alcalde de Zalamea.*

The simultaneous appearance of both subjective and objective Russian criticism on the comedia provided the technical background and emotional impetus for Russian symbolist innovators who wished to produce Spanish Golden Age plays. Very much in the way that the Russian symbolists reacted against realism in literature, Meierkhol'd, Evreinov, and Tairov rebelled against realism in the theater à la Stanislavskii. They felt that realism had destroyed the modern stage and that only by seeking inspiration from the great theaters of the past could they resuscitate the theater in early twentieth-century Russia. Among these was Spain's Golden Age Theater, and each one of the innovators saw something different in it.

Meierkhol'd was attracted by the naive folk elements in Cervantes' *Entremeses* and the Spanish itinerant theater of the sixteenth century. He preferred the simple two-dimensional stage on which these plays were originally performed because it brought the audience and actor into much closer communion. This closeness facilitated the religious experience which Meierkhol'd hoped to achieve from his theatrical productions in general. His fascination for religious themes and his contact with members of the Bashennyi Teater account for his productions of Calderón's *La devoción de la cruz* and *El príncipe constante.*

Evreinov became enamoured of the Spanish classical theater because of its *teatral'nost,* a term he used to describe man's natural instincts for acting and love of spectacle. Seventeenth-century Spain, in Evreinov's opinion, was an example of *teatral'nost'*, par excellence. Not only did the auto-de-fe reflect the Spaniard's love for spectacle, but according to Evreinov, the Spaniard lived in his daily life what he saw in the plays of Calderón and Lope. For the Spaniard, the stage and everyday life were one and the same.

In 1911-1912 Evreinov and his colleagues, Butkovskaia, Drizen, and Miklashevskii directed the Starinnyi Teatr's productions of Spanish Golden Age plays. They attempted to recreate the Spanish stage and the performance of these plays exactly as they had been performed in the seventeenth century. In their quest for authenticity and historical accuracy, the management of the Starinnyi Teater asked for and received the collaboration of Russia's finest theater scholars, composers, dancers, and painters.

Tairov, the director of the Kamernyi Teatr, chose to direct Calderón's *La vida es sueño* because it reflected his belief that the theater should be like a fairy tale, and also because it reflected his dislike for plays about psychological and realistic themes. These convictions led him to the realm of religious plays, oriental as well as occidental. On December 29, 1914, seventeen days after his production of Kalidasa's *Sakuntala,* the Kamernyi Teatr presented Calderón's *La vida es sueño.* Between 1910 and 1917 the Russian stage also produced many *comedias de costumbres* in the traditional manner. The role of Spain's Golden Age Theater in tsarist Russia, although very limited in the eighteenth century, became more and more important in the nineteenth century, and by 1917 it had played a significant role in the development of the Russian realistic and symbolist theaters.

Index

UNIVERSITY OF KANSAS PUBLICATIONS

HUMANISTIC STUDIES

Editor, KENNETH S. ROTHWELL

Volume 1: no. 1 *Studies in the Work of Colley Cibber*, by De Witt C. Croissant. October 1912. *

no. 2 *Studies in Bergson's Philosophy*, by Arthur Mitchell. January 1914. *

no. 3 *Browning and Italian Art and Artists*, by Pearl Hogrefe. May 1914. *

no. 4 *The Semantics of -mentum, -bulum, and -culum*, by Edmund D. Cressman. January 1915. 50¢

Volume 2: no. 1 *Oriental Diction and Theme in English Verse*, by Edna Osborne. May 1916. 75¢

no. 2 *The Land Credit Problem*, by George E. Putnam. December 1916. 75¢

no. 3 *Indian Policy and Westward Expansion*, by James C. Malin. November 1921. $1.00

no. 4 *American Indian Verse; Characteristics of Style*, by Nellie Barnes. December 1921. 75¢

Volume 3: no. 1 *The Relation of Ralph Waldo Emerson to Public Affairs*, by Raymer McQuiston. April 1923. 75¢

no. 2 *The United States, 1865-1917: An Interpretation*, by James C. Malin. January 1924. *

no. 3 *Home's* Douglas, *Edited with Introduction and Notes*, by Hubert J. Tunney. November 1924. $1.00

no. 4 *State Gasoline Taxes*, by Edmund P. Learned. March 1925. *

Volume 4: no. 1 *The Negro Character in American Literature*, by John Herbert Nelson. September 1926. *

nos. 2/3 *The Early Opposition to Sir Robert Walpole, 1720-1727*, by Charles Bechdolt Realey. April 1931. $2.00

no. 4 *The Liquor Question Among the Indian Tribes in Kansas, 1804-1881*, by Otto Frovin Frederikson. April 1932. $1.00

Volume 5: no. 1 *Public Intelligence; a Study of the Attitudes and Opinions of Voters*, by Seba Eldridge. June 1935. $1.00

no. 2 *Relationship of the Latin Facetus Literature to the Medieval English Courtesy Poems*, by Sister Mary Theresa Brentano, O.S.B. June 1935. $1.00

no. 3 *The London Journal and Its Authors, 1720-1723*, by Charles Bechdolt Realey. December 1935. 50¢

no. 4 *The Relationship of the Perlesvaus and the Queste del Saint Graal*, by Neale Carman. July 1936. *

Volume 6: no. 1 *The Kansas Labor Market with Special Reference to Unemployment Compensation*, by Domenico Gagliardo. February 1937. $1.00

no. 2 *El Secreto a Vozes*, by Pedro Calderon de la Barca. Edited by José M. de Osma. April 1938. *

no. 3 *A German Conscript with Napoleon*. Edited and Translated by Otto Springer. November 1938. *

no. 4 *Studies in English*, by Members of the English Department, University of Kansas. August 1940. $1.00

Number 25 *The Life and Works of George Turbervile*, by John Erskine Hankins. 1940. *

Number 26 *Medieval Latin Studies; Their Nature and Possibilities*, by L. R. Lind. 1941. *

Number 27 *Tennyson in Egypt; A Study in the Imagery in His Earlier Work*, by W. D. Paden. 1942. *

Number 28 *El Verdadero Dios Pan; Auto Sacramental Alegorico*, de Don Pedro Calderon de La Barca. Texto y Estudio por José M. de Osma. 1949. $2.50

Number 29 *Studies in Honor of Albert Morey Sturtevant*. 1952. *

Number 30 *Persecution of the Jews in the Roman Empire (300-438)* by James E. Seaver. 1952. *

Number 31 *L'Estoire de Griseldis*. Edited by Barbara Craig. 1954. *

Number 32 *Cooper's Theory of Fiction*, by Arvid Shulenberger. 1955. *

Number 33 *La Vie Monseigneur Saint Fiacre.* Edited by James E. Burks, Barbara M. Craig, and M. E. Porter. 1960. *

Number 34 *The Myths of Hyginus.* Translated and Edited by Mary Grant. 1960. $4.00

Number 35 *Six Studies in Nineteenth-Century English Literature and Thought.* Edited by Harold Orel and George J. Worth. 1962. *

Number 36 *Thomas Hardy's Epic-Drama; a Study of The Dynasts,* by Harold Orel. 1963. *

Number 37 *James Hannay; His Life and Works,* by George J. Worth. 1964. *

Number 37** "La Creacion, La Transgression and L'Expulsion" of the *Mistere Du Viel Testament.* Edited by Barbara M. Craig. 1968. $3.00

Number 38 *Problemata Varia Anatomica: MS 1165, The University of Bologna.* Edited by L. R. Lind. 1968. $2.50

Number 39 *The Development of William Butler Yeats: 1885-1900,* by Harold Orel. 1968. $3.00

Number 40 *The Nineteenth-Century Writer and his Audience.* Edited by Harold Orel and George J. Worth. 1969. $3.00

Number 41 *Mantillas in Muscovy,* by Jack Weiner. 1970. $4.00

* Titles marked with an asterisk are out-of-print.

** The number 37 was inadvertently used twice.